ROOTED

THE BEST NEW
ARBOREAL NONFICTION

INTRODUCTION BY
BILL MCKIBBEN

EDITED BY
JOSH MACIVOR-ANDERSEN

Outpost19 | San Francisco
outpost19.com

Published 2017 by Outpost19.
All rights reserved.

MacIvor-Andersen, Josh
        Rooted: The Best New Arboreal Nonfiction / Josh
MacIvor-Andersen
        ISBN 9781944853136 (pbk)

Library of Congress Control Number: 2016918545

OUTPOST19

ORIGINAL
PROVOCATIVE
READING

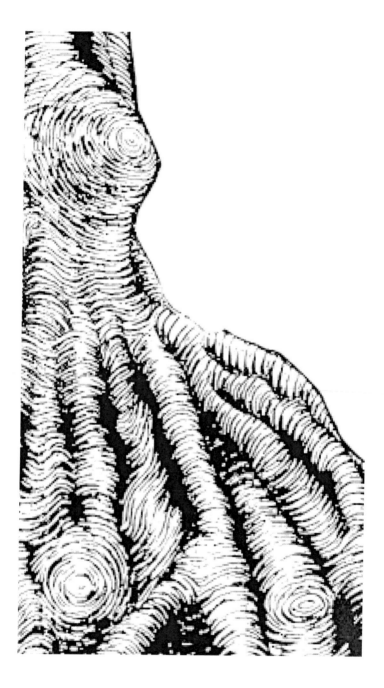

To Matthew Grewe,
for unbending friendship and faith

CONTENTS

FOREWORD
JOSH MACIVOR-ANDERSEN

As a professional and competitive tree-climber, my relationship to all things arboreal has been more intimate than most. I've known trees as scaffolding for removal, gymnasiums for fitness, courses for heated competition. I have saved trees with cables and killed them with powerful chainsaws. Hung swings from their highest branches and injected chemical cocktails into their roots, praying for new growth.

Yet the more I move through life with these unusual badges of labor and love, the more I realize how much I share with those who have never turned trees into paychecks. In fact, our human relationship to trees is not only foundational to our collective experience (read: each new breath), but remarkably rich narrative soil. Turns out I'm not that special. I've never met a person who didn't have an interesting story thematically tangled in a tree.

This is the spirit behind *Rooted: The Best New Arboreal Nonfiction*, and one that I hope will carry a reader through its unique, multi-faceted pages. Although trees show up in each essay, they are often merely the portals for deeper human dramas, the shadowy branches framing tales of love and life, death and discovery, longing, and learning.

See how many of us start with trees to articulate our spiritual selves.

See how many of us connect personal grief and illness with tree loss.

See the variety of tree species that have become integral to our lives—apple, birch, elm—and see Joyce

Kilmer, Prometheus, figs and growth rings make multiple appearances, in multiple continents, in disparate stories that strangely skein into the same patchwork quilt.

In this way, It's been more than a pleasure to collect these essays from both emerging and established writers and discover the wonderful overlaps we share with each other and our woody earth-kin. And it's exactly these connections that are so valuable these days.

Despite millennia of lessons to the contrary, we still find ways to sever ourselves from each other, at times with great animosity, vitriol, and violence—the erosion of relationship in favor of camps, compartments, our own worlds within worlds.

How lovely, then, to celebrate the simple shared roots, the connections, the story grafts that make of us a single human species, sharing the same oxygen, tethered to the same earth. May we all breathe together, and breathe deep.

September 2016, Marquette, MI

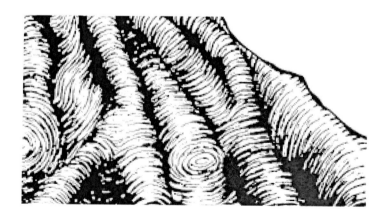

INTRODUCTION
BILL MCKIBBEN

In the middle of the place I love best in the world, a town in the hardscrabble and remote south-central Adirondacks, there is a mountain that rises a few thousand feet, and from its top you can see in all directions a considerable distance. When I first moved there, 35 years ago, I remember talking to an old man, a friend, who had been there his entire life. He said that in his boyhood—in the 1920s—you could climb to the top of that mountain and look out in every direction and not see a tree. He liked that world—liked the settled farming world spread out before him.

Now, when you climb to the top of that mountain and look out, you literally cannot see an opening, save for the ones created by marsh, pond, and lake. Every inch of those many square miles has grown back into the forest that once was there. I confess that I like that view.

I don't like it in contrast to the open farms of before; to each age its own glory. But the birch-beech-maple forest has always been my home, and I've come over time to feel very much at home in it. Its closeness attracts me: I like being able to disappear in a few strides, made invisible by the denseness of the forest. I enjoy, of course, its brief spasm of neon crescendo come late September; but I also like the deep leathery green of late summer, and the delicate light green of early summer. And I treasure above all the trees in what at this latitude is their default normal mode: the leaflessness that begins in early autumn and lasts well into blackfly season. A tree without its leaves is the essence of the thing, a sculpture revealed.

And though I enjoy trees in the aggregate above all, there are individual stems that call to me—high on this mountain, for instance, there's a hemlock that in my clichéd way I embrace each time I pass (half-hug, that shoulder pat of the slightly repressed male). So, tree-hugger. There are particular white pines that I climb each season, or smooth-skinned ashes that I seek out annually to see the bear claws heading topwards (and to make sure that the beech-bark disease hasn't claimed them since last I visited).

It is a pleasure to pick up this volume and find that there are others who have similar connections, and who have thought about them with more eloquence and depth. Trees are in certain ways our most obvious neighbors on this planet. They are, unlike say microbes, roughly our size: taller, but comprehensible. They are, unlike most animals, unlikely to flee at our approach. They are a way, then, that we come in contact with the more-than-human, a gate to the larger world beyond us. They are the opposite of a smart phone; they defy self-absorption. I am, I guess, strongly in favor of them, and hence eager to reread this volume.

TREEING:
NOTES ON LONG-LIMBED CREATURES
JOHN ROSCOE

Two of my brothers run a tree business in the state of Washington. They plant, prune, heal, and fall trees. When they drive around, every few minutes they pass by trees they've worked on. They point them out to me. Some trees they have worked on for more than ten years. They know some trees well enough to tell stories about them.

One brother tells me a story about a laurel tree he really admired. It had been planted more than a hundred years ago to celebrate a new baby. The baby lived her whole life near that tree. By the time my brothers began taking care of it, it was a massive creature with branches surging up and out like enormous anacondas. One day the laurel was mortally wounded by an ice storm. More than a ton of ice built up on the tree and finally it surrendered. Several of the main branches ripped right out of the trunk. My brothers saw the old giant broken beyond repair and they got their saws and finished it off respectfully, carting away a truckload of firewood and a truckload of chips. After four hours of work, all that was left was a stump and the mournful owner.

"It was an honor to work on that tree," says my brother.

•

My brothers edit redundancy and imperfections, lop off lively ideas heading in the wrong direction. They also provide guidance: by clipping in the right spot, they encourage growth somewhere else, somewhere better, like a parent nudging a child in the direction her gifts are most likely to flower.

They've been at this work for twelve years. They have planted and pruned thousands of trees and taken down hundreds of others. They have handled and hauled and chipped and split and stacked and burned tens of thousands of tons of tree. They know trees, love trees, climb and plant and examine and heal trees every day, and bring trees down when the landowner says it's time.

"Man, those guys even look like trees," a friend observed, and they do, both tall and long-limbed, with knots of muscle in their arms and backs and sandpaper hands and wood chips in their hair and sawdust in their pores.

•

One brother is a tall-tree specialist. For several years now he's been trying to find someone to train as his eventual replacement, but people with the muscle, stamina, and concentration needed to wield a chainsaw 120 feet up a 140-foot Douglas fir are not common. Even my other brother, as committed as he is to sharing the workload, finds it essentially impossible to function efficiently while clinging to the upper reaches of trees fourteen stories high. The brain plays tricks at that altitude. The chainsaw is a mad rattlesnake up there. The tree trunk that was solid as stone is now a loaf of white bread. The slightest breeze-sway makes you panic.

They tell me about taking down a group of sky-scraping Dougs that had been struck by lightning and were dying. Both men went up, roped in with harnesses around their waists and legs, chainsaws hanging from heavy leather belts. Up, up, up, limb after limb. Finally, where the trunks were no bigger around than their legs, they stopped and prepared to top. My tall-tree-specialist brother had to drop his top into a spot with a hedge on one side and a fence on the other. He studied the drop site, fired up his saw, made the wedge cut on the side facing the drop site, shifted in his perch, made the back cut, and when the tree started to go, gave a shove that sent the top floating down in a gentle arc, slowed by the wind in its branches. It landed smack dab between the hedge and the fence.

My other brother gripped his saw. Legs clenched around the thin trunk, he pulled the cord and winced as the chain rattled and snaked to life. He peered at his own drop site, an impossible sliver of ground 100 feet below. He squeezed the trigger. With his cuts complete, he shoved the top away and flung his arms around the trunk as it lurched back in reaction to having just been decapitated. He was suddenly perched at the very top of the tree, an angel on the point of a long wagging pin. The severed top, instead of drifting down under the parachute effect of its branches, caught the air wrong and began to flip and cartwheel, banging into the next tree over and wreaking havoc all the way down. When it finally landed, it jabbed into the ground upside-down, almost perfectly vertical. The force of its fall drove the tip deep, enough to hold it in place so solidly that no one could budge it.

"Had to climb down and fell that tree a second time," he says.

•

One brother has fallen from trees three times in twelve

years—from twenty, thirty, and forty feet up.

The first time he was saved by a brick wall. He was in an old oak and he grabbed a huge rotten branch and it sheared off and he fell thirty feet and landed right next to the brick wall, and the branch, which weighed maybe four hundred pounds, landed on the wall instead of him. The second time he fell he landed astraddle a split rail fence. He had been twenty feet up. He couldn't walk for a few days, and the bruise, like globs of fig jam under the skin, moved slowly from his amidships down the insides of both legs.

The third time he fell he was forty feet up, trying to go from one tree to another, using his weight to bend his tree into the adjoining one, but he leaned too far and the tree snapped in half right below the level of his rope, which then went sailing down after him like the tail of a kite. Luckily, all the way down he hit branches, which slowed him down, and he landed on his feet, still holding his chainsaw, right in front of the astonished homeowner. The undersides of his arms were bleeding but he climbed back up.

•

About half my native state is forest, and people and trees go way back here. People fall in love with trees, chain themselves to trees, worship trees, bring trees inside their homes, spend whole lives planting trees, build houses and schools and churches and playgrounds out of trees. We think about trees a lot here. Makes sense to me. Trees led the way out of the primordial slush. Trees and human beings are cousins, yes? We all breathe, we grow, we savor water, we have internal vascular systems, we sing in the wind, we lean toward light.

•

There's a bristlecone pine in California that is nearly 5,000 years old. There are coastal redwoods in California that are 400 feet tall. There was an Australian eucalyptus tree nearly 500 feet tall. There are trees two inches tall. The heaviest living thing in the world is a sequoia tree that weighs two thousand tons, ten times as much as the biggest blue whale. Some species of willow grow eight feet in a year, vastly outdistancing even adolescent male human beings. Intelligence? We've got $E = mc^2$ and Shakespeare, but they've got $6CO^2 + 6H_2O = C^6H^{12}O^6 + 6O^2$ and mangos. I'd call it a draw.

•

When I lived in Alaska I had a favorite tree, a little black spruce that stood valiantly in the front yard. The species is not the tallest or handsomest tree in Alaska. Visitors call the typically scrawny, stubby-limbed black spruces "bottle brush trees" and snicker at them. But I like the black spruce. Its short little limbs won't collect a big snow load and break off. The bottle-brush shape maximizes exposure to the low-angle winter sun here in the north, and it has learned to grow rapidly during the short, cool, gloriously sun-drenched summers. It's made for this place, adapted for it just like the long-legged moose and hibernating bear and wily ferocious wolverine.

•

At university, I remember reading old John Muir, who one morning found himself observing a windstorm through a cabin window and decided to get out and enjoy it. The top of a swaying 100-foot-tall Douglas fir seemed like a fine place to really get the full experience, so up he scrambled. "Being accustomed to climb trees in making botanical studies, I experienced no difficulty in reaching the top of this one, and never before did I enjoy so noble an exhilaration of motion," he wrote. "The slender tops fairly flapped and swished in the passionate torrent, bending and swirling backward and forward, round and round, tracing indescribable combinations of vertical and horizontal curves, while I clung with muscles firm braced, like a bobo-link on a reed."

A few nights after we read that passage a wind blew up the bluff and my buddy Dan Hutson and I climbed two big sequoias, slithering up the fat tapering bases, finally reaching the lower limbs, creeping higher and higher until competitiveness gave way to common sense and we settled in among arm-thick limbs to enjoy the ride. Even though it was more a bluster than a windstorm, and even though we were only two-thirds of the way up 70-foot trees, it was a thrill. We sounded our barbaric yawps (we had also been reading Walt Whitman) and pitied the dreary earthbound fools trudging off to bed far below. It was late at night but we could see trash and dust blowing through the splashes of lamp light in the parking lot below. The wind came in gusts, but it was warm and rhythmic, and the trees creaked and whispered and swayed back and forth, mothers calming their restless babies in the middle of the night, and we both found ourselves reluctant to come down. I still think about that night.

•

Reading this book, you are holding the remains of trees in your hands, and quite possibly you are sitting on milled chunks of dead trees as you read, and quite possibly the walls that surround you as you read are wooden, or cover a small treasury of wooden studs, joists, and beams, and have you ever wondered what sort of forest would appear if every tree that has contributed part of itself to your home and your life was reconstituted and resurrected, oak and pine and maple and cherry, teak and mahogany and fir and cedar, birch and beech and ash, alder and hemlock and hickory and ironwood, the siding and shingles and skeletal frame of your house, the beds and chairs and tables, the books and picture frames and junk mail and toilet paper and matches and salad bowls, the letters and cards, the photographs and Bibles, the windowsills and rakes and brooms? Every splinter of wood around us was once alive, living cells joined to billions of siblings that ate and drank and breathed and grew and one day died; and in one final way they are like us, that finally they too will return to the earth from whence they came, sent home into the ocean of soil, in which no energy is lost, but only harbored until resurrected again as the living.

TRIMMING TREES
DIANE PAYNE

Fledgings and nestlings started surfacing on the lawns soon after the tree cutters cleared the electrical lines, and mother birds squawked encouraging, yet futile words, like: I'm watching you, I'll bring you a worm, Don't worry, you're a big bird now, and the trimmers not only uprooted nesting birds, but they left trees looking lopsided and scarred, and neighbors stepped outside and said, "Glad I didn't have to pay for this; I get so tired of all these damn trees, wish they would've cut them all the way down," and others looked at the branches piled in the front lawn, awaiting the wood chipper crew, and said, "I never realized my neighbor had that huge metal shed in the yard; that's a bright white; guess I'll get used to it—one day," and when Hector watched a neighbor's cat swat at a baby bird, he said, "Damn, it's like 'Nam all over again."

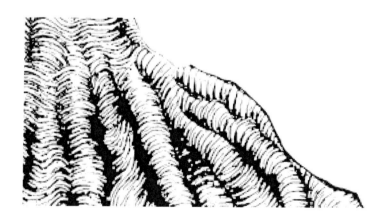

THE SPAR TREE
BRIAN DOYLE

One time I was in the woods near the ocean in Oregon
When I saw a truly immense stump looming in the sea
Of lesser green. Gray as bone, and shorn of everything,
It was still twice as vast as even the hemlock in ravines
Where they were safe from loggers without helicopters.
That's your spar tree, a friend told me. He was a logger
When he was young and strong ten thousand years ago,
As he said, mostly with a grin. Your spar, he's the boss
Of the woods, the strongest of them all, we'd knock his
Head off and set block and tackle on him and run cable
Through him for the whole operation, and then left him
Be. Sometimes guys would want to cut him too, finally,
Heck, there's a lot of log there, but that wasn't our way.
There was things done and not done from some respect.
Like a lot of things, the spar tree came to have meaning
Only after people didn't use it for work anymore, right?
So these people who don't know what they don't know,
They say it's a symbol of muscle and heroism and such,
But that's silly. For the guys who cut and worked a spar,
He kind of was the woods, you know what I mean here?
And you treated him with respect. The woods could kill
Guys and did so regular, and you wanted to treat it right.
This sounds like touchy feely stuff, but it was damn real
To the men in the woods. The woods was alive. It knew
Full well what was happening and if you worked casual
You got dead quick. This is why when we finished a job
Each guy touched the spar with respect, kind of a thanks,
I guess, for not killing guys, and for giving us the timber.
It was just sort of the thing we did. There was other stuff,
But it would take me another ten thousand years to tell it.

PROMETHEUS (1964)
M. J. GETTE

1. It was a leap year beginning on a Wednesday of the Gregorian calendar, a year much occurred on a human scale, when the Arab government of Zanzibar was overthrown by African nationalists in January, the Beatles hit #1 on singles charts, beginning the British Invasion in America with "I want to hold your hand," Greeks and Turks began fighting in Limassol, Cyprus, and Cassius Clay beat Sonny Liston to become heavyweight champion of the world. In March, Sean Connery began shooting *Goldfinger* and the next month premiered *From Russia with Love,* while Nelson Mandela gave his anti-apartheid speech "I Am Prepared to Die," receiving a life sentence two months later. Then in May, search and rescue teams found the bodies of two hitchhikers, Henry Hezekiah Dee and Charles Eddie Moore, two months decomposed in the woods of Meadville, Mississipi, while searching for three missing civil rights workers (two white, one black) and, after examining their two black and mangled torsos, concluded the boys were not who they had been looking for but had in fact been murdered by the Ku Klux Klan, one month before three more civil rights workers would be murdered by different Klansmen in another part of the state, one month before Lyndon Johnson would abolish racial segregation in the US by signing the Civil Rights Act into law, two months before Martin Luther King Jr. would become the youngest recipient of the Nobel Peace Prize, around the time the US military announced that Vietnam casualties had risen to 1,387, when goalkeeper Derek Foster of Sunderland

became the youngest-ever player in England's football league, aged 15 years and 185 days. On August 27, *Mary Poppins* premiered in Los Angeles, and, in September, 774 arrests were made during a Philadelphia race riot, riots which reverberated in Harlem, Elizabeth, NJ, Paterson, NJ, Jersey City, NJ, Rochester, New York, Dixmoor and Chicago, two months before Pete Townshend destroyed his guitar onstage in an act of auto-destructive art, two seasons before John Coltrane recorded *A Love Supreme* with his quartet and Che Guevara addressed the UN General Assembly in an effort to thwart US imperialism in Cuba. It was the year Flannery O'Connor, American writer, and Herbert Hoover, American president, died, the year Courtney Love, American musician, and Karina Galvez, Ecuadorian poet, were born, the year Jean-Paul Sartre received the Nobel Prize for Literature, a loaf of bread cost $0.21, and average rent cost $115, the year the first Ford Mustang was made, the most powerful earthquake hit the US (9.2 on the richter scale in southern Alaska), the US Surgeon General first suspected smoking may lead to lung cancer, and Jack Ruby was convicted of the murder of Lee Harvey Oswald, who murdered JFK.

2. Donald Currey, 30 years old and a graduate student at the University of North Carolina in July of 1964, was studying climate dynamics of the Little Ice Age on Wheeler Peak in the Snake Range in Nevada when he began taking core samples of Bristlecone (scientific name *pinus longaeva*) which grow in harsh environments at 10,000 or 11,000 feet where neither insect nor wind much affects the trees, which grow on a glacial moraine of quartzine boulders where the wind sweeps the trees unusually from

the northeast (not a southern or western exposure as most pine groves) leaving them to live without fear of predation. Bristlecone pines are some of the oldest living organisms on earth and are used to date archeological sites with hoisted wooden beams, comparing their wood (along with sea coral) to calibrate dates longer than 10,000 years. The trees also help the study of glacial changes over millennia. They look like the petrified fray of a woven shawl, twisted flames, corpses reaching out from their graves. Currey was studying them to put an end to the dispute over when the Little Ice Age began (some argued X while Currey was convinced it began in 2000 BCE, reasoning that the birth of the trees coincided with the date of glacial beginnings) and, using the techniques of dendrochronologists, he inserted a Swedish increment borer into the trunk to extract a core sample that would look like a narwhal tusk in shape and size in order to study the rings without harming the tree (because the tree lives in the flesh of its outermost bark, while its interior is dead). But after extraction, Currey found it difficult to count the rings due to tree's nodular and twisted bark, which is accustomed to living through thousands of years of brutal climate and a short growing season, a tree whose skin resists rot and bugs and erosion, but can be impaled by a human hand: Currey tried again. The expensive Swedish borer jammed in the pine's side. Afraid to lose his grant funding if he could not return the borer to the company which made it, Currey decided he could save the tool and get a more accurate count of the rings if he chopped the tree down. He could examine its cross-section. He gained permission from another Donald, Donald E. Cox of the US Forest Service, who agreed to fell the tree which looked so much like the others on the mountainside, who sent a crew from the Forest Service to accompany Currey, who assumed that among the thousands or millions of bristlecone specimens on the craggy wall they would surely not fell one of the eldest, who took a chainsaw to the body of one of the trees said to be immortal. He cut into it, then watched it collapse.

3. What is a millennium counted within a minute of time? What is two millennia over several minutes, three, or four?

What is 5,062 years of a non-clonal organism's life relative to human history, which has only recently begun to calculate its years on the Gregorian calendar with the suffix AD, the tree assumed to be born 3,047 years before this? (An estimation, as the bristlecone's old-growth pattern often skips years before it adds a ring, and the number could be off by one day or one millennium, depending who's counting.)

4. Every second today, a snail crawls 1 cm, a vulture flaps its wings once, 10,450 Coca-Colas are consumed around the world, the U.S throws away 2,011,216 pounds of food, a humpback whale song travels 5,085 feet through the water, and light travels 186,000 miles to fall upon my bedroom window.

5. Currey took a slab of fallen tree to the office to count the rings by hand.

He took one full day to count back 1000 years, when Yi Yuanji was born, whose paintings of roebucks and gibbons in Hubei and Hunan no one remembers.

Around 1000 years ago, the crusades began in the

interests of securing Christian access to Jerusalem, although 200 more years went by in a struggle for the Holy Land after most had assumed that in the year 1000 the world would end. (Today, most assume, neither the struggle nor the fear of the end has changed in twice as many years.)

It took another day for Currey to reach back to Pompeii, its Vesuvial grief, couples who had just died in each other's arms warm in shells of volcanic debris. The Anasazi painted petroglyphs on Utah sandstone.

Jesus of Nazareth walked on water, and before this, Romulus founded Rome. On the third day, Babylon faltered, Egyptians built the pyramids and pharaohs thought of themselves as living gods, American Indians grew maygrass and sunflower from buried obsidian, the Calusas built middens of shells and other refuse that aligned with the solstices, and Mayans entered the 12th Baktun.

The fourth day, East Asians abandoned crops of orange trees that would not survive the Little Ice Age, and instead continued to migrate, as they had for thousands of years, over the frozen Bering Strait (according to popular theory) becoming indigenous to the Americas. On the fifth day, the Indus river wiped out the Harappans and still, today, April 23, 2015, no one's solved the mystery of the Sarasvati.

6. On the last day of counting, in 1964, I imagine Currey did not rest but wept, no doubt reviewing these events in his mind, afraid that by chopping down the ancient witness he'd be cursed by it (so the legend went) and, realizing the tree he'd chopped was in fact much older than expected, that his life would be branded by this incident, that the anecdote of his study would be more significant than the

study itself, that from this moment, at 30 years of age, in July of 1964 (an exact date which has not been recorded) his name would be known for the destruction of the world's oldest living thing, that its broken trunk would lie prone on a mountainside after five millennia, enough time for each human soul to live an average human lifetime 85 times, the chopping act which, in the short time it took to complete, rearranged the scope of his own life that had as yet only been concerned with how we might survive another climate change, how he might survive 1964, what might surface during a second of an hour while he chops down a tree, the act of his destruction creeping on his awareness the way a glacier creeps over seasons to erase what attempts were made by humans to survive, the end which was the beginning, the alpha and omega, the rings: *I counted, I counted how long it took till the birth of the world was the time before the end of mine.*

THE SUGARING SEASON
ANNIE BELLEROSE

It's March on these 50 or so acres in eastern Vermont, and the days have been warmer lately, edging up towards 40 degrees, though the nights are still cold. There's sun in the sky and snow on the ground. In the maples, things are happening. Moving. Sweetness coming to the surface.

I'm out in the sugar bush every day. I'm the only one. Ian hikes out to work three days a week, and though Laura comes in from town most afternoons, and even sometimes in the mornings, I'm the one who gets up with the light and stays till it's gone. For a whole month. It's March and then it's April and I take the spring term off from school so I can be here. Every day. Because every day is what it takes when you're sugaring. Especially when you're sugaring the old way, like we are, with metal buckets and an open pan: no plastic tubing or big stainless steel evaporators or automatic heat sensors. You have to feed the fire every twenty minutes. And if you're not paying attention and the flames get too high, syrup can boil and fizz its way into sticky candy in seconds. When I'm alone there, standing in the little clearing of the sugar shed, it's so quiet, the kind of quiet where the sound of snow falling is audible, so quiet I can hear the sap pinging into buckets through the woods around me. When it comes out of the tree, it's only faintly sweet. It's clear and watery, and there's a little bit of metal in with the sweet. You can tell by tasting it that you're going to have to work hard to get it to taste like syrup.

That's what the last months have been: work. Hard work and winter. My boyfriend Ian and I moved to Barra in September. I'm nineteen and he's twenty-two. We live in a tiny house with no electricity and no running water. We have an outhouse up the hill and a Steinway grand piano that covers a third of the main room. We have, in this move, inherited a vegetable garden the size of a football field, berry bushes, and a little orchard. We're responsible for cutting eight cords of wood by hand, and for a root cellar that smells of earth and damp newspaper. When there's no snow, we walk in a quarter mile from the nearest road, and when there is, we snowshoe or ski a full mile. We are, now, homesteaders.

And there's the sugar bush. With over two hundred trees. Now that it's March, that's what's on our minds. It hasn't been an easy winter, for us or for the trees. In the last years, I've been struggling with a flattening blackness. When we get to Barra, it's not that the depression gets better, but that my survival suddenly depends on my ability to provide for myself. To have food, we have to harvest vegetables and fruit from the garden. We have to can them and store them in the root cellar so that we'll have something to eat through the winter. To have heat, we have to chop down trees, and saw and split them. There's a direct result to each action. When you live this way, everything takes effort. To go to the bathroom, you walk outside and up a zigzagging path to the outhouse, which has a shuttered front that you can leave open for a view of the distant Waits River and beyond, the tiny rope-tow ski area off of Route 25A. To fetch water, you gather up the metal pails from the woodshed, attach them to the shoulder yoke, and walk down the hill, around the garden, through the blueberries, and into the woods where, depending on the season, you must break the ice with a hatchet. And then you walk uphill with a sliding step, yoke over your shoulders, hands steadying the swaying buckets until you reach the porch and can dump them into Cambro coolers to take into the house. And you should remember to strain the water first, to avoid larger conifer needles, or leaves, or a spindly water insect. There is no easy flush, no turning of a faucet, no conveniences in the way most Americans think of them. No microwave or computer or furnace or chainsaw or music or phone or quick flip of a light switch. No ways to distract yourself from what's in your own head. It's a risk, moving to Barra, where Ian and I are suddenly isolated and faced with the daily work of self-sufficiency. But the alternative, to me, looks impossibly dark.

•

We're not the first, Ian and I, to wrestle with these issues on this piece of land. Nor the first to find more than one kind of sustenance in it. We're the last in a series of caretakers who've kept up the work at Barra after its creators, Guy and Laura Waterman, left in 2000 after thirty years.

Guy had been a speechwriter for Ford and Nixon, father of three sons, performer of ragtime piano. Himself the son of the head of the National Science Foundation, he'd eloped at eighteen. He met Laura after his first marriage dissolved; he was her instructor at a weekend rock climbing course. Laura, the daughter of Emily Dickinson scholar Thomas H. Johnson, had been working in publishing in New York City. Within a year, they married, began a life of serious climbing, moved from New York to Vermont, and had built the first building of the homestead, which they named Barra, after an island in the Hebrides where

Guy's family had immigrated from. Their story quickly gets complicated: first, in the early 70s, Guy's eldest son, Bill, vanished, last heard from in Alaska, a few years after losing a leg in a train-hopping accident. Then in 1981, his middle son, Johnny, died climbing Denali, possibly a suicide. In the meantime, Guy and Laura had climbed and hiked all over the Northeast, and had built Barra: not just the main house, but also a sugaring shed, extensive wood storage sheds, a timber-framed guesthouse, a shower pagoda by the stream, trails with steps and bridges and water bars. And they'd written huge tomes on the history of northeastern mountains, on hiking and climbing, and some of the very first books on the ethics of wilderness travel. Their life continued like this for three decades. The whole time Guy wrestled with darkness, though he never called it depression. Then in February of 2000, he climbed up New Hampshire's Mt. Lafayette where he let himself die. Laura knew he wanted to do this; it had been planned eighteen months in advance. Guy had helped her get started building a new house in town. Guy's frozen body was carried off the mountain several days later, and the funeral overflowed the East Corinth church, where special speakers had been carted in for people to listen to a recording of Guy hammering out Scott Joplin tunes. Laura left Barra that spring, and the first of the stewards moved to the homestead. Ian and I, in 2003, are the last itinerants before more permanent caretakers take over.

You can't compare one person's depression to another, but I know Barra sustained Guy in ways that another way of life couldn't have, and it's doing the same for me. And I'm beginning to realize this in a new way, since Ian and I will be leaving once sugaring is over, and I'll be faced with another kind of isolation (again, self-imposed): working alone in the New Hampshire backcountry. Really alone, this time, nearly five miles' hike into the White Mountains, without Ian, without visits from Laura, with only the occasional passing hiker. Barra begins to seem even more precious. Just the way there's that magic tenuous realm between 40 and 45 degrees where a tree produces sugar, I'm finding myself in a similarly precariously balanced spot where the yield in my life seems sweeter than it has in a long time. And it wouldn't be so sweet if the winter hadn't been so dark and filled with so much work and if we weren't about to leave.

•

Self-hatred can have a surprising tangibility, a hollowing out of your stomach, a tinny taste in your mouth. You want to squirm away from yourself. But you can't, and that's the thing. At its worst, depression lifts away all emotions but self-loathing and exhaustion and a murky indeterminate sort of sadness, so that you can look at a place or person you love and know you ought to feel something, some small happiness or tickle of love or recognition, but you don't. And then that lurking voice, that bitter taste, squeezes you tighter till you can hardly breathe and keeps whispering "*You* disgust *me*."

I was nine years old when these feelings started—the first time I remember trying to wiggle away from that hateful feeling inside myself. By the time I was sixteen it felt inescapable. That voice only hushed in moments of concentration or exertion. Alcohol didn't work, though I kept believing it would. Sometimes I'd have a month or several of brighter days, where the fog lifted, and the blue sky really looked that color to me. But then that light would seep away and only work—physical work—seemed to still my mind enough and even then, the "*You* disgust *me*" voice was simmering, always there, ready to strangle. On Thanksgiving Day at Barra, I swallowed down my first dose of a depression medication and tried to feel thankful.

Now that we're sugaring in spring Ian talks about my depression as a "funk," as if maybe the word "depression" sounds too permanent, as if I might snap out of it at any moment. He is patient, bemused, angry, hurt, kind. He sees me cry, sees my endless desire for sleep, my fierce and defensive anger, my lack of interest or sometimes even recognition of things I once loved, all encouraged by that voice, that twisting in my stomach, *You're worthless.* He writes me schedules: *Get up. Eat breakfast. Give Ian a hug. Saw and split wood for one hour. Do school work for one hour. Pull weeds for one hour.* We share so much here; we work together, eat together, climb and hike and ski together. We are hardly ever apart. But he can't share this. I can tell that he doesn't know what to do, and it scares him. And even though I can see this, and see that the parts of me he fell in love with are getting buried, I can't change. There's a gap widening between us: he moves fast and never gets tired. I'm moving slower and slower, conserving energy with every step because I never know when I'll need it next. I get tired walking up the hill from the garden to the house, yet our shared life has been built around long and difficult and sometimes foolhardy wilderness trips. Though we still make these trips, Barra keeps us closer to home, and I'm increasingly frustrated by a body and mind that won't cooperate: that little voice hissing *You're too slow, you can't climb that*, and a sort of numbing tiredness. Some days, I huddle up inside myself, don't want to talk. Some days I sleep every moment I'm not doing the chores I have to do. Something gets me out of bed for those. Something deep inside, instinctual, wants me to keep going, even if my body and mind resist the whole way.

•

Ian and I have been together a little over a year when we move to Barra. We met working at one of the Appalachian Mountain Club's huts on the southern shoulder of New Hampshire's Mt. Washington. And then, for the rest of the summer, we were always together. We went sledding in the June snow on Washington until the wind ripped our sled into Oakes Gulf. We hiked at night, ten or fifteen miles sometimes, to see the stars. We got caught in thunderstorms. We drank beer at nine in the morning to celebrate rare sunny days. We read aloud to each other. We took naps. We didn't intend to fall in love, but we did anyway. It was the brightest time I'd had in years. And then it ended. I entered my first year of college at Dartmouth, while Ian finished his last semester in Boston and then moved to northern New Hampshire. The geographic distance between us seemed untenable, but more than that, I was being swallowed up again. Straight up: I hated school. Or maybe my depression was what made it so terrifying, so suffocating. But it was Dartmouth that brought us to Barra in the end: a professor mentioned a field trip to Guy and Laura Waterman's homestead as part of her Gender and the Environment class, and something electric thrummed through me. It was the spring term of my freshman year—after some hard bargaining, I'd agreed to stay in school a year to appease my anxious parents, though I'd been pushing the idea of quitting for months by that point—and suddenly a light appeared when the professor said Laura was searching for a caretaker of the place, now under the auspices of early back-to-the-landers Helen and Scott Nearing's Good Life Center. A few phone calls later, Ian and I were at Barra, huddling under Laura's umbrella in the clearing. The white pines rose straight and tall, the house sank in against the hill. It was quiet and misty. I wanted it more than anything.

So we moved to Barra. Now we live here rent-free, in exchange for maintaining the garden, working up the wood, sugaring. We can eat all we want from the garden. Laura tells us what needs to be done, and we do it and she helps.

•

At Barra, I've had these electrifying dreams, vividly colored, night after night, as if I can only come alive in sleep. When I wake up it's a disappointment, the way it feels to get out of a warm bed into a frosty house, as if I'm pulling myself from something living and bright into something cold and still. But even so, I pull. And the reason I pull is the work. It's there even if I don't want to do it or don't feel like it or don't think I can. In the deepest parts of the winter, there's a stretch of a few days where I simply can't. It's the worst I've felt for a long time.

The work of Barra has slowed down now that the garden and wood are harvested, and I miss the time-driven intensity of needing to complete a chore before the first frost or a staying snow. Our daily chores are many: fetching water, splitting and sawing wood for the house, taking out the compost and grey water, building fires in the stoves and cooking. These help and I know that Ian needs me to do my share. But I need something all consuming, something that requires vigilance and responsibility, and sugaring arrives just in time.

Maple sugaring works like this: You tap the trees. It's a one-time deal. Then the routine begins. You collect the sap, slogging or slipping through the woods depending on the snow and ice, sometimes once a day, sometimes more or not at all depending on the temperature and the particular tree. Then you dump the collection buckets into the big evaporator; you need just an inch or two to start the fire and boiling. You have to pay close attention here. The evaporator can boil down and the sap scorch if you aren't adding more liquid or the fire gets too hot. Physics are paramount: the evaporator is separated by baffles into three connected parts, and the difference in viscosity between syrup and sap forces the syrup into the last baffled section, where it can be drawn off for finishing. So you're always watching, always peering into the pan, poking at the roiling liquid with a spoon, watching it get darker and darker as the sugar content shifts and the water steams away. Then, when you draw off the almost-syrup, it goes into an old aluminum pot, so crusted over with burnt sugar that it's black, textured like lava. Then you boil some more, stirring often, until the thickness is just right. Other operations might use a thermometer, but we use the old spoon test: when you can get two beads consistently to drip from a metal spoon, you can go ahead and can the stuff. And this whole time you can smell the syrup, smell it getting darker and sweeter. Even when you are pulling four-foot sections from the cords of wood in the shed—because there's always more wood to saw and split into the right size for the fires—you can smell it. Wood smoke and something sweeter underneath. The sugar-smoke stays in your clothes as you walk back to the house, shuffling in big Sorels or snowshoes, stiff with cold and fatigue in the late afternoon, carrying the glass jars of the day's work.

So that's what happens once the sap has left the tree. But what happens inside a maple, come spring, is even more complex and sublime. First, in the late summer and fall, the tree stops growing. It doesn't put energy into leaves anymore, but instead excess starch from photosynthesis gets stored in the tree's sapwood. When the wood of the tree starts warming up with spring sunlight, there's a magical sort of tipping point: the cells in the sapwood change from starch into sugar, right around 40 degrees Fahrenheit. At roughly 45 degrees, the cells' enzymes stop functioning and there's no more sugar, just starch again. It's a narrow window, five degrees worth of sun and shadow, snowmelt and late freezes. You might not even get a whole day of sugar; the tree can shift back into starch with a fluctuation of a degree or two, and the sap won't flow. So you just wait. And then, again, the rising temperature will build up pressure in the trees, and the sap will flow again, and then, if you've drilled a tiny hole into a maple trunk, and added a spile to funnel the sap, and hung a bucket from the spile, then the severed wood fibers inside the tree will drip their sap, and you've got the very beginnings of maple syrup. The *very* beginnings: forty gallons of sap will make roughly one gallon of syrup.

There's an amazing science behind all this, a remarkable kind of physics. The rise in air temperature creates positive pressure, forcing the sap out of the tree through its tap hole. And then when the temperature dips lower, negative pressure, a sort of suction, draws water into the tree through the roots while the sap drip stops. The tree replenishes itself, creating more sap for the next warm spell. Carbon dioxide and osmotic pressure create the force that pushes the sap out, though really it feels like spring itself. You can't have all warm days or all cold ones: the change in temperature over the month to six-week sugaring season is necessary. And none of it's possible without the long months of winter beforehand. Maybe that's what's happening for me, something rising, waking up a little, the way Laura crowed "The trees are waking up" when we first set out with our hand drill and spiles. The sun shines more and from higher up in the sky; the light is clearer and warmer. I feel necessary to spring's arrival, as if sugaring itself is ushering in the season and, with it, some return of my own self-worth. I'm collecting moments—the rustle of snowflakes landing on my jacket, the refracted sparkle of the icicles on the blueberry bushes, sliding off the sugar shed roof with Ian and Laura after a storm, smelling the smoky caramel of the boiling syrup. These moments build into a sort of quiet contentment: not happiness, exactly, but a precarious state where the voice of depression can't speak quite as loudly. I don't know what happened for Guy Waterman, if he also had these moments of startling beauty combined with the need to build and sustain the world of Barra, if both kept him alive until the weight of everything else, the volume of that depression voice, began to submerge them. To think of him defeating the voice gives me hope. To imagine him succumbing terrifies me.

•

Laura knows each tree by name. Guy and Laura tapped over 100 of them, but this year we tap only half that. As March begins, we watch the weather, waiting for the right combination of warm and cold. We're ready: we've shoveled out the drifts of snow in the sugar shed, a tenth of a mile's walk from the house. We've dug out the fireplaces and heaved twelve inches of compacted snow off the shed roof. We've banged bits of dead leaves and cobwebs out of the sap pails, located the spiles in the cellar, and toted over a couple saws and splitting mauls to the sugar bush woodshed. We're just waiting on spring. Then it comes, one of those glittery surprising early March days, the sun warmer than we've felt in months. And then another. And then Laura leads Ian and me into the sugar bush with a hand drill and a hammer and pockets stuffed with spiles. Each of us carries a green index card with the names of the fifty trees we'll be tapping. As we tromp our way through the sugar bush to each tree, I keep my card clutched in my mittened hand, trying to memorize their locations: here is Annapurna, here is D'Artagnan, here is Voltaire and Mad Dog, King Lear, Lady Walshingham, Ozymandias, all named by Guy and Laura. Once we're collecting sap from the buckets, we'll measure the amount each tree produces each time we visit the tree and note it on the index card, and then add the day's haul on a large chart at the sugar shed. I keep a chewed-up pencil behind my ear.

Laura shows us to each tree, reminds us of its name, if it runs early or late, slow or fast, and one of us drills into the trunk, looking for a good spot on the south or east-facing side of the tree. Laura is patient in her explaining, tiny and blue-eyed. She loves sugaring, and she loves these trees.

We can see some of the healed-over tapholes of years past; they look like bellybuttons in the tree bark. Some are down by our knees—years where the snow depth was low—and some are almost chest-height. It's astonishing to think that the twenty-eight inches of snow we're standing on will eventually melt; it's felt like winter for a long time. So we drill into the bark, shedding yellow curls of wood into the snow at the base of the tree, and then we fit an aluminum spile into the hole. We've taken turns lugging a stack of the pails to hang from the spiles. A friend of Laura and Guy's had passed them on after switching to pipeline, and they are painted a minty green, with gently peaked lids so the snow and rain and leafs will slide off and not collect with the sap. It's exciting, this drilling. Something is coming. I've taken the next eight months away from Dartmouth and this feels freeing, the constant weight of my unhappiness at school lifted for a time. And it's companionable to work together with Ian and Laura, to be learning a new skill.

To collect the sap, we follow the snowshoe-packed warren of trails radiating out from the sugar shed, galvanized metal collecting pails in each hand. Laura, 63 and nearing a double knee replacement, uses a wooden yoke that fits across her shoulders. We desperately try to avoid sloshing out even the tiniest bit of sap. Ian and I have had months of practice—it's the same gliding-step technique to get our drinking water from the stream. Some days there's fresh snow, and we use snowshoes. Sometimes, we can tromp our way along the packed paths just in boots, which works as long as you don't stumble off into the deep snow beyond. And as the weeks go by, the paths become the last lines of white in the woods; the hard-packed snow the last to melt. This is physically tiring work: up and down the hilly paths, lifting heavy buckets, using the crosscut to saw up logs as wide around as a dinner plate. It helps, being worn out at the end of the day, makes my mind go quieter.

Because the sugaring season is so short, six weeks at the very most, we have to take advantage of every day the sap runs. Gone are our days of climbing and skiing away from Barra. This is a full-time job. So in the mornings, as if we're traveling far from home, we stuff extra layers and water bottles and lunch into our packs, pull on wool pants and down jackets. We'll be gone for hours, though only a few minutes' walk away from the house. There's that sense of necessity again, that our work is needed: syrup for ourselves, for Laura, for the caretakers who will move in just a few weeks from now. Though I hate to think of that, having to leave. Something crumples inside me.

•

The sugar shed itself is two buildings in an L-shape, hunkered low on a little domed spot in the middle of the sugar bush, a tenth of a mile from the house. It's really a shed, a timber-framed lean-to attached to a big, open-sided storage area, big enough for four cords of cut wood and a sawhorse for splitting and sawing. Guy and Laura established The Hall of Fame, awards distributed each year on wooden plaques and nailed up in the lean-to: Tree of the Year (usually Mad Dog), Tree of the Decade (mostly Mad Dog), Tree of the Century (Mad Dog again). Guy's presence is everywhere here; in the names of the trees, in the exacting index card system, in the neat black-Sharpie handwriting on our measuring sticks. He's been dead just three years this past February. I think often about what it would have been like to meet him, and how Ian and I are such a small part of the history of this place. Barra will leave a longer impression on us than we will on it.

In the inner corner of the shed's L is where we make the syrup. There are two fire pits, one taller and longer, one shorter and squatter, both made from rocks mortared together with cement. The evaporator with its crusty, burned-sugar edges tops the taller fire pit, which can be fed from both sides; logs up to two feet can be shoved in. If the fire burns hot enough and you cover the coals before heading home for the night, with a little stir in the ash you can get a good blaze started up again the next morning. But not always. That's my job, since I'm the first person to the sugar shed most mornings. I've lit a lot of fires at Barra: in the woodstove we use for heating the house, in the woodstove we use for cooking, in the brick oven outside we used for baking in warmer days. I can light a fire in my sleep now. I'm always singed, my jacket sleeves pocked with burns, my hands grimy with soot. On the lower fire, there's a grate like on a campground grill, and two pots with blackened sugar-smoked outsides. That's where the sap-syrup goes when it's boiled its way to a certain consistency. You turn a little nozzle at the far end of the evaporator and the almost-syrup gushes into the bucket. Then you boil it some more in one of the blackened pots.

If you look out from the cozy nook of the L, you see the slant of the hill and the tall trees, seventy, eighty feet tall, the height of a three- or four-story building, and the blue shadows from the trees that lean down or up the hill depending on the time of day. There's undergrowth, skinny beeches with transparent brown leaves still on their branches, and maples growing up into the next generation of sugaring. But these are managed woods, carefully harvested each fall for firewood, and it shows. Through the trees, splotched with green and gray lichen, you can see the mint-colored buckets with their silver or sometimes snow-covered caps, reminding you of your work. I watch these stripy shadows in the mornings and at midday and in the late afternoon, when the hillside gets dim and the sky smudgy with color. The light stays so much longer now, hours more, than it did in the deepest part of the winter. It feels glorious. These mornings when I walk over to the sugar bush, it's cold, the kind of cold where your nose runs and your hands ache so that you have to whip them in the air to warm up, so that any delicate endeavor —unbuckling a snowshoe, writing with a pencil—requires some fumbling. The trees' buckets each have an icy disc in the bottom from the sap that dripped after we stopped collecting the night before. I have to wait for them to melt. I'm good at being cold, and anyway, hard work warms you up. Five minutes of whaling on a piece of wood and you can break a sweat. And it's surprising how warm 40-some degrees can feel with some sun. Some days, though, we're boiling while snow flings itself sideways, squinting into the finishing pots while the wind gusts the flames up against our legs. The fires get hot enough so that the tiny metal rivets on my Carhartts burn me in little moons, even through my long underwear, while the rest of me shivers.

•

Laura introduces us to syrup tea. She splurges and buys us a quart of half and half from the store, which we splash into a mug of the boiling sap and top off with a packet of black tea. It's a deadly drink; it makes your teeth ache and your pulse zing. We drink it every day. We make toasted cheese sandwiches on the grill. These can be dipped in syrup too. Hot dogs can be boiled in the evaporator but only Ian will eat those. We wrap vegetables from the root cellar—beets, carrots, heads of garlic—in foil and tuck them in the coals. We carry over little glass jars of salt and pepper from the house and leave them there. It feels a little like a party, a chilly picnic, every time we stand under the eave of the lean-to and eat our lunches. A chance to uncurl our frozen hands and watch the fire and talk about books or climbing or the day's highest sap producer. We dip our fingers in the sap-syrup to taste it. We look for shapes in the billowing steam of the evaporator, like watching the clouds.

Though there's more brightness in my day-to-day life, it doesn't take much to sink into something dark, the way you can slip-slide blithely down a packed path until you fall into the deep snow and then have to decide whether to lie there in cold, damp defeat or to flounder yourself out. I always flounder myself out. Eventually. So far. Some days I wake up with self-loathing needling at me before I even get out of bed, *Why bother, you're a waste*, or maybe I get the splitting maul stuck in a chunk of hop hornbeam, *You're incompetent, you're weak*. Sometimes I'll watch Ian carving beautiful telemark turns, lit up by the moon, between the fruit trees on the hill out the east window and I'm so tired and locked inside my own head that I can't bear to put on my skis and join him, and the voice doesn't say anything, it just squeezes till I'm breathless. It's that five-degree difference between sap and stasis in a tree. A few degrees one way or another.

Other than Ian, my parents, one professor, and doctors, I haven't told anyone about my depression. How do you talk about it, anyway? How do you say it? I have depression, I'm depressed, I suffer from depression. I don't like any of them, and I'm not good at talking about what I feel even when I feel good. Ian has to wheedle it out of me: How do you feel today? I dunno. Not good? Yeah. Can I do anything? No. Those conversations never really go anywhere. But it comes up, finally, with Laura, one day while she and I are taking turns sawing and splitting wood and stirring the evaporator. She brings it up after reading an essay I'd written for a class at Dartmouth. I didn't know, she says, and I say Yeah, I don't really talk about it. And she says Guy didn't either, and then we both go back to work. Later, when I'm standing over the finishing syrup, steam and sticky golden foam rising up around my stirring spoon, I tell her that if it hadn't been for Barra, I would have dropped out of college, and I'm not sure what else. I want her to know what Barra has meant to me, even though I think she already does. Work is medicine, that's what I'm figuring out. Laura knows this: her shared life at Barra with Guy is proof of that.

•

Syrup held up to the light is magnificent. It looks alive, glowing. Thicker than water, but not as thick as honey. We use last year's yield to sweeten our bread and cookies and jams, to pour on pancakes and oatmeal and winter squash, to stir up with canned rhubarb. It's the only sugar we have. It's

33

magic to watch it darken as it boils down: clear to pale gold to wheat-colored to something coppery and then roiling and rich, like a big Southern river, cloudy with air bubbles. When those bubbles settle, you strain the liquid through a sieve into a Mason jar, and watch the color deepen. Syrup comes in grades, from the lightest Fancy through Grade B. Here at Barra, the syrup is dark and weighty. Grade D, we joke, and agree that it tastes best this way.

Part of what is making me feel more alert, alive to the world, is the discovery, the wonder of this process. This sap, this science! This syrup! This miracle! It's humbling, what happens in the spring, astonishing what rises to life inside a maple tree. I can recognize everything that is beautiful and good, see it for what it is, and these things—the jars of syrup, the stacked cord wood, Ian's face, Laura's laugh— are made better because I had to work so hard to see them, to keep pulling the cloudiness away from my sight. Here, we don't take syrup for granted; we're not buying it off the shelf. We know exactly what's gone into it—our time and frozen fingers and burned sleeves and sore muscles—and that's true of my life. I have to work hard for it, fight for it, drown that *You're worthless* voice with the whirr of a bow saw and the crunch of boots on an icy snow crust.

It's a lot for two people to sustain, when one person is uncontrollably sad, so unreachable so much of the time. But Ian tells me one afternoon that I'm more myself, and that means a lot to me. I've worked hard for that these last months. I'm also discovering that it's the smallest things I can lose myself in. Find myself in. A task that's concrete, tangible. To just stir the steaming syrup, watch the wooden handle of the spoon go around and around in the pot. To just saw, listening to the squeak of metal in cold wood. To see the fire blazing through the trees and the snow when I walk back with full buckets, and to think, I built that. These can keep you anchored to something human when you've become so unmoored, when you've come to the end of yourself and your partner and your family and friends and medication and you don't have anything higher, as I didn't then, to turn to.

●

As sugaring winds down and new miracles of grass and robins and branches knotted with buds appear, I don't feel the incessant fear of leaving. Instead, there's a sense of mourning, balanced by peace and satisfaction. I will never come back to Barra in the same way, or know these trees as intimately. I will no longer have these necessary chores. Something in me grieves not just the loss of Barra but knowing that only now I'm waking up and wondering what I have missed these last months, so often locked inside my own head and the rigid routines of physical labor. Can't I do it over again, have it back? Be kinder and more awake? Live without that constant voice of *despair, despair, despair?* But really I know that Barra had to be what it had to be. That its beauty and its work kept me going in a particular time in a particular way. There's no going back now, but maybe I can carry something of Barra with me. Because I'm also learning that what gives me the most peace costs me the most: the physical exhaustion, the isolation of a homestead or the backcountry. Places that sometimes terrify me, where my ability to survive depends on my ability to do the work.

The temperatures are rising into the fifties now.

On the day we hike out of Barra in mid-April, I wear a t-shirt. I take a couple jars of syrup with me as if I could bottle up the goodness of that last month there, the first tastes of sun and sweetness. What I was only beginning to understand then, I know well enough now. That some seasons are sweet, and some are cold and bitter. But they cycle through again. A sugaring season can be slow for two weeks, then run like mad for the next three. Because that's what they are: seasons. They come and go; fluctuate within themselves. I didn't know, at Barra, that the saddest and most terrifying days were yet to come. Nor did I know that the same would be true about the most beautiful ones. The maples don't know either what each season will bring; they just keep growing, and wait.

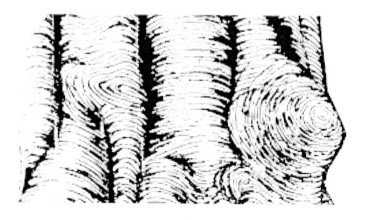

THAT WINTER
SARAH BATES

I used to think about stars dying. I'd lie awake and imagine white specks exploding into black, stellar winds pushing their twinkle into tiny windows. Then nothing. I was twenty-two and the closest thing to God was the closest thing I could see from the shores of Lake Superior.

Some days the deep lake would hang above my bed like dead figs stuck together. Some days the deep lake was the only thing I saw before the sky went black.

For weeks, I stayed up for Northern Lights. I set my alarm to the sky and waited for it to go green. For weeks, I wanted to believe in unfinished maps. For weeks, I walked the shoreline alone believing the front yard's moss would weep for thirty years.

930 miles North of the Japanese cherry tree my dad planted when I was five is 3,000 miles of granite gneiss. Here, I watch strangers search through smooth rocks for red-brown. I watch strangers with their heads bowed for hours until the snow starts to fall. Here, on top green glass and agate, I waited.

I waited for his shoulders to weaken, waited for water to seek water. I waited for needle to reach satin, scattered pores exchanging gas for air. Here I waited for five-petalled flowers to sour.

I started measuring time with trees. I can't tell you what this had to do with dying stars, with planetary nebulae lit up for 10,000 years, or the central star cooling, or rings of dust tracing where the new stars form. I only remember counting leaves until they became soft. I'd watch white pine scatter, then scraps of red in between white. I'd watch colors brighten, dull. Here was something like an animal running around death. The last week of September, I stared so long honeysuckle became mountain maple.

The problem with pain is the sun going flat. Finding out there is a butterfly that only lives for five days. The problem with pain is I was standing on the shores of flickered gneiss when I realized it was the daisies I'd pulled.

When I was little, I told you that of all the trees on our way to the river, I'd be a birch. I decided this with my right index finger, how it followed a stream of warm sap down the tree's golden bark. Looking up, its yellow leaves were the only things I could see on top of daylight. Looking up, how I believed in rain falling to feed flowers. How I dreamed the trees would fall asleep to dusty cocoons, caterpillars circling dark clouds, different ways than sleeping stars, than my father and me.

In the Upper Peninsula of Michigan, half a year's winter. When I moved here, it was mid-July and 55 degrees. Walking the lake that morning, I hated the pure air and its chill. *But look at all the flowers*, you said, as if to change my mind. You were leaving the next morning so I smiled at placed petunias and painted brick as if you had.

But you couldn't. In a couple months, the bright greens and red-orange that lined the highway would be dead and dry and gone. I wanted mountains again, to be home on riverbanks standing under the yellow birch's shade. The same yellow birch you told me God put there one Saturday morning. When you said this, the smallest star shook. When you said this, a language of birds.

For months, it stopped raining. For months, I stopped thinking about the light pink of cherry blossoms, how they piled themselves on top half broken blue jays every spring, and of God.

Gaston Bachelard says we comfort ourselves by living memories of protection. That something closed must retain our memories while leaving their original value as images. And when the image is new, the world is new. Unlike my father, Bachelard liked to hide in the slump of ravines. I imagine it was thick wood that kept him from sad cities, the sound of dying stars.

And so, winter came. I remember telling the joke about loneliness. The walk to willowy bodies where I'd laugh just to weep. There are too many pines, I wrote one morning in a journal you'd sent. There were bible verses all over its front pages, how you wanted me to remember words like wind and bones.

For months, I listened to the hardness of water. For months, all I could hear was Andromeda asking shorelines for ore.

I thought if I could put it all down, I would find what I wanted in the shadows of freezing sap.

I thought then, I might fall asleep to the stars putting the sky back together. If I kept reaching for the yellow birch's limbs, one morning I'd wake to a face in the trees.

In 1852, miners stumbled across a grove of giant trees in

Northern California's Calaveras County. Word of the tall trees spread east to San Francisco and it was George Gale who first rode out to see the giants. Among the 92 sequoias in the 160-acre valley, Gale came across what he thought to be a cedar, a tree measuring 321-feet high and 92-feet around, she was perfectly symmetrical. *Mother of the Forest*, Gale named her one morning under altostratus. Inside his body, the soft tissue where his hands had opened the fox's chest, as he named her.

This was the age of freak shows. Barnum nights full of speculators and gold. In the 1850s people circled the tallest trees reading newspapers, foreign fingerprints grinding on fallen acorns. Gale saw the Mother of the Forest and sensed a commercial opportunity, shards of crimson meant for Vaudeville.

And so came exploding stars, falling asleep to things dying, things washed away. I started to imagine my life ending, and all the strangers stopping with arms full of rocks to watch my knees stare out of me. *Every loneliness dies here*, I'd say until I fell asleep.

Ruaan Kellerman has written a logical theory of trees. He says trees occur naturally in mathematical settings with their paths representing different histories. He believes that every tree is a forest, and every forest is a union of trees. I read this to you in between Christmas and the new year. I want an answer to my loneliness, to give the animal a name. *For every burning star, eight elms dropping. For every well-rounded tree there is an ordered path...*

You tell me how they talk to one another, how one came down in October and no one could cross the river for weeks. That winter, you don't remember the time I was a birch.

Another morning I wake to the sky still dark and a line from Maggie Nelson's *The Argonauts*, *because nothing you say can fuck up the space for God.* Because nothing I said could make the moss empty sidewalks, because that winter there wasn't any room in the house for three hundred nights.

Because I waited like a field of statues.

I walk through the forest's sassafras and frozen gale and find a spot on the ice where there used to be sand. Into the waves, I drop down earlier parts of the year when I listened to God standing under Virginia dogwood. Into the waves, I ask if the map is still unfinished.

There has to be a way through the woods, I wrote underneath Psalm 37:4. *Delight yourself in the Lord and He will give you the desires of your heart,* I filled in with blue ink just in case there was somewhere my life existed. I miss the rain, I wrote on the page's bottom left corner. I was halfway through the forest when the sun picked what was left of a hemlock. That morning I sat on the old hemlock's stump and said nothing.

Every morning for months, I'd watch the kids next door play underneath the silent pine and fill bright orange buckets to make snowmen. They'd play through winter's sun cup and firn, and I couldn't remember the last time I felt someone's hot hand behind me. The tallest snowman was still there in April when I used to plant daisies in the front yard.

It took three weeks and five men to cut through the tree's

2,000 year-old trunk. Even after she was sawed through completely, the tree remained upright. For twenty-five days, men forced wedges into the cut with hammers and sledges, her trunk smashed by a nearby battering ram. For twenty-five days, the Mother of the Forest stood still. For twenty-five days, she continued her song to monkey flowers and Abe.

I held onto Bachelard as the snow fell, "a creature that hides and withdraws into its shell is preparing a way out." I held onto seasons changing, how summer would come and I'd leave for fields of frozen buffalo.

Every morning I worried I'd messed up the map coming here. My image was a fifteen-foot pine with needles for a floor. Moss floor taken up by three feet of snow and floating birch.

Three months before moving to Michigan, I went home to the river and all its trail. I couldn't remember it ever being that green. It was morning when you asked me to pull weeds from the front yard's flower bed. You can barely make out the spots curling the top of its dying limbs. That morning I watched the smallest tree shake off its top layer and shrink.

Some say that the yellow birch is the most important of its kind. A species of lower elevations, it's a slow-growing, long lived tree. A single trunk with yellow-bronze bark, it is best solitary, when it can develop its broad, open shape.

Still I'd listen to the others, "if we remain at the heart of the image under consideration... by staying in the motionless of its shell, the creature is preparing temporal explosions, not to say whirlwinds, of being."

The yellow birch is meant to be alone, I would write over and over until it was true.

For months, I tried vanishing into the outline of pine. I'd reach the water's edge and be glad no one was there to watch. Slowly, and then all at once, I sat under the soft, simple leaves and stopped talking to God. I'd tell the branches next door about the elbows of black-eyed susans instead.

How they'd line the riverbank's edge just as the gravel began.

It wasn't until strong winds, the dead of night, that the giant tree finally began her groan and sway. Sounds of the crash carried fifteen miles away to a mining camp, the Mother of the Forest burying herself twelve feet deep into creek bed while a family of stellar jays and a junco watched.

Gale's men stripped most of the tree's bark, some parts of her two-feet thick. His plan was to piece the tree back together for display. The tree was so immense and stored enough water that five years passed before its leaves turned brown and died. Once reassembled, she stood fifty feet high, thirty feet in diameter, and ninety feet around, a piano was placed in the middle of her.

The junco was dead. Only two of the jays surviving.

For years, guests danced to the sounds of rotting bark. For years, someone else's lyric sunk into her skin. In December 1866, all that was leftover was lost to a fire.

But when I tell you I hated it here, I don't mean the abandoned boats falling apart, the sound of the ice cracking. I hated my loneliness. I hated the frozen lilac outside my kitchen window. I hated how my knees stared out of me at 2 a.m. I hated the trees for watching.

There were so many stars, and all I could think about was Andromeda's branches falling into the deep lake with all their collected rocks. 40 degrees down, one hour to the right, I'd watch the Chained Lady spill across November's skin.

Gertrude Stein says anybody is as their land and air is. For months, I was iron. For months, I was the maple. The sky. Thin circling lines in the agate. For months, it was winter.

No one ever told me how loss felt godless. This is what I say to you when you ask if I've been praying. No one ever told me how the trees would stop explaining and I'd be standing by the deep lake alone.

That summer I left the shores of granite gneiss for taller trees. I wanted to stand beneath time, I wanted to drive across seasons, and forget. I pressed my hand against the window while it rained and asked cities I'd pass to explain. Stein would have named this season first.

Your joy is your sorrow unmasked, I read to black hills and herds of prairie dogs, missed trains, and thaw. I'd traded in Bachelard for Gibran. Staring at Lincoln's chin, *the deeper that sorrow carves into your being, the more joy you can contain.*

For days, I felt my life exploding in stone, my sorrow described underneath mountains of pine.

The first time I drove through redwoods, there was still snow on the ground. My feet got cold and I thought about the strangers digging for rocks. I thought about the silver walls of my kitchen sink and that sad February. The first time I drove through the tallest trees, I thought about God and the junco that watched her fall to the forest floor.

2,363 miles from the shores of Lake Superior, I watched rain skim the top of trees, I watched rain hit my right index finger and then leave.

Standing under the Mother of the Forest, I saw my life in fire-blackened bark. I saw marks made when her skin was cut away, a dead tree 100 feet tall still standing. I saw someone else's life peeled into piano.

I forgave myself when the blues went white, when I realized it was the daisies I'd pulled.

The sky exploding slowly. Slow enough for the smallest galaxies to collide, tidal tails of long, thin stars forming above birch. Slow enough for blood-root to reach sun, slow enough for Orion to notice the red-orange fuzz, growing like a fox hole, just below his hip.

TREE EATER
STEVEN CHURCH

If Joyce Kilmer were alive he would say: "I think that I shall never see / a man who eats a lovely tree" as Jay Gwaltney eats an 11-ft-tall birch sapling. He ate branches, leaves and the 4.7-in.-diameter trunk over a period of 89 hours to win $10,000 as first prize in a WKQX-Chicago radio station contest called "What's the Most Outrageous Thing You Would Do?" As he finished he said, about the taste, "as far as trees go, it's not bad" (Guinness Book of World Records 1982, 505).

The picture in my 1982 edition is black-and-white, so it's difficult to tell the full truth of this moment. But I suspect that young Jay Gwaltney wears a powder blue tuxedo, white shirt, and matching blue bow tie—something his mother helped him pick out from the JCPenney catalog.

I want to believe Jay was a lot like me. I see his yellow rose corsage, the bouquet of roses on the table. He is seated in a metal chair with vinyl padding. He's tall and broad-shouldered, maybe an oversize boy with obsessions and compulsions that set him apart from the other kids.

On the table sits a side plate with a saucer and spoon—maybe filled with some thin soup, a salty chicken or beef broth, something to wash down the wood. There is a coffee cup and a large, empty dinner plate. Jay's blond hair shines in the camera flash. A banner hangs behind him on the wall, the only visible word, "Chicago."

In his right hand he holds a sprig of birch sprouting seven or eight leaves. With his left hand he pulls at one of the leaf stems. He is ready. He does not look at the camera.

He has made his decision. He stares down at his hands, eyeing the last remnant of his eleven-foot dinner sapling, perhaps wondering if it is worth the ten thousand dollars. It must have taken some time, some real commitment. He couldn't have done it all at this table in the picture, not wearing that pretty powder blue suit the whole time.

•

I imagine Jay's commitment, his own obsession. He's in the garage of his parents' home using Dad's power tools to grind the sapling down to sawdust. He sees a new image of himself reflected in the eyes of others, a heroic image, and he doesn't care about what they might whisper.

He's shoveling handfuls of birch shavings into his mouth, washing them down with buttermilk. His mother bakes sawdust pies with graham-cracker crusts. She mixes sawdust into milk shakes. She makes salads from the leaves and drenches them in dressing. His father cheers him on from the sofa. They'll do anything for their baby boy, anything to help him succeed, anything to get him out of the basement, and I'd bet Jay is dreaming of a Camaro or a catamaran, a ski trip to Aspen, a motorcycle, or a camper truck with a propane heater.

I doubt that he, like his mother, is dreaming of college or investments in the stock market. But it could be more than the ten thousand dollars. Maybe he knew Guinness was watching all along. Maybe he knew I was watching. I suspect Jay understood the immortality of the page, the legacy of living in a book so full of heroes and freaks. He could've been a lot like me, a misfit boy striving for identity in strange ways. Or maybe he just liked the taste of wood.

•

If I could find Jay Gwaltney today, I'd ask why he chose the birch tree. Was it the paper-like quality of the bark, the soft wood? Did his Norwegian grandfather tell him stories of the Old Country and how they used to drink birch tea? Did he consider soft pine or ruddy dogwood, hard oak or red maple with its fire leaves?

I'd ask him if he loved the Guinness Books too, if he'd seen the pictures of Shridhar Chillal and Michael Barban, maybe Benny and Billy McCrary. I'd ask how he made the step that I couldn't—from voyeur to participant, from off-the-page to on-the-page. How did he turn chance into choice? I'd like to see the moment he heard about the contest on the radio, that DJ's voice surfacing from the noise, and how it came to Jay as if it were a voice from God. I wonder what made him think that he could eat a tree, an eleven-foot tree, and that this would be enough for the rest of his life.

I think a Guinness World Record would be enough for me. I think I'd be proud of my accomplishments if I were Jay Gwaltney. But perhaps he never chose this path. Perhaps it was some emptiness inside he was trying to fill. Perhaps he graduated to eating forty-foot trees, redwoods, railroad ties, or untreated telephone poles. Perhaps eating wood pulp was all he knew, the only fulfillment he had.

Jay might have spent his prize money on a bungalow in the old part of town, where the cottonwoods towered overhead, and bought a wood-chipper right off the bat. When he worked in the yard, he might've put a pinch of sawdust between his cheek and gum.

He'd never fit into the neighborhood—no matter how

hard he tried—standing out there in his Carhartt overalls and his safety goggles, feeding everything into that damn wood chipper. He'd frighten the children and old ladies who stopped to watch, because now Jay's yard must be naked and brown, emptied of green and punctuated with stumps. He has worried the trees down to nothing. The neighbors point at annual rings, the shadow arcs of lost time, lost history.

He has planted a new grove of birch, and he says he's trying to cut back, but they are still angry about neighborhood character and the loss of shade. They're angry because their own children have begun to eat strange things too—twigs and paper, nuts and washers, entire boxes of Hot Tamales cinnamon candy, and several number-2 pencils. They're angry because Jay has a way of getting under your skin. Shridhar Chillal too. Michael Barban, Benny, Billy, and the others. He just follows different rules, different rhythms than everyone else.

If Jay Gwaltney were my neighbor, I'd join him for a pinch of sawdust on his porch. I might ask him to autograph my Guinness Book. I might ask him about commitment and obsession. I'd let him hold my son on his lap, and we could just sit and talk about nothing at all. I might do anything I could to help him fit in with the normal neighbors.

STUDY WITH CREPE MYRTLE
LIA PURPURA

Say *"Once there was a crape myrtle tree . . ."* and right off, it's a tale, a story with shape, and it moves toward an end.

I know there are other ways of saying, like:

"What the hell *happened* at that moment . . .?"

"Let me never . . ."

"Still Life With Thing Indifferent To Me"

"To You Who Do Not Need My Eye to Complete You."

I've racked up here, as approaches go: inquiry, petition, title, dedication.

But I'm thinking that a simple letter (lost form, so little used these days) will be best in setting the right atmosphere, in how it leads and wanders, weighs and comes upon thoughts. In the receptivity it assumes: someone settled in a comfortable chair, unsealing the envelope, unfolding the pages, creating a space into which words can seep.

Dear (if I may),

A few weeks ago, walking home with the dog, I took the street off to the side of the college. At the bend is a grand, one-story house, and in its front yard, a spectacular crape myrtle. (The spelling varies: you'll see "crape" and "crepe"—though neither the flowers nor leaves are particularly crinkly or ribbon-like.) A c.m.'s deep pink, firm, hardy blossoms gather in clusters like fat bunches of grapes held upright. (Being from New York, too far north for c.m.s, they're still new to me, here, in Baltimore.) As is the tradition, the trees are pruned to be bare lower down, though c.m's seem naturally inclined this way, and then encouraged to fill out up top. Maybe you know that sketch by Picasso, "Hands Holding Flowers," popular in the 60s as an emblem of peace?—that bouquet-in-fist captures exactly the angle of flare on a c.m. The trunks remind me of the brown arms of a girl, sleeveless in summer. But none of these images came to me then.

What filled the space of a pause so long?

I should've been able to think *something*—a relief to say "what a beauty" or even stop short with an *Oh* of surprise. But it would not come forth as a specimen. ("It" most surely isn't right at all.) And that was the very immediate problem: the tree could not be *called* anything, and resisted a name. Not "crape myrtle." Not even "Tree." The simplest, singular sounds weren't working. I stopped and looked and heard just my own breathing. And being reduced to standing and breathing produced a wave of something fearsome. Cliffs rose, the air sharpened and chilled between us. In the steepness, I was unshimmed, root-cut, insubstantial as pith. The seal the tree closed around itself was—what? Solitude? Pure being stripped, ungrazed, unsnared? Insistently *here*. While I really wasn't anywhere. I dissolved. The tree in its quiet unspecialized me. To be pinned and bored into, gnawed back to a core, to feel myself going, crumpling, shedding, splintering into something with edge would've helped. But there was the tree. And there I wasn't. Not on a fringe. Not in a web. Unfixed in a sight and in nothing's arms.

I hadn't expected this at all. I hadn't expected anything. Certainly not to be so rattled. I was just out for a walk with my dog.

●

Yesterday, nearly a month after this, I took down from my shelf Martin Buber's *I and Thou* (I knew my encounter would be close to his thinking) and when I opened the book—I haven't since college, the pages were kind of crumbly, and I had to endure my marginalia—it was to a passage, then sentence so absurdly exact, "I contemplate a tree," that I laughed out loud. (The coincidence, I realize, is pretty wild. What it might *mean* is another issue altogether. I simply present it here as fact. And writing of this to *you*—the relief of that!—I can imagine the anxiety I'd feel writing to one who didn't know me at all, who might suspect a convenient fiction, a sleight of hand, or strategy employed to heighten the moment. I am grateful I don't have to defend myself to you.)

Buber writes that while he could have, he did not "accept the tree as a picture or feel its movement: the flowing veins around the sturdy, striving core," he did not "assign to it a species and observe it as an instance with an eye to its construction and its way of life." He did not overcome its "uniqueness and form so rigorously that [he] recognized it only as an expression of the law." He did not "dissolve it into a number, into a pure relation between numbers and eternalize it." The c.m. was (as he says of *his* tree) "no play of my imagination, no aspect of a mood" and "it confronts me bodily . . .." Certain modes of apprehending, or seeing, or contemplating (a taxonimizing of forms, for example), aren't *bad*, Buber says—just that it's not necessary to move through such intervening steps, in order to be in relation to a tree. It's just that *relation* is something different. Not a thing manifest, but a commodious state, disordered even. Not a sense of a hasp worked open—just . . . open. Terribly, amazingly so.

And there was this, too: I felt if I didn't *make* something of the moment—the sight of the tree, those sensations—it would be gone, and the feeling, the fearsomness would evaporate, be erased (I didn't exactly want to keep or stay close to the feel of not-being the tree kindled up in me). My impulse to exert in response to the tree was powerful—and also very fully resisted. So there I was, with the certainty that what I do in the face of moments I can't understand is make something of them. Not fashion a scene. Not "capture in words." More "the mind in the act of finding what will suffice," as Wallace Stevens said, but even that's not exactly right. Whatever it was that happened for me, none of these ways of saying pertained. None of this mattered, as far as I could tell, for the tree.

And right there, the gap opened up (as I said, it's been nearly a month now since I could even approach my initial notes, so mured around was that moment, so unnerved was I by it). It's that seeing-and-making was not sufficient. Not adequate-to. A puny gesture. You know how a gnat will hold on in surprisingly fierce winds? (trying blowing one off your hand and you'll see.) Well, on a wind scale of 1-10, this gnat was caught in a Beaufort 8 ("edges of waves break into spindrift, foam is blown in well-marked streaks; walking against wind becomes very difficult. . ."). That's what the past month felt like whenever I recalled the scene.

How accustomed I am to being emplaced.

The tree's crown wasn't enormous, its height not imposing. Nothing about its blossoms was weird the way orchids in their pouchy seductions beckon, suggest you dip a finger in, or imitate, right out in the open, all the sweet parts we keep covered. To have felt part of a system then, a minor part of the tree's constitution would've helped: to be a beetle evolved to feed on the one flavor of aphid that lives at the heart of a c.m. flower, and who, at the moment of the flower's opening, and to keep the blooming going, chomps down the offending aphid. To be a thing suited to its one task. Built to take part. To have a confirmed way of being with the tree. But I was outside the composition. I had nothing to offer the very closed system-that-was-the-tree. How to be so unniched, not of use, not needed? How to be more than unto-oneself—since *oneself* pretty quickly doesn't much matter, does it? Is not of much consequence, is it?

If trees release phytoncides—a class of airborne chemicals that protect from insects and decay—then the thought of a being so complete, one that has nothing at all to do with me, is in yet another way, accurate. What I suspected was a closed circuit, is indeed that. But then, I read, too, that these substances also benefit humans (one study showed an increase in white blood cells that lasted a whole week in people who took a single forest walk. I guess I knew this, but only as the feeling of relief I get, walking among trees).

Just recently I received a postcard from a friend (imagine! while thinking about these things—but I am growing more comfortable with extended forms of conversation with those I cannot see) (though do not for a moment think I am not also grieved by the absence of my friends) (of course absence and grief, each in its way, are also forms of presence). The card read: *I could spend my life making stuff no one cares about, not even me, really—except that I like making things. And walking down to the hardware store, I was thinking how much I really liked <u>that</u>—just walking, being in the sun, alone. Just being in the sun alone. You know? How nice that is?*

How you can feel that's the whole reason to live? And it's enough?

I, too, have had, at other times, that same experience: that *I see a thing* is absolutely steadying, precisely *enough*: Rome, Via Appia, those dusty, resinous pinenuts on cobbles, and lines of dew drying in chariot ruts; while ironing, the wrinkle in the landscape of a sleeve laying down like a time-lapse geological event; a just-picked fig, warm in the hand, heavy as an egg, with a milky bead of juice at the stem. Here, though, when I angled toward home, when I turned and stopped looking, I could sense the tree easily going on being—not at all caring that I was seeing. The effect made my seeing equal to ceasing, and the tree so much more than my speaking of it. Before last month, in another life, before that walk, a feeling or sensation might have been very directly received; *oh, beautiful tree!* was sustaining, proper, all that was needed.

Let me say (and how thankful I am that you're there on the other end, having opened this letter in your special way with your very own envelope-splitting techniques which of course, I can't know and only imagine you practice, you who I believe to be reading this slowly, having first cleared a space for settling)—let me say, this impulse to make something is coming forth only now as I write to you—and it is, indeed, a saving gesture, a conservation of energy, a *circulating*, a renewing. But the initial emptying out of the form of me? Shattering.

I suppose in response I'll get to work on a word for "the shattering calm that being formless brings." "The fear that accompanies invisibility." "A recognition that causes one to slip while standing still." "Absence digging out a core in one's presence." "The bright air of ceasing, its watery savor . . ." which if I had to name more precisely

(I promise to write you again soon) is very much like a vein of iron, one I located in that moment deep in me as if banded in rocks lodged once at the bottom of the sea, formed back at the beginning of the world as we know it—and which tastes, when swallowing hard (as one does when frightened or moved) uncorrupted, raw, free.

STACKED FOR FIREWOOD
DIANA HUME GEORGE

CHILDHOOD TREE,
WRONG ABOUT ALL OF IT
In the recurring dream the grizzly bear lopes down Route 39. He's coming after me. He knows who I am. I'm the little girl in polka-dot pedal pushers sitting on the wooden rope-swing that hangs from the branch of the old horse chestnut tree. I'm listening to the locusts drone. He's not just any grizzly on a rampage; he's the bear that's come to get *me*, but I don't know this at first so I have stayed too long on the swing, trying to remain still, thinking I can become invisible. Then I realize he's known all along where to find me. I leap from the swing and run past the circle of dirt underneath it and through the tiny patch of grass onto the asphalt because I can run faster on pavement. Now I am fleeing downhill on Route 39 and he can see me in front of him. He roars, picks up speed. He's gaining on me. The bear looks just like the one that attacked my hero Cheyenne in that Warner Brothers western, so maybe Clint Walker will appear on horseback to save me. But he doesn't. The bear is snarling in my ears now. He will rip me to pieces and then shake his head back and forth with parts of me dangling from his maw.

The story of the horse chestnut spans half a century and includes my grandparents and parents, my first husband and my son, and some of my long-dead friends from the Seneca tribe of the Iroquois Nation near where I grew up in western New York state. The tree is gone now, as are most of the people who could confirm my memories of it. But the dream that took place under the tree and recurred throughout my childhood is with me still. We don't know, when we are young, that some places and people are only for the moment, and others will return to us in repeating patterns coded in our psyches. I found myself back at the horse chestnut at crucial times, always on that swing, the breeze fluttering the leaves, the sound the chestnuts made as they fell to the ground around my feet, the locust drone of August. Do you ever imagine what images might appear to you from your deep past when you're dying?

The tree stood in front of Grandma and Grandpa Russell's old house in the tiny hamlet of Perrysburg, New York, just a few miles outside of our own town, Gowanda. I went to the Russell homestead sometimes on weekends from when I was seven until I was almost twelve. They were my stepfather's parents, so different from my real grandparents who came from stilted gentility—there was a maid at my real grandparents' home in Ohio, where my grandmother the composer sat straight-backed at her piano, making music that was her passion, she who in all other matters remained rigid. Her husband Fred was one of those candy dish and mints-in-his-pockets grandpas, and anyone could see he loved her dearly. But his ardor was wasted on her. Their home ticked with orderly clocks that kept the time tense with small explosions that would never detonate.

But the Russells were step-grandparents, and thereby not quite real. By the time I knew him, Eber Russell was a stately old presence, somewhat severe, a storyteller whose Native American artifacts had made him a respected historian and scholar. A white man thought to be one-eighth Indian, he'd been made a member of the Seneca Wolf Clan for his efforts on the tribe's behalf. The upstairs hall floor of their creaky woodframe house was filled with display cases of arrowheads and stones and other objects he had found over a lifetime of local digs. I had no knowledge at the time that his collection would later be housed in museums, catalogued and authenticated by archaeologists, and I knew nothing of his theories connecting present-day Senecas to the moundbuilders and pottery-makers, then to the basketmakers, and eventually to *Sandia* man in an archeological line reaching back 30,000 years. Those arrowheads held mythic significance for a seven-year-old. Back then I'd never seen "a real Indian," but the pig-tailed white girl stroking those smooth flint surfaces would later marry a Seneca, and by the time she'd leave the reservation, her life would be in ruins. Some ruins hold no magic. They're just ruins.

Ruth, my step-grandma, was practical and warmly detached, the matriarch whose roast beef dinners fed crowds of relatives on Sundays, always permissive about giving grandchildren the run of the house and the big gardens out back, with vegetables and tall sunflowers and old sheds. But I preferred to go by myself to the horse chestnut in the front yard. Swinging idly beneath the shade of its leaves in the summertime, I felt freer than I ever could at home. When I first see myself swinging there, toeing fallen chestnuts with my sneaker, twisting the rope of the swing and then twirling while it wound down, it is about 1955. Summer is eternal and no one is supervising me. At home, my mother barely took her eyes off me because my real dad had thrown himself out of an 11-story window, leaving her with two young children, no money, and vigilant anxiety. Only at Grandpa and Grandma Russell's was I free of the abiding fear that made my mother my prison guard.

We ran around the yard and into the tall weeds as we wished, coming back covered with burdocks. In my memory, I am mostly unaware of my brother and my stepbrother and stepsister, all older than me. They could be anywhere. I am always alone under the horse chestnut tree, swinging, and nothing is happening. Nothing at all. I am idle, a thing unpermitted at home. There's magic in the air around the tree, a sound of heat and late summer, with only a small foreboding that never materializes. The drone is comforting. The source of the magic is the locusts all around and in the tree. They make their deafening buzz, their perfect empty shells appearing on the bark of the tree and on the ground. Locust shells—that's what we called them—were the first scary thing that I learned not to be afraid of. They looked spooky with their humped backs and eye holes and segmented sticky legs, but they were empty inside, so when some boy-cousin tried to scare me, sticking one in my face, I'd reach out and grab it.

The live locusts themselves remained frightening, but even if one buzzed by your head, making you crazy inside for a second the way June bugs did, they never went after you and they didn't sting. So it was possible for something to look monstrous, yet be harmless, a good thing to figure out young, especially if you were a minister's daughter who'd heard the word locusts associated with end-times and the apocalypse, featuring plagues and the wrath of a righteous god upset at immoral acts, probably sexual sins, though I didn't know what that meant. If I'd taken an equal and opposite lesson from the locusts—a thing can look beautiful, yet be harmful—it might have helped me later.

It turned out I was wrong about all of it, even the name of the tree—I had always called it the chestnut, but a horse chestnut isn't a real chestnut at all. Its name probably originated from the mistaken belief that its nuts, or conkers, would cure horses of chest problems. The confusion is understandable because the conkers, inedible to humans but poisonous to horses, appear almost identical to actual chestnuts. This tree was almost certainly the genus *Aesculus hippocastanum*, common throughout America. It had the white flowers of the *Aesculus*, which would bloom suddenly, then fall apart on the ground in Spring, entirely covering the area around the swing. I was similarly wrong about the insects—they weren't locusts, but cicadas, probably genus *Tibicen* that emerge in July and August, which is how I know, over half a century later, what months it must have been that I was most often at the Russells' house on Sundays. But to me they remain locusts.

What I most loved about the tree were its beautiful seednuts. If you got them at the right time, split from their spiky green shells, you could harvest a collection. I'd gather them up, take them home in my pockets, stare at their glossy brown skins gathered under my pillow in bed. They kept their sheen for months. I thought them of inestimable value. I still do. A lifetime later, I picked up chestnuts near the tiny Istrian hamlet of Cerrato, just south of Trieste, Italy, at a memorial dedicated to fallen World War II partisans of that village. I stood under a chestnut tree with my friend Luciana, who'd been a child during the war. She pointed to a lamppost from which as a tiny girl she'd seen a young partisan hanging by the neck. It was said partisans had assassinated a high Nazi official about 30 miles north of Cerrato. The seventeen-year-old boy had been held in Luciana's family's home, which soldiers had occupied, right above where I slept all those years later as a guest. Luciana was told he died under torture, and that they hanged his corpse for three days as a display to terrorize the village. How unlikely that she had returned later in life to this place of early fears, with someone for whom the gleaming chestnuts at our feet were reminders of a protected childhood a world away. I thought it odd that the very tree that meant so much to me also lived here in Croatia. It wasn't until I began to write about it that I discovered *Aesculus hippocastanum* was actually native to the Balkans, not America. I filled my pockets with shiny talismans and brought them back across the ocean.

TEENAGE TREE, CYCLES OF 13 AND 17

I stopped going to the Russell homestead when I was barely 12, when my mother left my stepdad and hauled me from New York to California to divorce him. New York didn't recognize "irreconcilable differences" but California did. Mother and Dad, both widowed and with children, had loved each other madly at first. I remember them dancing in the living room, gazing into each other's eyes. But something went wrong and after only a few years, she wanted out. I despised her for this, for taking me from the dad I loved, my own father having been dead since I was five. In my mind my actual dad lay forever on that hotel sidewalk in Cleveland, arms and legs shattered, head caved in. I had only a few memories of him alive—his morning glories, his stamp collection, the smell of bacon frying when he'd make breakfast, the way he'd cut the grapes in half, scoop out the seeds. I'd loved him dearly but he was gone, and this man who'd taken his place, Eber and Ruth's son Louis, was a wondrous father. He was a dog person, and I loved dogs as much as Mother loathed them. The collie-shepherd puppy he snuck into the basement became the first dog-love of my life. Dad took us hiking in Zoar Valley, a vast gorge in western New York where he let us go barefoot under the tall trees, finding swimming holes among the rocks. Mom leaving him was not thinkable. What did I care that she was miserable with him, and he with her? I threw tantrums all the way across the country to California. It would be decades before I'd recognize how gutsy she had been to drive across the continent at the end of the pre-feminist 1950s with two kids in tow to teach school and manage an apartment building.

Those two years I was in middle school in Los Angeles, I remained hungry for home and for Dad. I cried until she gave up and brought me back, but she must have had other reasons to come back to Western New York after the divorce. I don't know, and it's too late to ask her. She died at 96, not always knowing who I was. I didn't have the sense to ask her these questions when she was still herself. We don't always think to ask what we will later find it needful to know until it's too late, when the ones who know are gone, their memories buried alive in them even while they live, until they themselves are buried deep in the ground.

But not necessarily as deep as the cicadas that can burrow eight feet to gestate. The cicadas I saw on the bark of the horse chestnut tree don't emerge from the tree, like I always thought when I was a kid. That song they sing in summer is the male calling out from the trees and from plants all around, but once his mate has come to him, she cuts slits into the bark of twigs and deposits hundreds of eggs. The newly hatched nymphs drop to the ground and burrow deep, feeding on the root of the tree. After a year or two or five, their strong front legs tunnel them to the surface, where they attach themselves to leaves or bark to molt, abandoning their exoskeletons. *Blue Velvet's* beetles teeming below the surface of a manicured lawn are as nothing compared to cicadas, who burrow back up in staggered generations, yearly and at 13 and 17 year intervals, depending on what kind they are. The numbers figure just about right in my private numerology, because the story of me and the horse chestnut recommences in my 13th year.

I returned from California to western New York to a transformed world. When I'd left, we were all in elementary school, and almost everyone was white. When I came back, my peers were entering high school and the Thomas Indian School had closed, so the Senecas from the reservation outside of Gowanda came to school with the children of the white farmers and businessmen. This was a change on the order of school integration in the South. I too was transformed, far more worldly than my classmates. No more the geeky straight-A student of grade school who never did anything wrong, I wore heavy eye make-up and traded on having lived in LA. My grade school friends might have grown into student government leaders or cheerleaders, but I was now a breed new to me, a bad girl. Rejecting what my mother insisted on calling "dates" with the good boys, the clean-cut sons of lawyers and insurance agents, I hung around with Seneca guys. Those dark-skinned, high cheek-boned boys exuded an aura of excitement even when they weren't fueled by alcohol. I didn't drink, but I liked to act as though I did. I disappeared onto the reservation every time I got a chance, hitching rides in their old Chevies and

Pontiacs. Sometimes they'd go to a swimming hole where a tree reached one long limb over the water, and they'd jump from the rope, often drunk. Sometimes we'd find a house or a tar-papered shack where no adults were home or no one cared, a bunch of us gathering inside its wood-and-lath walls. My ninth grade guyfriends were all native boys, Doug and Richie and Dave, not near as tough as they made themselves out to be. Two of the three would be dead by their forties, because the start they got in high school was also how they later ended.

A white girl hanging out with "those Indian boys" in 1960s small-town America upset the white parents and teachers, who were full of racist fears of recent integration. It also angered the native girls. Only two other white girls in high school hung out with Seneca boys—one was exempted because her boyfriend was a football hero, and my best friend Nancy's Indian love was in the Marines. But when I elbowed my way into local territory, the tougher Seneca girls didn't like it. A few pushed me into lockers or followed me into the john to shove me up against walls and sinks.

One of them, Jane, lived at the intersection of white and native worlds. Her mother was a single woman, a widow with a good job who had taken Jane to live off-reservation. Although I didn't realize it then, Jane probably had to be tough exactly because she didn't live on the reserve. Seneca boys might want to meet me after school to neck under the bleachers, but Seneca girls wanted to meet me after school to beat me up, and one Friday, Jane challenged me to meet her outside town on Route 39 the next day to fight. Terrified but weary of being bullied without defending myself, and needing to uphold my new rep as bad-girl, I agreed to show up. It was just down the road from Grandpa Russell's.

I don't remember how I got to the scene of the fight. I probably stayed overnight with my friend Nancy, who lived on Route 39. I can't check with her about that because she's dead. Almost everyone in this story is dead now, but not because they were old. They died young from how they lived, of diabetes or alcohol poisoning or addiction or early cancer or car accidents. Or of broken hearts: Nancy became a rape crisis counselor in Florida, and I will always believe that absorbing her clients' pain caused the cancer that felled her in her forties.

Jane and I started fighting, and we somehow ended up the road in front of my step-grandparents' house, not far from the horse chestnut. I was grateful that no one was home. How we moved that far up the road I do not know. At first we faced off, then Jane moved forward to shove me and I shoved back. We clawed and punched at each other until we fell down and rolled right into the road, where we could easily have been hit by a car. All the fighting experience was on her side, all the desperation on mine. She outclassed me, but somehow I held my own. I didn't win, but I didn't lose badly. I looked worse than she did, but at the end we both stood back up. I don't remember our words, or what names we called each other, but I remember our breathing, labored, exhausted—and then I collapsed onto the tree-swing and started laughing. I couldn't stop. It was the first of many times in my life that I'd burst into that laugh born of anxiety when I was in physical danger. It began as a suppressed giggle and became helpless. Jane, too, began to laugh, bent over, hands on knees, looking down at the ground, then up at me where I sat on the swing of my childhood.

That fight was the start of a friendship that lasted from then until I left the area six years later. In school, Jane had enough authority to cause other native girls to back off. She'd come into the john with me and say *She's all right* or *Leave her alone*. Even then I knew that a friendship born of holding my own in a fight was based on something sick in the culture and in both of us, but our bond, forged in a rage of race and class we had no way to understand, was strong. Now I had a protector among the people who were the victims of my people, the whites of a small town in an era when prejudice against Native Americans was as bad as prejudice against blacks in the south. That sounds extreme, but it was true. She no longer treated me as the interloper I actually was. I thought I was dedicated to racial equality for its own sake, but really I was just a white girl with a bad case of Wannabe, in love with a dumb idea of primal nobility crossed with an element of real danger that I longed to court. I'd pay for that perversity later, but not yet. At the end of that school year, Jane and I went to a Beach Boys rock concert, two teenage girls entirely oblivious of any of the seven generations of irony attending us there. In the car on the way back we sang "In My Room" and "Little Deuce Coup," her weary Seneca mother frowning behind the wheel, asking us to keep it down.

Soon I would present no problem to the native girls, not because I lost interest in their boys, but because I'd met the one who would dominate my life for the next five years. Lennie is not his name but it's what I've called him in other things I have written about us. He dropped out of school in the seventh grade. At 20, he was a man, not a boy. He ran the Ferris wheel for a carnival outfit. Jane knew his reputation for drinking and womanizing, and she didn't like or trust him. When both of us graduated from high school two years later, I was pregnant. In 1966, age 17 and vastly with child, I married Lennie. Jane pretended to be happy for me, but she knew I was headed for trouble.

One kind of cicada crawls out of the ground after 13 years, another after 17, and that one brings blight. Which takes me back to my stepdad and grandparents and the tree. Grandpa Eber heard about my impending marriage from Dad, who had stood by me through my mother's attempts to force me to go to a home for unwed mothers. Scarcely able to credit that such a thing existed, I toured the "home" with budding journalistic interest, taking notes while matronly women in uniforms showed me the clean, sterile rooms where I could live with other unfortunate girls until the birth of my child, which would then be taken from me for adoption. My stepdad defended my right to love whom I wished, to marry, to have this baby. "You leave that girl alone," he told my mother on the phone when I went to his house weeping. He even prevented my mother from trying to put me on a plane over a state line to force me into an abortion.

It would be decades before I'd do the same thing my desperate mother did, when, as a very young grandmother, I was afraid that my barely grown granddaughter would follow in my tracks. "But why shouldn't I have a baby when I'm a teenager?" she asked. "You were pregnant with Daddy when you were 17, it didn't hurt your life, look at you, you're a professor." *Oh you poor child*, I thought, and trundled her off to the abortionist's. Soon she was pregnant again.

I have a dim memory of my talk with Grandpa Eber, the only one-on-one encounter with him I remember— grandchildren were beings over whom he cast an aloof and undifferentiated group eye, except that time he took us out to plant evergreens for our future—and it took place under the horse chestnut tree in the Spring, when those white flowers with their tiny red spots covered the ground like blossoms strewn for a wedding. He pretended to be happy that someone in his family—I was still vaguely family, despite the divorce—was about to marry into the Seneca nation, to whose history he had dedicated his life. He must have realized what kind of man I'd thrown in with, and how it would end up. Probably he knew he wouldn't be around to see the end of it because he was already old by then, and he was right. Standing there picking at the bark on the tree, uncomfortable in the private presence of this majestic, kind of scary old man, I noticed for the first time that, despite the lovely flowers, the tree's leaves were not whole, and not a healthy green, but green mixed with brown, all wrong for Spring. Its canopy seemed thin. Had it changed? Had it always been like this? Perhaps it had been dying all along, blighted by cicadas or some other invasive occupant during the short phase of its long life during which I knew it.

GROWNUP TREE. WRONG ABOUT ALL OF IT AGAIN, MAYBE

What happened to Jane by the time our lives parted ways a few short years later was always hard to think about, so I put her out of my mind. As a writer, I have prided myself on confronting everything, but there are a few people in my history whose futures I have managed to avoid lifelong thus far. Jane is one of those few. All right: she's the only one. My husband was a drunk who later turned out to be a serial rapist. That's an awful thing to slowly discover when you're a young mother, but the man Jane ended up with was far harder on her. He beat her relentlessly, even when she was pregnant. She began to drink to deal with her dismal life in a shack on the reservation with no running water. She had no money, no car, no outside support, and like so many beaten women, she'd lost the fierce sense of self that had once defined her.

We didn't live far from each other, so now and then I'd drive my old Buick to get her and her baby, and take them to stay with me in our off-reservation apartment for a couple of days. Jane had become alarmingly thin, her face a mass of bruises and black eyes more than once. I could not understand why she stayed, even as I myself was unwittingly with a man no better. I didn't know that yet. But she did. Lennie always insisted on taking Jane home at the end of her visit, saying he didn't want me driving the reservation roads in the dark. Later I understood why she'd ask me to ride along. I'd decline, because I'd have to bundle up my own baby. Later I realized that at least one time when he took her home, with her own baby right there in the car, he had raped her, and she, in that time before women's services, had not known what to do but to remain silent.

It was a hell of an end for those two girls who'd sung "In My Room" together just a couple of years before, but a common one for women before battered women's shelters and rape crisis centers of the kind that Nancy would later work in. It would be decades before I'd truly understand why Jane stayed with that man, how she could have lost the strength of spirit I'd thought was bone-deep in her. It's only now that I comprehend it, through my own granddaughter, the one who finally did have a baby when she was still a teenager, who for years would not leave a man who broke her bones.

When I left my husband at the age of 19, I took my young son many miles away from the reservation, not to remove him from other natives but from prejudiced whites. I'd tried life off the reservation but close by. It didn't work. The farmer's wife across the road would let all the other kids come in for cookies and milk, but my son had to stay outside and drink from the hose, because "half-breeds" were "light-fingered." So I moved near a college town farther away, and before I was thirty, I was clear of the kind of danger that had once defined my life. Teaching at a college of Penn State, I wrote books that seemed remote from my life, but were really all about my personal issues, disguised as scholarship. My books on poet Anne Sexton were my effort to comprehend suicides, my father having been one. I began to write my own life, especially my time among the Senecas, moving toward an always unfinished book that still has one missing segment, the one about Jane, the one I'm moving toward here among my memories of the horse chestnut.

For years I've written about white appropriation of native culture, my own included, and about the dangers of romanticizing the remains of genocide completed by suicide among native tribes. With respect for the resurgence of Native American identity, I've tried to take a clear look at both white America's romance with indigenous American people, and at the downside of native reclamation of cultural traditions if they primarily take the form of re-enactments for tourists. Most of the Native Americans in my world didn't know who they were, yet as the 20th century drew to a close, white America wanted to become them, falling in love with the ruins of colonization, as I did. I've written about all those people I grew up with and loved—all except Jane. For a person as dedicated to digging up my personal arrowheads as I have fancied myself to be, for a research-based writer and editor of books, this is a stunning omission. My fear is partly rational: when I seek to find out what has happened to Jane during these intervening decades, I might discover that she, like the rest of them, is gone. As long as my fear keeps me from knowing anything for sure, I can also hope. Maybe she's still out there. Slowly, haltingly, I began to look for her.

I found online traces of several women with her name living in western New York state. Their ages are about right—like me, she'd be in her sixties. One of the addresses is on the Seneca reservation. It could be an old listing by now, but maybe it's her, maybe it's my Jane, maybe I'll find out that like me, Jane escaped long ago, not into death but into a life free of fear. Maybe. Vicky, the postmaster in my tiny Pennsylvania town, called the postmaster in the town on the reservation where someone of Jane's name is still, even now, listed as living. But my postmaster was referred to a post office miles away from that address, because the house number on that road is not any longer a postal address at all. The other postmaster knew that road, but he didn't have any idea if a person of that name lives there, nor can he legally say whether his post office has a box number held by someone of that name. "A lot of those people," he tells Vicky, "don't want to be found."

Well, maybe so, maybe not. I know better than to trust white people's perceptions of native people, so finally, *finally*, this year I drove to the reservation, to that road, that address, myself. The woods seemed unbroken on that side of the road my first few passes, and then I spotted a slight indentation where a pull-off might once have been. But no house. Only the subtle remains of what was once a clearing, where a house might long ago have stood. New growth trees have taken over. Whatever might be my next step toward finding Jane, I haven't taken it yet.

•

I will never know many things about the horse chestnut, since it lives now only in my memory of that childhood nightmare, which still comes back to me more than it should. In some corner of my mind, I must have known that the freedom and the safety of that tree was illusory. A bear was coming to get me. There's often a bear coming to get you if you don't move out of harm's way. And you never know who the bear really is.

I used to pass the Russell homestead on the way to visit my mother. I gasped one day years ago at the sight of the old tree felled, naked and raw. The next time I drove by, it was cut into logs, and the time after that, it was split and stacked for firewood. Later still, the firewood had disappeared over the course of a winter, the whole tree gone without a trace. Each time I went by throughout my forties, I'd imagine that tree whole in my mind before I saw the gap, the empty circle that met my eye, and all my idle summertime swinging came back, and the cicadas, and the bear, and Jane.

Writing memoir is a fearsome thing—you have to tell the truth and after you do, you have to fact-check yourself ever since David Carr published his memoir, *Night of the Gun,* for which he found he'd misremembered many events. Like this: why did I have a dream so terrifying, set in a place so safe? When I set out to discover its sources, I assumed they had to do with the Warner Brothers Cheyenne western. I would have liked that to be true. It would mean I early internalized the myth of the white man who wants to live as a native, venturing into the wilderness with the skills and even the buckskins taken from the native, which would connect to my own appropriation of indigenous culture. But it turns out that "Night of the Grizzly" wasn't filmed in the mid-fifties when I first had my bear dream. It was made in 1966, not when I was eight years old, but when I was 17. So it cannot be as I remember it. I must have invented that first dream-bear.

The tree is gone, the people who knew it are gone, and I won't ever know if my cicadas were the annual ones of August, or whether, one year, they were the blight-bringers that arrive every 13 or 17 years. I can't even know of a certainty if my tree was a horse chestnut. The circumstantial evidence says it was, and so does my brother David. But things are never quite as they seem, nor as we wish them to be. All along here, I've said the tree was in the front yard. But now David says it was the side yard, and when I had my sister Marsha draw a map of where she remembers it, she said side yard too. I don't know how I could have been that wrong.

Further fact-checking led to a news article about Eber Russell written in 1963 by Joyce Ferris Swan, where one sentence brought my connection to Grandpa Eber full circle. "One eighth Indian himself (the first deed of his Irish great-grandfather upon stepping on American soil was to marry an Onondaga girl), Eber Russell had an inherent faculty for observation." I'd just transcribed it, feeling moved, when my unsentimental brother David emailed me that the story about Eber being part-Indian is probably false. Quoting Eber's daughter Ruth Smith, a meticulous historian, David tells me that when Eber said he was part Indian, his Aunt May would tell him not to say that, "for taint true." But wait—although being part-Indian would have been a point of pride for Eber, in an earlier generation, native heritage in a white family was more often a thing to hide, and who can tell if Eber's Aunt May, a generation removed from his, would have been of that fearful racist persuasion? It didn't become a badge of honor among whites until much later. To find out more, I'd have to pursue the family tree, as well as the horse chestnut. I still haven't.

But wait. What if I never had that dream in childhood? What if I had it in 1966, the year the Cheyenne movie was made? What if I was eight years old in the dream—I know I was—but not in real life? It would account for thinking I first had it when I was eight. "It cannot be as I remember it," I told you a while back, "I must have invented that first dream-bear." And suddenly it hits me: 1966 isn't the year I was a little girl running away from the bear. That's the year "The Night of the Grizzly" was made—and the year I married Lennie.

(Note: To protect the privacy of people whose identities I have no ethical right to reveal, I have changed the names of the two people called Jane and Lennie here.)

SAVING TREES
JACQUELINE DOYLE

When I am among the trees,...they give off such hints of gladness.
I would almost say that they save me, and daily.
    —Mary Oliver, "When I Am Among the Trees," *Thirst*

1

My younger brother and I tuned out our parents' continuous bickering every night at dinner and escaped the kitchen table as soon as we could. "May I be excused?" we asked the minute we'd cleared our plates. Permission granted, we bolted out the back door, screen door banging, clattered down the rickety wooden stairs, ducked under the low hanging branches of the maple trees by the back porch, and swung around the corner to race across the back yard to our tree-house in the large apple tree.

2

I grew up in New Jersey, where Joyce Kilmer wrote his poem "Trees." We had to memorize it in school. "I think that I shall never see / a poem as lovely as a tree."

3

The tree house in our back yard was just a small platform nailed into the boughs of the apple, and some scraps of wood nailed into the trunk that served as a makeshift ladder. My brother and I liked to sit there, cross-legged, hatching our plots for forays into the woods. In spring, fragrant white blossoms surrounded us like clumps of snow.

4

Kilmer wrote his poem in Mahwah, New Jersey, now designated an EPA Superfund site because of millions of gallons of paint sludge and other industrial waste dumped in the abandoned Ringwood Mines by the Ford Motor Company.

5

In the front yard, an oak tree surrounded by damp green moss towered over the road and rained acorns on the ground every fall. I could see it from my bedroom window, a stalwart sentinel. Lilac trees lined the yard, their blooms lavender, their trunks ancient and gnarled, propped up with two-by-fours. I inhaled their heady scent in spring, when I escaped the house to sit and daydream and read in a sheltered corner of the side yard, leaning against the slender trunk of a dogwood tree.

6

In the 1950s, no one was talking about pollution or global warming or toxic waste, at least not in New Jersey. We studied photosynthesis in school, but we didn't learn why we needed trees to absorb carbon dioxide and store carbon, or that deforestation contributed to greenhouse gas emissions. We didn't learn that carbon dioxide levels in the atmosphere had risen over 40 percent in the past century. We were studying the *Weekly Reader* and learning about the perils of Communism.

7

My brother and I endlessly explored a large wooded lot

behind the neighbor's house. Three older boys from the street behind ours liked to climb trees in the lot and throw rocks at us, so crossing the woods was a hazardous adventure. Farther down the block we caught crayfish and tadpoles in a tiny stream, dipping our hands in the cold water. Sometimes we lugged large rocks home for the metal tub in my brother's room, where we kept turtles and frogs.

8

When I recently zoomed in on my old neighborhood on my computer, I was surprised to see that the wooded lot is still undeveloped, though some of the surrounding houses are worth over a million dollars. As children we didn't think the woods belonged to anybody. It's hard to tell from the aerial view on the screen, but it looks like the gigantic oak tree by the road out front and the hemlock tree outside my bedroom are gone. My brother and I used to shimmy down the hemlock at night to prowl the neighborhood, so changed in the moonlight. The trees cast long shadows over the neighbors' yards.

9

In the summer we got up early and rode our bikes to the dense woods surrounding Birchwood Lake, where we roamed all day, unsupervised. The ground at Birchwood Lake was damp and covered with a thick cushion of brown pine needles. Tall trees filtered the sunlight, and we clambered over fallen, rotten birch trunks on the narrow paths. Brushing away clouds of gnats, we squatted to peer at green-striped jack-in-the-pulpits and yellow lady slippers, poked at bulbous mushrooms amidst feathery green ferns, stepping carefully to avoid red-tinged poison ivy. We climbed trees and we swam in the lake and we caught frogs and turtles and fish. Sometimes we roasted the fish on campfires, each small sunfish about a mouthful after it was deboned. We never seemed to get tired. Or sated.

10

By high school my brother and I had lost the intimacy of the woods. He hung out with the popular kids in the cafeteria and drank every weekend. I hung out with the outsiders in the art classroom and read all the time. He moved to the Midwest, became a beer-drinking good ol' boy. I moved to Ireland, then Germany, the East Coast, the West Coast, became a professor. We didn't have much in common any more, including geography.

11

Lady slippers and jack-in-the-pulpits are on the endangered species list. Birchwood Lake is still there, but the small town we grew up in has changed into an enclave for the very rich, who have felled the large oak and maple trees and demolished the old three-story stucco houses to build new mansions over the old foundations.

12

Now, I live with my husband and son in northern California. Developers keep felling trees in our neighborhood. An unincorporated area of former chicken ranches, Castro Valley has long narrow lots with room to build houses behind houses. One developer built two oversized houses with no yards behind a modest house on our block. We could hear the chainsaws after dark one night, as workers cut down the protected trees without permits from the county. The light felt too bright the next day, the sky empty until we got used to the missing canopies.

13

Where I live now, the pomegranate tree behind our 1930s house flourishes, and the orange and lemon trees alternate between abundance and a meager output. When they bloom in the spring, the fragrance of the citrus trees is overwhelmingly sweet. The white blossoms on the apple tree in our side yard remind me of my childhood tree house. The tree overproduces tart green apples, only good for cooking. They attract animals, and one night my son woke to a deer peering into the window at the foot of his bed. The two towering blue pines in the front yard are home to squirrels and mourning doves and robins and finches and humming birds. Red-tailed hawks soar in the sky and perch on the highest branches. At night we sometimes hear the soft hoots of an owl. The two trees are gigantic, as if they predate human beings on the planet.

14

The oldest redwood on the Pacific coast is an estimated 2,520 years old, the oldest giant sequoia 3,200 years old. A bristlecone pine in the White Mountains of eastern California, over 5,000 years old, is believed to be the world's oldest living tree. The trees dwarf man's written histories and puny achievements. "It took more than three thousand years to make some of the trees in these Western woods," John Muir wrote in *Our National Parks*, "trees that are still standing in perfect strength and beauty, waving and singing in the mighty forests of the Sierra. Through all the wonderful, eventful centuries ... God has cared for these trees, saved them from drought, disease, avalanches, and a thousand straining, leveling tempests and floods; but he cannot save them from fools."

15

Recently, scientists at Yale University estimated that there are more than 3 trillion trees on Earth. At the present rate of attrition, however, they may all be gone within 300 years.

16

Now, I lie on the couch on our porch, looking up into the two giant pines in the front yard. Boughs sway and rustle in the breeze. Squirrels chitter as they chase each other up and down the trunks, leaping from branch to branch, their tails twitching. Hummingbirds dart in and out of view. I can hear the whine of a buzz saw down the street, someone's lawn mower in the distance, our neighbor's leaf blower closer by, the twittering conversation of birds and the jeers of a blue jay between pauses in the combustion. The smell of new cut grass reminds me of my brother, summer days running through the sprinkler, tree sap sticky on our palms.

17

Now, my brother is dying of cancer, two thousand miles away. He tells me the experimental chemo has poisoned his body and killed his teeth. "They're going to start breaking off," he says. "That's what the dentist just told me." There are no treatments that will save him, no more treatments to extend his life. He doesn't know how long he has. I remember meeting under the stars on the sleeping porch that connected our second-story rooms to escape the house together at night. How we leapt onto the hemlock tree, arms outstretched, ready to grab the rough trunk. Pine needles and twigs scratched our arms and faces as we carefully shimmied down, testing branches under our feet, one by one, hugging the tree as we made our thirty-foot descent. Usually I went first and helped my little brother as he lowered himself to the ground. This time he's gone before me.

HECTOR IN THE REDWOODS
MATHEW GAVIN FRANK

It is ill-advised to stroll aimlessly around Weckman Farm at night. I suspect this is the same with most marijuana farms. Charlie the Mechanic, the guy who fixes the one-seat tractors that haul the trimmed weed to the curing sheds, fancies telling stories about the "Great bloodbats of the redwoods, brother. Suck yer neck limp as a rubberband."

I think of airborne rodent teeth traveling at considerable velocity and bite at my fingernails. But there are certainly worries more logical. After all, in darkness, I am a human shadow, easily mistaken for an intruder—government official, militiaman, neighborhood raider. There's a sniper about. I'm friendly with the daytime sniper, an insect-hating sweetheart named Hector. But Waldo, Hector's graveyard-shift replacement, remains a mystery. Rumor has it he's an epileptic. With a rifle. Waldo is somewhere up in these trees, having scaled the rope ladder to the sniper station—a misappropriated tree fort of sorts—surely staving off a fit by massaging the trigger. This does not for peace of mind make.

We have fled, my wife Johanna and I, to small-town Northern California, to seasonal jobs as, respectively, a massage therapist and bud trimmer on a medical marijuana farm after having spent the last year living in my parents' house on the outskirts of Chicago, nursing my mother through her battle with cancer, our marriage desiccating in my old childhood bedroom. We have fled from something definitive, and toward the sort of cultural underbelly and marital nebulousness that manifests itself as intoxication on the local plants, and crew of recovering drug addicts, ex-cons looking for a second chance, doctors, alternative healers, pseudo-hippie kids looking to earn enough money to spend on a season of hotel rooms and restaurants, revolutionary war veterans, people who used marijuana to weather illness and who now want to give back, and limbo-bound assholes like us. Neurotically, we have been overusing the word, *recover*.

•

Tonight, I have to walk. My heart needs calming. I already realize that Johanna and I will not be staying until the end of the harvest season. We already have the gasoline in our veins, the conversations about leaving the farm, that can not be undone. Somehow, we've been branded flighty, the iron having left its mark on more that just our skins. I don't know where we're going to go after this, and it's not necessarily back to Chicago. Maybe we'll return to Taos, New Mexico, where we lived a couple years back, out of our tent along the ski valley road for the summer, bathing in the frigid Hondo River with environmentally-friendly soap and shampoo, shitting in a pit toilet where the only paper were the Subway sandwich napkins that a neighboring squatter left as a courtesy and mark of his day job. Maybe we could get our old restaurant jobs back at the Sagebrush. Maybe we've lived that life already.

So I am compelled to wander the night-Weckman, I think, as a way of collecting goodbyes. Tonight, it recalls the lullaby of a children's book: *goodbye redwoods, goodbye crops, goodbye food tent, goodbye sniper tower...* I have to walk. Johanna is not happy about this. Now, she rests on her side in our Coleman Cimarron back in the Residents' Camp—the community of tents that house the seasonal crew—hopefully rediscovering sleep. I had the dream again, of my mother drowning in a volcanic lahar, frozen into position, a Pompeii refugee, exiled to Illinois. As always, natural disaster has quite a reach. Tonight has been nothing if not pyroclastic.

I woke with the typical cold sweats, something manic, but moribund in my chest, and the need to walk the dream off as if it were a cramp. A good night's sleep remains a marathon's distance away.

"Please be careful," Johanna whispered as she retraced her steps back into a good dream—maybe the one she always has about canoeing in Sweden along the Kalix and Angesan Rivers, on the back of a benevolent roan cow.

Unzipping the tent tonight is the loudest thing in the world, the Residents' Camp draped in a chorus of snores. The nose whistle must be Bob. The grunting must be Charlie. The low moony moans must be Lance and Ruby, finding, in sleep, the open spaces of each others' necks, and some dream-meadow lit up in lunar white.

I find the wind tonight only by walking. The air at this hour is an otherworldly brine, the moon pregnant with the Pacific and wetting its bed, the dampening sky rewriting the tide tables in fatigue and discomfort. Each star is a blossoming rash. I imagine the longhorns a few miles away, their snores not unlike Charlie's, their heads resting on each others' spines.

And beyond them, the matchstick cemetery, the dead so modest under this leaking moon. Tonight's light is one of outlines, the shapes of trees perfectly edged, but their middles murky. Tonight, like expensive linen, is lined with silver. Tonight is the optimist's wet dream. In it, a lone crow calls out to the lost murder, who do not answer, underlining its loneliness with beak-yellow highlighter.

I pass Hector's tent. It lies in place like a carcass. By the way the wind caves it in, I can tell that it's empty, its ribcage picked clean by the vultures. I wonder where he's gone tonight, envisioning a red-eye shift as a soccer coach, a wayward and lengthy drive into an all-night Los Angeles; the push to make it to Mexico. Where does he go? I imagine the laminated postcard on his tent door, autographed divinely:

Dearest Hector,
Best Wishes!
The Virgen de Guadalupe

•

I turn from the tent and walk beyond the Residents' Camp, turning from the crops and toward the redwoods, standing like pillars on a plantation house for bloodbats and their caged birds. Across from the trees, Lady Wanda's mansion sits dark and quiet, a mere footnote at the bottom corner of this forested page.

The night, even in the trees, is blissfully mosquito-less, the insects likely having latched onto Hector, carried out of Weckman by the magnetism of his sweet blood. The redwoods rock slowly as if in genuflection to the night, creaking with history, haunted and antique. Surely, in these trees, and in their nighttime ability to frighten by swaying, nothing bad can happen. Surely, in these trees, the world is safe, all wayward bullets absorbed into the warmth of their trunks.

Lady Wanda, reefer heiress and owner of Weckman Farm, has been employing snipers since 1997. Though an avid gun collector herself (her antique gun collection includes such weaponry as an 1865 Belgian cavalry snap hook and an 1891 Argentinean navy nickel-plated rifle—both fully badass), she used to be anti-firearm on Weckman, believing their presence would provoke violence. After the passing of the Compassionate Use Act in 1996, Lady Wanda was the victim of a governmental and grass roots backlash.

During 1996's harvest, Weckman Farm was twice invaded illegally; once by CAMP, California's Campaign Against Marijuana Planting, a division of the Department of Justice and Bureau of Narcotic Enforcement; once by a private vigilante militia, whose guns were neither Belgian nor Argentinean, were not from the 19th century, and were not safely locked behind Lucite. According to Lady Wanda, these private militias are increasing in number, staging armed raids on numerous marijuana farms both commercial and medical. For security's sake, she brought in guys like Hector and the clandestine Waldo, both, according to rumor, ex-military.

I stand, one inch tall, at the bases of the redwood trunks, roots thick as a pipeline. The marijuana crops flitter in the distance, trying to sneak me the exit key. But tonight, I don't want to be sprung. Not just yet. I embrace these trees over sleep; their scariness has nothing to do with my sick mother. There is no real grief in putting oneself in danger. *Goodbye grief...*

In these trees, their tops muddled in darkness and a soupy moon, I listen for the cocking of Waldo's rifle. In these trees, I imagine the clicking of a weapon could be nothing but gentle. I tread lightly, in these trees, listening. I hear only the wind. I wonder if Waldo has fallen asleep at his post.

Tomorrow is another day in the fields. I think of this past year, our fleeing from Midwest to West, lopping off a prefix as if decapitating a stage in our lives. Strange, when the same thing sickens and heals us. After that stint in Midwestern realism and all of its spiritual bratwurst, California seemed to us the physical manifestation of a cosmic high-colonic. The cleanse, unfortunately, didn't fully take. For Johanna and me at this point, whimsy has gone the way of my mother post-chemo, having drowned in my parents' suburban Chicago sump pump, seeded green into their manicured lawn. Their birch tree is dying. The one I climbed as a child, fell out of, carved vulgarities into. They're going to have to call the city to remove it. The neighbors have been complaining.

What else can I do, but handcuff myself to this melodrama as punishment, as, perhaps, protection. It is my wetlands, my glossy ibis, and I stand between it, and the flock of tractors who want to turn it into a megamall.

But the redwoods, if not that birch, seem to have the power to resurrect whimsy, as do the marijuana crops and encampment of tents, the sleeping bodies inside breathing small contentments into larger eccentricities, all of us as plastic and immobile as Resusci-Annie, waiting for some holy drunken paramedic to crack our sternums in the name of heroism.

The seasonal crew: In all of our desires to escape— from alcoholism and Vietnam, AIDS and cancer—we find a collective empathy. Maybe this isn't whimsy per se, but it's something whimsical, dissolved into our fucking up.

I run my palm over a redwood trunk; dig my fingernails into its meat. In it, I find a wetness, old rain or sap, the moon's diesel. I breathe and hear behind me a snapping—not of a twig or of a gun shifting its bullet, but of a bottlecap twisting open. I'm sure of it. I hear a sipping sound, the wet smack of lips pulling from a glass mouthpiece; a swallow followed by a tired exhale.

Aaaaaaaahhhhhh...

I am nervous, but oddly comforted, in a parental sort of way. Before he became the sad man standing over the blue wastebasket of his wife's shed hair, my father's personality was embodied in his flamboyant *Aaaaaaaahhhhhh...* after a long sip of Diet Coke.

I want to call, *Hello?*, but don't. My voice freezes, my breath pumped cold and smoky from my lungs. Instead, in an act that calls equally on self-preservation and destruction, I weave through the redwoods toward the sound. I half expect to see my father, thirty-five again, doing push-ups between the trees.

Soon, against the base of a medium redwood (which, for a cypress would be like 10XL), I see a strange shape floating about three feet off the ground. In this light, or lack thereof, it appears to be a giant disembodied brain, something that broke from the oversized pickling jar of a 1950's B-movie and hid out here, filtered through Gabriel García Márquez, on the outskirts of Weckman, protected by an epileptic sniper. Is this guilt made manifest? Some ghostly return of the Latin *contritus*, ready to grind us into pieces, crush us with the weight of our own skewed decisions? If so, it looks pretty fucking small, not up to the task; I hope this isn't one of those sci-fi cases wherein the beautiful siren, when approached by the lusty man, morphs into a larynx-ripping alien with a thirst for frontal lobes.

I squint into the trees, and the shape mutates into something less solid: a plume of seafoam escaping the moon and the ocean. Stepping closer, the shape shifts once more. I can see now that it is a head of hair, and that it is Hector's. He's sitting against the fat base of a redwood, sipping from what in outline appears to be an Erlenmeyer flask. This is a surprise.

"Hector?" I manage.

His hands fumble with the air between them. He loses his grip on the flask, then regains it. I think I can hear his heart stutter.

"Oh, fuck it," he cries, trying to scramble to his feet before settling again into a seated position, "You scared the shit outta me, man. My God..."

"Sorry. I couldn't sleep," I say.

I don't think he hears me yet, the blood beating in his ears.

"What are you doing out here?" he asks.

"I couldn't sleep."

"Yeah. Right," he says, his breath and his heart calming down, "Well, you're welcome to a slug of this."

He raises his bottle. It is Agavero, a tequila liqueur of sorts, infused with fermented damiana flower tea. I sit next to him, the girth of the redwood trunk more than enough to accommodate us, and three conversion vans besides. Hector exhales again, still in the process of regaining his internal peace. Given his unfortunate insect magnetism, I'm shocked to find that the air around him is mosquito-less as well. The Agavero must be a repellant. But not to me. Not tonight.

I sip from the bottle this thick mixture of cactus

nd petal, running over my throat and into my belly, a
desert snake slithering with satin skin. I exhale. Like the
snake, I want to rattle. Hector begins telling me how the
ancient Mayans in Mexico used the damiana flower as an
aphrodisiac.

"They would smoke the flowers, man, and go, go, go,"
he says.

"Wow," I muster, my throat regaining its elasticity.

"Good shit, right?" Hector asks.

But he knows the answer. Anyway, though he can see
only the outline of my head, I nod.

"You could find a lot of shit in New Orleans, man, but
you couldn't find this," he says.

He raises the bottle and toasts the moon.

"You can't hide, you fat white fucker!" he shouts, and
I wonder if anyone in the Residents' Camp wakes up. I
know Johanna can sleep through anything. If she sleeps.

"New Orleans?" I ask.

"Yeah," Hector says, and takes another sip.

He passes the bottle to me. In the moonlight, the
bottle is green-black, skinny at the top and flared into a
sphere at the bottom. Tonight, in these trees, Hector has
attached a siphon to the globe, and is sipping from the
core. If he chooses to share this delicacy with me, I can
not, in these trees, say no. I take another swig and feel
poisoned, poisonous.

"That's the good thing about California," Hector
continues, "You can find almost anything you can find in
Mexico."

I cough agave sugar.

"Well, not everything," he clarifies, voice trailing.

"What were you doing in New Orleans," I ask as soon

as the Agavero loosens its grip on my throat.

Hector exhales. His breath tumbles over itself, balled up lace in the cool, and the white of the moon.

"Livin' there, man," he says.

He exhales again, a shorter breath this time.

"I lived there," he says.

•

It is ill-advised to dwell on the bark patterns the redwood trunk has burned into Hector's forearms. They cycle his wrists, scribbled highways devoid of blood, a testament to the impressions, sometimes ditches, nature digs into us. More to the point, I'm getting drunk, and the struggle to see such patterns makes me nauseous. At any rate, I'm thankful to the cosmos for granting me this strange goodbye.

I picture Hector in his treetop perch, having scaled a rope ladder to get up there, this wooden fort, large enough only for a barstool, a tattered movie poster of Russ Meyer's Supervixens, Hector's boombox. He tells me he listens to Dr. Judy on the radio, that advice show that duels between medicine and morality.

"Have you heard this shit, man?" Hector asks, "It's unbelievable."

The sniper station: just enough room for this, and the gun. Hector never had to shoot anybody. Not here. Never spotted a trespasser. In the sniper station, he reads all the bestsellers about lawyers and doctors and serial killers and detectives. He comes to his job ready to commit himself to plot mechanics—stationing his gun in the corner, sitting on his stool, putting his lunchbox on the floor, taking in the panorama, turning on the radio, pre-tuned to Dr. Judy dispensing bad relationship advice. He reads a paragraph, looks around, reads another paragraph, looks around, takes a bite of BLT, looks around... his daylight hours spent at the treetops, with the birds who fight and love and fuck and feed there.

He hoists the bottle of Agavero and talks about it. By *it*, I mean this:

Hector was one of those rooftop shadows the Hurricane Katrina relief helicopters passed over. He waved a soaked white sheet that twisted in on itself like a braid.

He waves a moth from his hair and says, "It was like a fuckin lead vest, man. That X-ray shit. That's what they don't tell you. That everything was heavy as shit."

As he says it, I can hear his voice thickening. Or maybe that's my ear. I'm getting pretty wasted. He nods, folds his fingers into what may be a prayer, and bobs them back and forth, fishing for God without a lure. The wind is cool and, as if we were candles, nearly blows us out.

He lost two daughters, six and eleven, and a wife who was threatening to leave him.

"She never got to do it," Hector says, his breath deflating in the air. He drowns it with another sip of Agavero.

He was going to community college, wanted to be a guidance counselor at a high school. I imagine the smaller trees he drove under on the way to class—the Southern magnolias and live oaks, the Cherrybarks and Sawtooths, the Overcups and Cows—trees I will never get to see. Katrina, Hector tells me, wiped out two-thirds of the city's trees. Certain wards lost every one. In the aftermath of the hurricane, in regards to the decimation of New

Orleans' urban forest, Tom Campbell, spokesperson for the Louisiana Department of Agriculture and Forestry, summed it up with all of the gentility a Midwesterner could never muster, "It looks like the dickens."

Here, the wind curls among the redwood trunks, carries with it the sound of a false piano, the smell of false roses. If it wasn't for these trees, I could close my eyes, be at a Preservation Hall funeral. The electrons between us shut us out, close the door on an atomic orgy, ions passing into an opium coma. The littlest of things, having the time of their lives, abandon us. I pat Hector on the thigh, thick as the roots under us, but not immune to uprooting. Hector pats me back with a great social worker's generosity.

"Lady Wanda found me in Phoenix," he says at last.

"What were you doing there?" I ask.

"Family," he says, "I have some family there. Distant family, but, you know. And I stayed with them for a bit before moving to this refugee camp, set up in the Coliseum there."

He pauses, runs his index fingernail over the ridges in the Agavero bottle. The sound is like the sound of chains dragged over a tile floor. The stuff of ghost stories.

"All I took," Hector says, "was this white laundry basket. Plastic."

"Why a laundry basket?" I ask.

"It was what I kept my things in."

Phoenix, like many American cities, turned their gymnasiums and concert halls, fairgrounds and basements into refugee camps for those displaced by Katrina. In these camps, people slept and woke and ate donated food, drank donated water, their sweat asserting itself more every day, children becoming restless, clothes getting dirtier. In these camps, people died for lack of medication and medical supplies—no insulin or IV drips, tetanus shots or Tylenol. People died of minor cuts that grew with infection.

The number of people who had yet no bid on a future reached approximately 1.4 million. Local people tried to give what they could, crowded the animal shelters, adopting dogs with names like Gumbo, Jambalaya, Beignet, Po'Boy. A culture dying. A language surviving in the names of its rescued pets.

Much of the federal relief went to the restoration of New Orleans hotels and casinos, chemical plants and (as we all know by now) upper-class, predominantly white neighborhoods, while Hector and many, many others waited in hours-long lines to get into buildings with names like Sky Harbor and Superdome. I wonder what he thought of Phoenix's relative treelessness. I wonder what he thought of the saguaros.

"We had to wait outside in the rain for like five hours, while they searched everybody," Hector says.

Inside, people staked-out their places in chairs or on floors. The spaces against the walls were particularly sought after, where people sat and rocked, missing things like a glass of milk. Unlike Johanna and me, these folks were not granted the luxury of choosing to flee.

I picture Hector in Phoenix, in the Veterans' Memorial Coliseum, lying in a hallway crowded with survivors, a cavern that once hosted Bruce Springsteen concerts. I picture him deep into a sleeping bag against a dark and caged concession stand, its beer taps empty, popcorn machine unplugged. I picture his trying to find sleep amid the ghosts of his family, beneath a neon banner sign advertising Pepsi. It's been much more fun picturing him in his sniper tree.

"You can't even imagine the bathroom situation, man," Hector says, mustering a laugh.

"I hadn't even thought about that," I say.

"It's nothing to think about."

He swats an insect from his ear, feebly. The more Agavero he drinks, the more tolerant he becomes.

He says something about lying down there, this four-year-old kid stepping barefoot over him. I look up to these giant trees and the giant sky beyond it, and imagine a tiny bare foot in their place.

He hiccups on the liquor a little, but doesn't make a sound, like he's hiccupping in a silent movie. At any moment, I expect Charlie Chaplin to descend from the treetops and fumble with a parachute, reminding us how hilarious and precarious all of this shit is.

It's too dark to see, but not dark enough to miss the Coliseum, how he struggles to sleep there. The rustle of the displaced and misplaced drops over him like leaves. Children pad the hallways, climb over arena seats. Local volunteers plastic-wrap a metal tray of white rice, refrigerate it for tomorrow's breakfast. One-hundred and fifty women wait behind a velvet theatre rope to see the ob-gyn nurse, on duty for another forty-five minutes. The next shift comes in for the night, taking the flashlights and key rings from those who are going home to empty apartments and houses full of families. These nights: no stage or light-show, no rounds of applause. The encores are across the country, buried under water.

Into this arena and many others like it, came the farm owners of the American West, hiring these former Louisianans as apple pickers in Washington, cannery workers in Alaska, snipers in California.

Hector exhales.

"Lady Wanda herself came in there recruiting. A lot of people running marijuana farms came in there, offering jobs...and not for shit pay, either. Without her, man..." he says, shrugs, shakes his head, unzips his neck with the back of his finger, "This industry helped so many Katrina victims, man. It's fucking generous."

He sets the Agavero bottle between his feet. The glass catches the moon, lights up like a crystal ball. In it, I see tomorrow's hangover, the nauseating cling of marijuana resin to my hands. I see Hector putting together his rifle as if a toy, a hobby horse, a remote-controlled car, long since running autonomously, without a battery in the world. We sit. In this silence, I realize how exhausted I've become, my mouth petalled with alcohol, a cactus rung out.

"Oh," Hector says, breaking the silence like a bottleneck. But he doesn't go beyond this. This is the sound, an old writer friend of mine once said, that is at the center of all poetry and, therefore, should never appear in a poem.

I wonder about Johanna and me. About my family. About what is and what isn't inherent in us. Somewhere, beyond these trees, Lady Wanda's mansion lies dormant and dark, and beyond it, the food tent, the curing shed, the tractors asleep like gorillas on their feet. In this inventory is some kind of abundance, or its surrogate.

Hector, by my side, reaches once more for the bottle between his feet. I think, together, in these trees, in this dark, we're trying to feel full. The shit just keeps heaping itself on. Drunk, I lean my ear into Hector's shoulder, giving him an awkward hug with my head. He's as sturdy as a menhir, warm with booze.

"Well, like they say..." he says.

I nod.

"So what's next?" I ask him, lifting my ear from his shoulder.

He holds up the bottle.

"Let's finish this little bit and head back to Camp," he says, "I'm tired."

I picture his big empty tent. The Virgen de Guadalupe postcard whistling in the wind. I picture Johanna splayed diagonally across the floor of the Cimarron. I feel lucky for such pictures.

"I mean," I clarify, "Where are you going to go from here? After the season?"

Somehow, I think his answer may help to inform mine.

Hector pulls from the bottle, tilting his head back grandly. I silently pray he will howl at the moon, give me an excuse to join him—two guys being stupidly, happily male. He just holds an upturned palm to the sky. The night lights dapple his arm with shadow, the redwood tops draped over him like vines.

"The moon, man," he says, "I'm motherfucking Neil Armstrong."

TEMPLE
ANGELA STEWART

If I speak in the tongues of men or of angels, but do not have love, I am only a resounding gong or a clanging cymbal.—The Apostle Paul

I've read that there is a proper way to eat a fig. You're supposed to take it by the stump, quarter it, then pop the sections into your mouth whole. Delicately. What you're not supposed to do is take it in hand, squeeze it and split it at the seam, because then it's difficult not to notice when it opens red and bursting and wet that it looks like a vulva. Some people are uncomfortable with eating vulvas in public, and so they quarter them instead. But no one is really fooled. Figs look so much like vulvas that the slang for vulva in Italian is fig. And in popular Latin. And Greek.

There are wild figs growing all over the tiny island of Cyprus that floats below Turkey and to the southeast of Greece. A friend who lived there once told me that the trees are two thousand years old—that they sprouted in the same years that the Holy Spirit flamed in tongues and told the apostle Paul to catch a boat to the island and go evangelizing there. The story goes that Paul liked figs so much that he planted a trail of trees behind him from what was left when he was done eating, and the saplings popped up from the ground like a line of green converts.

I know the apostle Paul. I grew up going to a church that sat on a tall hill between the city and the country and that preached Paul from the pulpit nearly every Sunday. I loved church, even as a kid; I stayed upstairs to listen to the sermons instead of going down to Sunday school with its stupid paper crafts and songs we had to sing in a too high key. It seems like a miracle now, but all I remember learning in church was that God loved me and that God loved everyone the same. It took me a while, though, to wonder why none of the people telling me about this love from the pulpit had a vulva of their own.

Paul wrote thirteen books of the twenty-seven in the New Testament. He said that our bodies are a temple for the Holy Spirit, and that we should honor God with them. Less beautiful are some of the other sentiments credited to him:

A woman should learn in

quietness and full submission. And

I do not permit a woman to teach a man.

And

Wives, submit yourselves to your own husbands as you do to the Lord. For the husband is

the head of the wife...

Paul never married. He said it was better to be single, unless you couldn't control yourself, and then he said, Let them marry: for it is better to marry than to burn.

I went to a Bible college that my church sponsored the year after I graduated high school because I wanted to learn about theology and the mystics and how to shape my life around love. But it was a place where the girls read books on how to picture themselves as spiritually male so that they could be "sons of God" and sometimes, we were asked to stay after class while the wives of visiting teachers taught us about how important it was to allow men to be the "heads of our households" and how filling it was for them to submit to this kind of arrangement. And though I knew enough to argue with them, I did not know enough to not worry that I was wrong.

The unmarried principal with flappy lips and a belly bigger than her breasts threw Paul at us like a firefighter hosing down hell. Marriage is good, but single is better, she'd quote, then press her lips together and widen her eyes as if we were now all in on the secret. But she did not know that we were torches. Burning together between the library stacks when she went home and the lights went out. All those Bible concordances watching on with greedy eyes, moans pressed between their pages like dried flowers.

When the apostle Paul was wandering Cyprus, it was during the time when the worship of classical Greek and Roman gods was in full swing, including forced temple prostitution to the goddess of sex. Besides figs and Paul, Cyprus is credited as the birthplace of Aphrodite. Uranus' genitals were sliced off, thrown into the sea, and the goddess of sex and love and beauty rose up from the foam on its beaches. It was Aphrodite's home long before it was Paul's. So when I heard about Paul's figs on Cyprus, I imagined him walking the dirt roads and standing on the beaches, spreading the good news of the love of God and the need for purity, while Aphrodite laughed at his sticky mouth, sweetened from all those vulvas.

But apparently not everyone thought it was funny. Paul preached out against temple prostitution and was tied to a marble column and given forty lashes for preaching there. Some tourists travel to Cyprus just to see that column.

I saw a lot of wild fig trees the summer I spent in Greece, though it wasn't the season for fruit. They were strangler figs, which means the seeds germinate when they are dropped into a crevice of a host tree. As it grows, it sends down long, vinelike roots that prop up the stem and eventually bind together to form something that looks like a trunk. The fig grows around the host and sucks out all its nutrients and steals the sun and rain for itself, until the host dies from starvation. Eventually, all that remains is a tree-shaped hollow in the center of the fig's trunk.

What I know about fig trees is that Moreton Bay figs are the most beautiful of them all. Their roots are so enormous that you can stand between them and lean your head against their curves. They snake out from the trunk onto the ground like a fluid thing frozen, or like a woman's dress pulled into peaks around her while she sits in the grass. They are decidedly feminine.

When I first discovered Moreton Bay figs I wanted them to be Paul's figs, as if he left a string of daughters behind in his puritanical wake. And that maybe they wept for him when he left them and the island. And that maybe they were afraid. Maybe some of them died. Or some of them made a life of waiting for his return. Some of them sat around all day getting fat and watching TV or some of them starved themselves to grow thin, but both did it for the revenge of not knowing what else to do. And maybe some of them eventually stopped waiting, skipped out on temple duty and hopped a ferry. Lived abroad, drank tequila, wrote dirty stories. Maybe the Moreton Figs stopped moving, got jobs, families, raised money for literacy, and then, finally, returned to their old island with gnarled knuckles and tales of giant sequoias and the scent of pine in the winter, their ghost spaces still hollow after all those years.

But I don't know what kind of fig Paul ate, I don't know what grows on Cyprus, so I asked my friend if he remembered. Tell me again about Paul and the figs and those vulvas that he ate and then threw to the ground, I say to him one day.

Figs? He says. They weren't figs, they were olives.

And it occurs to me then how much I still resent the apostle Paul, and how much I want to shame this very dead man for all the centuries of shit he brought women with his writings. And what the hell, I wonder, do I do with olives instead of figs?

So Paul the apostle loved olives. He traveled Cyprus preaching the love of God and eating olives. But olive trees belong to Athena, patron goddess of Athens, known for her virginity, and the goddess of war. She earned Athens in a contest with Poseidon by offering the city a better gift than he did. She smacked the ground with her spear and an olive tree sprouted; Poseidon smacked the ground and a spring of saltwater gushed. The people chose the olive because who needs more saltwater when you have the Mediterranean? Her tree is said to stand at the Acropolis still, and the Greeks like to claim that every Greek olive tree can be traced to a cutting from that one.

Olives are the oldest of all fruit trees, and they've been cultivated in the Mediterranean since at least 500 BCE, but have been pickled in salty brine and pressed for oil since 3500 BCE. It was an olive branch that Noah's dove brought back to the ark, olive twigs that decorated the heads of Olympic victors, olive oil that Homer called liquid gold, olive groves that Jesus wept beneath before his crucifixion. He said that a tree is known by its fruit. And that tree, daughter, is an olive.

The olive trees I saw in Greece had hard, smooth berries hanging in the branches, not yet ripe for the picking or the shaking down onto the tarps spread beneath them The apostle Paul must have known these trees too, or their great grandparents at least. Perhaps, after he had preached in Athens at the Areopagus he wandered over to the Acropolis and saw Athena's tree. But what does a virgin goddess of war have to say to a man like Paul? Maybe they could have chatted about how great virginity is. Or maybe he reached into her leafy folds with itchy fingers and plucked her ripe fruit. Or at least wanted to.

They could have talked about sexual purity at Athena's tree, and maybe talking about sex would have almost been a substitute for sex, like it sometimes was in the Bible college, and they would have become hot and lusty and intimate without nudity or sin or guilt, and maybe they would have grown tender and vulnerable, as sometimes happens after sex, substitute or not, and maybe they would have unfolded those dark places they kept hidden and also talked regret. And war. And violence. Paul could have told her about his past, and of how he had learned to want nothing more than to put an end to this new cult that had sprung up around Jesus; and how he had approved and stood watching as other Pharisees had hurled rocks at a follower named Stephen; how Stephen's face had glowed until it was battered and his nose pushed to the side, how his last words had been the same as Christ's. And Athena could have laid her pretty white fingers on Paul's dusty arm, tenderly, virginally, and chosen which of her murders she would tell him about, landing on the worst, the one where she had lost her temper and killed her childhood friend. How she had been so grief-stricken that she made a wooden statue of her and wrapped her in the aegis and set it up on Olympus. And Paul would have felt compelled to say that there was only one true God, but that he understood regret and sorrow, that you don't always grow older and wiser, but sometimes just older and sadder. Athena's warrior shoulders would have softened, Paul's stiff upper lip relaxed, and they would have sat in the shade of the olive together, sex having done what it does best.

I only stayed a single night in the city of Athens and missed Athena's sacred tree. I was on my way through to Istanbul with a friend, and after dinner, we lay on the beach in the dark with Cassiopeia, Orion, Cepheus and the great Cloud of Witnesses looking down from their night sky. Later, we walked back to only one bed in a room for the two of us who had never shared a bed and hadn't planned on doing so. I made a joke of it with his face beside me on the pillow—that I would tell everyone at home we had slept together. He smiled, we lay still under the sheets for years, and then we did. Paul and Athena frowning down on us from their pockets of heaven.

Had Paul visited Athens at the right time, he could have witnessed Athena's feast of Arrhephoria. Two young girls were chosen to live on the Acropolis for a year and tend Athena's olive tree while they wove a new robe for the goddess. At the end of their year, they were given a secret package by one of Athena's priestesses, which they carried on their heads to a sacred underground room. Neither the priestesses nor the girls knew what the package contained, and when they arrived at the room, they left it there and brought back another secret one. Scholars today aren't exactly sure what this feast meant, but they know the name Arrhephoria comes from two Greek words meaning "mystery" and "I carry."

I like to imagine that the packages were empty. And

that the girls had sometimes been curious enough to remove the wrappings and found only air inside. As if they could have known that all girls for all years had carried a space that was made sacred by their presence around it.

Paul was uncharacteristically gentle in Athena's city. It was there he said that God is not far from anyone—close enough to be found by everyone. Named among his followers in Athens are women, at a time when women were rarely noticed, let alone named and recorded. It was his third journey by then and perhaps he had learned some things as he traveled. He would be arrested soon after, and the path to his execution by Rome set with no chance for turning back.

There is debate about whether or not the apostle Paul really wrote the book of the Bible named Second Timothy, but if he did, some of his last words were, "Pursue righteousness, faith, love and peace." He said that in God we are all equal—male and female, we are all the same in Christ. He talked a lot about love near the end. I guess we probably all will.

They closed down the Bible college a year after I left, and most of us married in our early twenties, tired of all the burning and before we had learned we could live differently. Some of us lost our faith, some of us became insufferable evangelists, many of us are ashamed of the things we used to believe. Years after we left the college, getting together with friends we had made there seemed like group therapy sessions, like recovering from a trauma. We laughed together nervously and wondered what had happened to us that year. How we could have been drawn into such small and sad ways of living. How sometimes the old guilt came creeping back despite the decision to turn from it.

A friend recently accused me of cherry-picking my faith. She doesn't like the way I throw away the theology I don't agree with anymore and yet still profess belief. I guess I do cherry-pick. It seems like the most responsible way to live out a faith. I'm still only interested in hearing about love.

In Bible college, we were told that everyone had a space inside of them that could only be filled by Jesus. They called it the God-shaped hole, as if we were all strangler figs and had taken root in the divine and sucked the nutrients out of it, until we had sent down such limbs and strength as to stand on our own and were left with the ghost shape of where God once lived. It was an odd way of seeing, I thought, even then. As if God couldn't also be the emptiness itself.

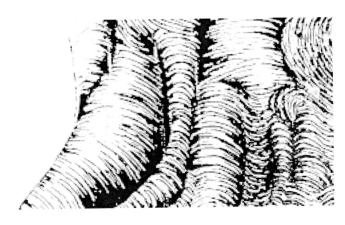

QUAKIES: *POPULUS TREMULOIDES*
AMARIS FELAND KETCHAM

The quaking aspen are a medium, not the message. Don't mistake an aspen's tremble for the wind or a showy yellow leaf for autumn. Wind shivers through them, just as a wave is not the water, but force shoving the lake to lap the shore.

On the flesh of the medium, shepherds have written clues for the flock, directions, and preferences for willing women. These notes won't last longer than papyrus, sandstone, or your url. They will outlive bathroom graffiti, written in Sharpie, along the stall walls at the High Noon Saloon.

The aspen are also a message, not the medium. Like a scab of the mountains' recent wound, they pioneer a new colony after each forest fire. Aspen share a single root system, a net of suckers a thousand years old.

Each colony its own clone; each tree identical to the next; each a trunk of the same organism. And if the message is dieback, shared vulnerability etched in their rhizome? Every aspen you've seen could disappear at the same instant. So through the smooth white bark scarred black; let leaves tremble in your wake.

ETIOLOGY
THOMAS MIRA Y LOPEZ

Whenever my mother and I drive to her house in Pennsylvania, she asks me to take a look at the Ohio buckeye. It's a ritual I'm familiar with by now. I carry the bags inside and leave them on the kitchen counter, then move the food from cooler to refrigerator. She takes the black poodle out of his travel crate, praises him for being so patient, eyes him closely as he romps around the field, and when I have slid the ice packs into the freezer and the poodle has discovered for the hundredth time the hundredth smell at the base of the pine, she will call to me through the screen door. "Come, Tom, come see Dad's tree."

She doesn't know how much I begrudge this ceremony. She does not know that, after two hours in the car next to her, all I want to do is open a bag of tortillas chips, pop the seal of a jar of salsa con queso, and stand over the counter dipping a dozen or so chips into the cheese. Or, rather, she does know this: she's my mother. If I eat too much, she knows the next thing I'll do is take a nap. The poodle's walk is timed so that she can call out to me before I become too involved in the process of dipping and chewing, before I feel full enough to grunt a refusal and shut the door to my room. She might even know that I do not care about the buckeye, that I attach no particular importance to it. She is my mother. Maybe she knows that she has only to expose me enough to it in order for me to care—like the way when I sit down to eat take-out with her on Monday nights, she has only to refuse to change channels and I will watch *Dancing With The Stars.*

In Pennsylvania, I trudge outside and around the house and walk up to the tree. I circle it and give the trunk a hesitant pat, squeeze its diameter, unsure of how to touch it just as I'm unsure how to pet the dog. "It's beautiful," she'll beam, standing there, watching me. "It's grown so much."

•

There are five rivers in the Greek underworld: the Styx, river of hate; Acheron, river of pain; Cocytus, river of lamentation; Phlegethon, river of rage; and Lethe, river of oblivion. I like to think that, taken together, these form a rough Kubler-Ross model for ghosts. In their enumeration, Lethe comes last, the final stage of grief. Its waters serve as a general anesthetic—all those who drink from them forget their former state, their joy and grief and pleasure and pain. This potential, this river of morphine and drowsiness and opiates, sounds quite tempting when poetized, when it becomes, as Ovid writes in the *Metamorphoses*, the place "where dream-haunted poppies grow, hanging their heads above wet ferns and grasses...and weighted eyelids close each day to darkness."

Yet my uncertainty about Lethe stems from its source. Arriving in English from Greek via Latin, the word is rendered as either oblivion or forgetfulness. To me, speaking the English that I speak, these two words mean different things: oblivion is a permanent state, forgetfulness temporary. I would like Lethe to mean the latter—a soporific that acts nightly not just to erase all memories of pain and suffering, but to restore those memories upon arising and transform them into something acceptable, into a new and peaceful state. But I suspect it's really the former: that once you drink these waters there is no going back, no middle ground or middle island upon which to stand.

•

My father planted the Ohio buckeye in 2004, the year my parents bought this second house in northern Pennsylvania, fifteen minutes south of the Delaware River. What makes the buckeye impressive is that my father planted a seed, not a sapling or nursery tree. The seed, brown with a lighter spot in its center, resembles the eye of a male deer and so gives the buckeye its name. By 2006, it had grown to a four foot sapling. By 2012, my mother estimates the tree at twenty feet tall. Buckeyes grow to a height of forty-five feet. Their diameter measures fifty centimeters. They live for eighty years, a human lifespan. That is, the lifespan of a lucky human.

It's crucial for my mother that this buckeye not just live, but flourish. She'll scoff at the afterlife, yet all the same, animism and reincarnation grow within this tree. She's assigned it a spirit and wished it a narrative to fulfill these beliefs.

That spirit, of course, belongs to my father. The body is his as well: the hands that scooped out the pocket of earth and laid the seed to rest are now the buckeye's leaves, his limbs the branches, the mind that decided to plant the tree exactly there are its roots, stretching ten feet downhill from the squat evergreen, thirty feet from the house so that my mother may gaze at it from the window above the kitchen sink.

•

One does not need to pay for passage across Lethe. Charon the toll collector ferries the dead only across the Styx or Acheron. As payment, the dead must each give Charon an obol, or he will not allow them to cross. An obol holds little value; the coin is equivalent, roughly speaking, to a worker's daily wage in ancient Greece. If Charon does not receive his payment, the soul cannot cross and is fated to spend eternity in limbo between the world of the living and the world of the dead. To prevent this, families would place obols in the deceased's mouth, under the tongue or on the lips. This became Charon's obol: a viaticum, bus fare and a bag lunch, provision for a journey. The otherworldly narrative one can conjure from a small circular object, seed or coin, grasped in a hand.

•

My father's seizures began in 2003, the year before he planted the buckeye. They were minor, except when they were not and my mother and I spent the night next to him in a hospital bed at Mount Sinai. Medication could treat them, except when it could not. The seizures kept recurring and, by the summer of 2006, my father no longer worked in the garden or the field. He complained of his right hand cramping, of losing dexterity in his fingers. He no longer drank black coffee in Duralex glasses, the way he had growing up in Brazil, nor did he have a glass of Sandeman port after dinner, the way his mother did. He did not drive and this frustrated him. When I visited, I drove him from New York to Pennsylvania and he remained silent, watching the speedometer.

I wasn't around that summer—I worked on a farm near my college, weeding by hand, complaining of the straw that would scratch up my arms—and so I didn't witness these regressions. I could hear them, however, if I chose to. His voice had started to slur by then, his lip a little twisted, and so he sounded over the phone as if he had just woken up from a nap, disoriented, not entirely in his present state. I wasn't around that fall either: it was junior year and I went to study abroad in Rome.

In September of 2006, my father suffered a massive seizure while visiting his mother in Brazil. Two surgeries later, the right side of his body was paralyzed and he could no longer speak. By October, he was back in New York, flown twenty-four hours in a Medevac plane alongside my mother. She told him, when she was planning the evacuation, that he would be able to recover in the country, that they could watch the mother-of-pearl sunsets together and count sheep on the opposite hill. I nodded along. My father did not say anything. In November, after a little over two months of silence, he died.

•

Once one crosses the Styx and Acheron, there is still a ways to go before reaching Lethe. The dead, Plato writes in *Phaedo*, are sentenced to different parts of the underworld according to their earthly acts. Murderers, for example, are sent to Cocytus; those who have outraged their parents to Phlegethon. Once they have served their time there, the current brings them to the Akherousian Lake, where they must call out to those they have wronged and ask to be set free. If their plea is accepted, they may leave; if not, they are borne back into the rivers. These rules are meant for the dead. Yet if the living may travel to the underworld, if the living sometimes search for loved ones or drink from Lethe, I wonder if they can be judged as well. Why don't they float in the waters of Cocytus or Phlegethon?

•

Unlike other memories, the buckeye does not decay or fade, but gains in strength over time. It's tangible. My mother can mark its progress and measure its height as if it were a growing boy. She perceives its existence as remarkable, just as she perceives mine as such—her only child, born to her at the age of forty-two, unlikely life after a miscarriage. She nurtures it, this memory of my father before his illness—the scientist who loved trees, who loved experiments like burying seeds in the ground or sifting through bear shit he found on the road, oblivious to the implication that the bear and its danger might lurk nearby. She sees this and envisions a new, sturdier body, a body that grows skyward without shaking or collapsing.

Yet still, despite the buckeye's heartiness, she worries. She thinks of razing the trees around it, the squat evergreen and the weeping willow, holdovers from the previous owners, even though they don't steal the buckeye's light, even though the buckeye, in fact, robs theirs. She fears she won't be able to sustain its life or keep it healthy, that it owes its vitality to itself, to whatever magic my father's hands held that could create a living thing.

My mother worries, in particular, because she believes herself a hopeless gardener. "Not just hopeless, I'm cursed," she'll say. I don't want to believe her (how could the woman who swaddles the poodle in a towel after his bath to hold him in her arms fail at nurturing?), but the evidence exists. The plot I weeded the year before is overgrown as ever, the sole mark of success a transplanted petunia bush. When strangers politely inquire what she grows, she snaps back, "I grow weeds." It's not immediately clear that she's serious. Rumors of her inadequacy have apparently spread. The gardener who lives down the road does not return her calls. She does not know why. "I'm cursed, I'm doomed," she'll say. She has left several messages, asking for his services, offering him to name his price, but he has not called back.

Given the chance to keep something, someone, healthy all over again, she's enlisted my help. I weed the base of the buckeye, lay down mulch and wood chips. I build a wire fence around its perimeter to keep out rabbits. We both have no idea what we're doing, but these acts are of utmost importance—if I refuse or complain, the tree's life hangs in the balance, we could lose my father all over again— and so we walk out and admire it each visit, as if we were visiting a living tomb, as if we were trying to grow the thing on good karma alone.

•

In 2008, as the buckeye was making its ascent, my mother bought a tree in Central Park also in memory of my father. A horse chestnut, specifically. It stands in the North Meadow, along the path my father walked each morning to and from work. Standing beside this tree, you can see Mount Sinai to the east. The hospital's medical center, a large black building, fills the skyline. My father worked in this building as a cell biologist and was transferred there as a patient after my mother flew him out of Brazil. It was where he died. Adjacent to the horse chestnut lie the fields where he watched me play soccer growing up—I was the goalkeeper, he the assistant coach by virtue of his being Brazilian. Nearby, a five minute walk away, are the trees where he buried the pet hamster and cockatiel on his way to work, after we found them at the bottom of their cages.

•

I read about Central Park and a man named Elmaz Qyra one morning at my mother's kitchen table. The *New York Times* is profiling the dangers of the city's trees. Like my father, Qyra liked to walk in the park after work. When he had finished his shift as a busboy, he walked a few blocks north to the 59th street entrance and headed to Poet's Walk. One time in late February, 2010, he went for a walk after a heavy snow had fallen. At 3:00 p.m., the *Times* wrote, if there was any sunlight, Poet's Walk must have been wondrous. The park, his wife said, reminded him of his childhood home, of his parents' farm in Albania. What Qyra did not know, as he walked alone along the promenade, was that one of the trees above him was due to be removed. The year before, a limb had fallen from it and damaged another tree. A five-foot cavity swelled within its trunk and fungus infested it. Elmaz Qyra passed beneath and a fifteen-foot limb as heavy as a refrigerator fell, split his head open, and killed him.

•

After my father was hospitalized in Rio, I visited him there. I flew from Rome and stayed for two weeks. Over those two weeks, my father in then out of the ICU, I gained between five and ten pounds. I liked the food in the hospital cafeteria and it killed time. There wasn't much to do: hold my father's hand, read Graham Greene, watch soccer or CNN, masturbate, nap, wipe the sweat from my father's forehead, play solitaire on my iPod. Staying overnight in the hospital room, I would sleep from eight in the evening till ten the next morning. My mother did not. She lost fifteen pounds and started smoking again, exhaling a lot, smoke or sighs. She sighed so audibly and so out of the blue that I thought she did so on purpose, wanting my attention or awaiting my comment, but she said she didn't even know she was doing it.

My father lost even more weight, thirty pounds if I had to guess. Around a half pound came from his skull. A human skull weighs a little over two pounds and doctors removed a quarter of my father's to perform their second operation. They did not install a plate and so the left side of my father's head looked deflated. There seemed nothing separating brain from skin. The skin, hair shaved to a stubble, flapped and breathed of its own accord. If I pressed hard enough with my finger, I thought it would sink all the way in until it touched brain.

Needless to say, my father didn't have much of an appetite. I began to eat the soft, warm foods off his tray: macaroni and cheese, apple sauce, mashed potatoes, flan. The nurses who brought in the meals would do a song and dance each time as to how delicious the food looked, how hungry my father must be, how he needed sustenance to get his strength back up. I looked on while they did this, picking out which food I would eat first, the nurses little knowing that they were performing for me.

To eat and sleep, of course, is its own form of forgetting. If you were not awake for it, it's hard to say it really happened.

•

I cannot see the buckeye the way my mother sees it. My father does not stand tall within it, this ugly, puny thing choking the water and stealing sunlight away from the evergreen. Its growth is not representative of his spirit or his hand. There are few memories for me of my father in the country, none of his working the land. When my parents first bought this house, during the visit when my father planted this seed, I stayed in New York. I was still in high school then and their overnight trips meant that I could have friends over and hotbox the bathroom.

Still, I yearn to see it and him with her eyes. Now he rises balanced, where before there was asymmetry and paralysis. Now he grows and feeds on water where before he shrank, withered from the inability to retain fluid. Now bark armors the pith within his trunk, where before nothing encased his cerebral tissue or separated it from his skin. Now the wind rustles through his leaves and sometimes it even howls, where before there was only silence.

This is all, I suspect, just another way of forgetting. Or of remembering only what we want to remember. The river of Lethe runs underground and feeds the buckeye. By placing my father in this tree, my mother chooses to remember him as she preferred: as strong and healthy, flourishing instead of decaying. I do not fault her for that—it dulls the pain.

Form, however, collapses. My father's body, my mother's superstitions. And what happens when that balance breaks down, when the surface level can no longer hide the structural frailty underneath? Trees rot, desiccate, become infested, drink too deeply from poisonous waters. Oblivion lasts until it does not, until a branch snaps and falls in anger at its being forgotten.

•

Forms indeed collapse. Within her own memory, my mother has begun to mix-up names. She calls me Rafael. She calls the dog Tom. She calls my father Tom or Celso, the poodle's name. Sometimes she says your grandfather, when she means your dad. What's more, she no longer catches the slip. I used to correct her every time, jumping on the chance of being right. Now I let it slide.

Her memory is sharp in other ways. "Do you visit dad's tree?" she'll ask me, meaning the horse chestnut she purchased in Central Park. I tell her not so much. I rarely have reason to pass it—I no longer play soccer or baseball on those fields, I have no desire to cross the park and visit Mount Sinai. I read a book underneath it once, Salinger's *Nine Stories*. "No, Mom," I'll say, "I was a mile away." I ask her if she ever visits and she says she doesn't often end up around there, it's out of her way and a bit hard to get to. She means she can see that big black building in the east. But she's glad the tree's there all the same.

•

I read the *Times* to learn of more cases like Elmaz Qyra's—dozens of incidents over the past decade, at least ten lawsuits against the city stemming from them. In 2009, the year before Qyra died, a thirty-three-year-old Google engineer, father of two, was struck by a 100-pound branch from an oak thirty-seven feet above him. He suffered traumatic brain injuries, paralysis, and damage to his spinal cord and lungs; his lawsuit, still pending, is worth 120 million dollars. In June of 2010, a branch fell on a mother and her six-month-old daughter outside the Central Park Zoo, killing the infant. This lawsuit is also still pending. What seemed highly improbable—a fate for those with bad karma, for the superstitious to fear—has now entered the realm of possibility. The realm where we no longer have to assign divine or spectral cause, where we should be more careful about what hangs over our heads.

Adrian Benepe, then New York City Parks commissioner, made a statement that the only way to prevent falling branches would be to cut down all of the city's trees, a measure that would do more harm than good. The Central Park Conservancy writes: "The trees of Central Park have an important impact on the urban environment. They improve the quality of our air and water; reduce storm water runoff, flooding and erosion; and lower the air temperature in the summer. This is why Central Park is called the lungs of New York City." Benepe further added after Qyra's accident that "There is no reason to believe anything else might happen like that."

•

At my grandparents' house growing up, my cousins and I

would play a game called Monster under my grandfather's horse chestnut tree. My father would chase us around the yard, his face twisted into a rictus, lip upturned into sneer. "Now I'm coming to get you," he would shout, once he had given us enough time to reach safety. If my father found and caught us, he would wrap us up in his arms and the game would be over. To avoid him, we hid under the canopy of the horse chestnut tree. When we heard him coming, his stomp and growl, we began to climb the tree. We climbed a limb near the tree's edge, one that ran along the ground until it rose upwards again. My father would palm open the curtain of leaves and scowl, feigning disorientation, giving us time, pretending he did not know we had run to where we always ran to. For reasons unexplained, he could not climb the tree so elevation proved our safe haven. If we climbed beyond his grasp and kicked free of the hands that grabbed at our ankles, he could do nothing but look up at us—our chests breathing against bark, arms hugging the tree limb, feet dangling— and glower. Then the game would end.

Eventually a branch necessary to climb this limb snapped off. It was our first foothold and, without it, we were helpless. My father nailed a two-by-four to the trunk where the branch had been. Our feet could not wrap around it the same way, but it remained fixed and we could climb the limb again. I know that even if this limb were to continue growing, this two-by-four would stay in the same place and persist, at the perfect height for a four-year-old's step. This, to me, is stable memory, oblivion's antithesis. That is, until a new owner decides to prune the branches, or lightning strikes the thing, or hurricane Sandy or Amelia or Rachel or Alexandra or Hannah moves in off the Atlantic, or the branch just rots and poisons the tree and I die.

•

The last time I heard my father's voice was on my birthday. I was in the shower, in Rome, and my cell phone rang. turned off the water and answered. It was October and m mother was at Mount Sinai, my father Medevaced on a 1 hour flight back to New York. He raised his fist in victory when he was rolled off the plane in New York: he didn' want to die in Brazil. She wished me happy birthday and put him on the phone. He was doing better and could form a few sounds. Mostly sighs. The word *hey*. He made it half way through *happy birthday*. I waited on the other end, head leaning against the tiles, naked, dripping wet.

The last time I heard him speak a sentence was at the airport. I had an evening flight to Fiumicino and he was to fly to Rio de Janeiro the following day. I don't remember what he said, but it must have been along the lines of: "Be safe, Tom. Remember x, remember y. Love you. Be safe."

I asked my mother why they didn't call me from the hospital more often, if my father could manage a few words. She said she didn't really know. "Dad was tired," she said, "It was very hard for him. He preferred silence." Now it's hard to know how he felt about us, if he was mad I was not there, if I were acting the right way or hurting him further. We could have just remained speechless over the line but I do not say that, just as my mother does not ask me why I did not call the hospital myself, why I stayed in Rome.

•

The above is not exactly true. The last time I heard my father's voice was not on my birthday or at the airport, but a few years after his death. He had recorded the message on the answering machine at the house in Pennsylvania. I would call from time to time, when I knew my mother was not there. His voice sounded distracted, caught off-guard, because either my mother or I had just walked into the room. You could hear the kitchen chair creak as he leaned in when the recording began. I didn't tell my mother I did this, but I am almost certain she did the same because sometime later, when I was away or abroad, she changed the recording to an automated message and erased his last remaining words. Though I wouldn't have done so, I only hope the agony of deleting his voice, the willful choice to forget, weighed less for her than the pain of its reminder.

•

While there's no account of what Elmaz Qyra heard before he died, others describe the sound of a falling branch in various ways. It can sound like a thunderclap. Or the creak of a floorboard in a horror movie. A booming. A loud crack or snap. It is something. It is a warning or a taunt or a condemnation.

•

Trees rot because of fungus and internal decay. A tree suffers a significant wound, anything larger than three to four inches in diameter, and fungi will establish their presence in the time it takes it to form a callous over its injury. It's a common phenomenon for a tree to suffer significant injury: lightning can strike or a thunderstorm can break a limb; roots can be damaged underground or insects can infest it; there's human harm, say someone who prunes one large limb instead of several smaller ones. As a defense mechanism, trees will compartmentalize their decay to maintain structural integrity. That is, fungi will only rot away the dead wood in the center of the tree. A tree can sustain the hollowing of its core as long as new rings are forming and widening around its circumference; its structure can bear a central emptiness if there is something to compensate. Just as humans—my suffering mother, my sick father—will do. Some trees do a better job of compartmentalizing decay than others. Oaks, for example. Some trees do not. Hackberries. Ash. Horse chestnuts.

•

Technically, my mother did not buy the horse chestnut tree in Central Park, but an endowment for it. The Tree Trust of the Central Park Conservancy offers New Yorkers the opportunity to "create a living memory that will last for generations to come." In exchange for a donation, the Conservancy will engrave a paving stone in honor of the endower along the southern end of Poet's Walk. The endower also receives the more or less false sense that he or she owns a tree.

Donations range depending on the tree endowed. For $1,000, you can purchase a new sapling. For $5,000, a remarkable tree and an engraved granite paving stone.

For $12,000, a tree cluster family. For $25,000, a historic tree, planted 150 years ago at Central Park's inception. For $250,000, you can purchase groves or allées. Groves are a cluster composed of four or more trees of the same species. Allées are "a unique arrangement of two or more rows of the same species." The example the Conservancy gives is of the majestic American elms along Poet's Walk itself. With these come an engraved bronze plaque.

My mother purchased a remarkable tree. Her engraved granite paving stone, must read somewhere on Poet's Walk: *"Endowed by JUDY THOMAS in honor of RAFAEL MIRA Y LOPEZ."* But I am not sure. I've never visited.

•

I flew from Rome to New York in early November. I landed on a Thursday and was to fly back on Sunday, but my father died that Sunday night so I stayed. That day, around noon or one in the afternoon, a doctor told my mother and me that my father would not last very long. I told my mother I would be right back. I took the elevator down the eight or nine floors from the ICU my father had been moved into the night before and stepped out onto the street. Across Fifth Avenue was Central Park and I began to run. I ran into the park, past the dust field, past the North Meadow, past the horse chestnut where my father's spirit would later reside, out onto the Upper West Side and north ten blocks until I reached the Cathedral of St. John the Divine. I entered and told the man behind the donation booth that I would like to buy the $3.95 candle. I handed him a twenty and he told me he could not make change and pointed to a sign. I left, bought an Apricot Linzer cookie at the pastry shop next door, came back, put a five dollar bill on the counter, took my candle, and threw the cookie at the man. I walked down the nave until I reached the bed of candles by the altar. I lay the wick in a neighboring candle's flame and placed mine among the others. Written on the glass of the other candles were messages and well-wishes for loved and lost ones. I did not write anything, but I did make a wish. A wish that, if I were to say what it was, I'd be afraid wouldn't come true.

I took a cab back to the hospital. I watched the New York Giants lose to the Chicago Bears and that night, figuring things would hold, I told my mother I was going back to the apartment. I'd have a bite to eat and get some rest. My aunt had just driven down and we ordered take-out, General Tso's Chicken and scallion pancakes. The food arrived and a call came from my mother. "You should come back," she said. I did. When I arrived, my father seemed the same and I fell asleep in an armchair at the foot of the bed. The overnight nurse came and left and, after she did so, when his breathing began to shallow, my mother told me, "You should come to the bed, Tom."

•

A remarkable tree is an interesting name for a common horse chestnut, especially when one considers that the Conservancy is naming things that do not know they have names. But a remarkable tree is exactly what my mother believes this chestnut to be.

Endowments help ensure the maintenance of Central Park, but the Conservancy does not inform you what happens if your particular tree is damaged or destroyed.

This is a valid concern. On Halloween in 2011, an unexpected and unprecedented snowstorm damaged 1,000 trees in Central Park. Earlier that year, Hurricane Irene destroyed 100 trees.

Before these, a thunderstorm downed more than 100 trees in the park on a single day, August 19, 2009. Hundreds more were damaged, many fatally. This was the most severe destruction the park's trees had sustained in decades and it was concentrated in the northern third of the park where my father's horse chestnut stood. The storm was a microburst: straight-line winds reached speeds of 70 mph. "Central Park has been devastated," said Adrian Benepe, then Parks commissioner. "You have personal relationships with certain trees and now they are gone." "We're not going to be around in 80 years when they grow back," said Donna Castellano, director of operations of the cardiology department in the big, black building at Mount Sinai.

The storm lasted from around 10:00 to 10:30 p.m., a time in years past when my father would be walking home from work, when I would be in another part of the park, getting high with my friends. The storm destroyed another horse chestnut close to my father's, near the entrance at 100th street. The city temporarily closed the fields at North Meadow because of safety concerns. Yet no one was hurt, strange when one considers that, after such a storm, the likelihood of a falling branch causing serious injury would increase. "I have good reflexes," said a jogger the following day, when asked if he was concerned.

My father's chestnut went unscathed. "It was terrible," my mother reported to me, "but what a miracle. Nothing happened to Dad's tree. How lucky." It survived with only a few broken branches. It had earned its remarkableness.

•

After you watch someone die, an odd minute passes when
you are unsure what to do next. It's a minute removed
from time's flow, even though you are very sure of what
time it is. When my father died, this happened. The nurses
were not yet informed, the hall was silent, it was 11:11 p.m.
There was not much for us to do. I did not know whether
I was allowed or supposed to touch him. What I did—with
the knowledge that one day I would look back, hovering
over myself to scrutinize these actions—was take a penny
from my pocket and place it in my father's hand. This was
not easy; *place* is not the precise verb. I had to uncurl his
hand (his right hand, the one that had been paralyzed,
though now it made no difference), stick the penny against
the palm's flesh, and then close the hand again. But the
penny would not stay put, his hand did not want to close,
and so I wedged it in between his index and middle fingers,
near the lowest knuckle.

Why I did this puzzles me. I knew it would at the time
and I believe that was part of the reason. It wasn't Charon's
obol exactly—I did not open my father's mouth and lay the
coin on his tongue—but it was an act of superstition. I'm
not a pagan or a polytheist, I don't believe in Hades or the
underworld. I am the son of a scientist. But, all the same,
I told my mother as I struggled with his hand, "He might
need this."

I believe now that this was not just superstition, but
forgetting. Passage paid for not on Acheron or Styx, but on
Lethe. I was, in a way, trying to obscure or distort memory,

to make surreal or unreal what I would otherwise have to account for as the truth. I was not being me, but watching myself be me. That bad old habit of pretending you're a character in a movie: this is one way of dealing with a situation you are unprepared for, to watch what motions you will go through as if from a distance. I watched myself put a penny in my father's hand because I knew I would later replay that moment and not what happened the minute before. I ran a mile and a half to the Cathedral, for example, when I could have taken a cab because to run was more cinematic.

Milton calls Lethe "the wat'ry labyrinth, whereof who drinks, forthwith his former state and being forgets." I say Lethe because, when I look back upon that day, I see someone other than myself going through those motions. I see someone who, when not eating or sleeping, was wrapped up in the business of being another; who already then was planting a seed to obscure the past; who was busy constructing a labyrinth of oblivion. I see a boy who was prepared to wave happily goodbye to memory and father if it meant circumnavigating the rivers of hate, pain, lamentation, and rage. I see someone content to lose sight, to let the boat slip into slick still fog, if all it left him was a penny poorer.

•

The trees Elmaz Qyra walked underneath were the allées, the American elms of Poet's Walk that can be purchased for $250,000. "These elms," the Conservancy writes, "are one of the largest and last remaining stands in North America, and one of the Park's most photographed areas." It goes on: "They form a cathedral-like canopy above the Park's widest pedestrian pathway." The American elm that killed Qyra, the one scheduled to be removed, the one within which a five-foot cavity swelled, was given a special name for the way it always appeared bathed in light. It was called the Ghost Elm.

I called my mother to find out what she inscribed along Poet's Walk and discovered I had it wrong. She said she did not buy an endowment for a horse chestnut. She wanted to but they had none available. She had bought an endowment for an American elm.

•

Midway through *The Aeneid*, Aeneas descends to the underworld and reunites with his father Anchises. When the Greeks sacked Troy, Aeneas fled the city carrying his elderly father upon his back. Before he reaches what will become Rome, before even Dido and Carthage, Aeneas lands at the city of Drepanum in Sicily. There, Anchises dies. A year or so later, Aeneas breaks off a golden bough, gives it as a gift to Proserpina, and wins entrance into the underworld. When eventually he finds his father there, he sees a multitude of people drinking from a river and asks Anchises what they are doing. Anchises tells him the following: "They are the souls who are destined for Reincarnation; and now at Lethe's stream they are drinking the waters that quench man's troubles, the deep draught of oblivion…They come in crowds to the river Lethe, so that you see, with memory washed out they may revisit the earth above."

•

So, you see, I had it backwards. The living do not drink from Lethe; the dead do. It is not my mother and I who drink for oblivion, but my father. Its waters wash his subterranean roots, wipe out all memories of pain and agony and paralysis and monstrosity, and perhaps, I hope, restore him to balance and peace. A tree that readies itself to grow and survive, to stand in symmetry, to speak in whispers and wind but to speak nonetheless. He would, of course, in his preparation for earthly life, forget all else. He would forget us, his wife and child; he would have to. It's a fair trade, I think. The most my mother and I could hope for is something animate, something spirited and numinous to pass between us, some flash of sun to glance off the buckeye and catch my mother's eye at the kitchen window, or some pattern of light and shade to fall across the pages of my book as I sit on a rock underneath my father the remarkable horse chestnut.

But maybe that is not so. Let us pause on that rock, that tree, that American elm that survived one thunderstorm and more to come. Let us stage another cinematic scene. Imagine an incision of more than three to four inches in diameter, imagine a fungus creeping in, imagine decay and rot and the loss of integrity. Imagine the penny was needed, but it fell loose from his hand. Imagine that Lethe was the wrong river all along, that really we are still stuck on the Styx or Acheron or Cocytus or Phlegethon, that the waters still bubble with hate and pain and lamentation and rage. Imagine there is no end, no true forgetting, that whatever already happened will continue to gnaw and plague and eat away at me and my father and mother. Imagine that

that's how eternity works. And now imagine that I have actually come to visit my father's tree, that I have come to sit on the rock underneath its branches and read a book and occasionally look out at the children playing soccer and, farther away, the large black building where he died. And imagine what if I have it all wrong—what if, just what if, the sound I heard before the branch fell and split open a quarter of my skull was not the boom or crack or thunder or creak others described hearing, but a voice, his voice, his deprived voice, and it was mad as all hell and it said to me, "You motherfucker, you monster, you tried to sleep and eat your way past me, you tried to pretend I wasn't there, you piece of shit, you stayed away while I was dying, you ingrate, you fuck, you ordered Chinese food two hours before my death, you asshole, you masturbator, you were content to let me go if it made your life easier, you selfish son of a bitch, you, you, you, you, you, it's always about you. But now I'm coming to get you."

THE DECADENCE OF GRAPEFRUIT
TOTI O'BRIEN

It was the first thing I noticed when I paced in front of the house, waiting for the real estate agent. I had found the house on the internet—very cheap, undersized even for my basic needs, quite a fixer-upper and marginal in location. But I needed a place, right then. And by instinct I knew this was the one.

The tree—so enormous it obstructed the view—calmed me down. Soothed me.

I had never seen such a tall one, though I was raised in a citrus orchard. Our grapefruit trees were small and uncared for. My grand folks traded in oranges, lemons, and tangerines—those were taken seriously. Grapefruit were an exotic plus for the family and thrived on their own, spare and kinky, overlooked.

This one, though, doubled the house. Its branches spread over the roof, loaded with yellow spheres. The fruit bunched up in clusters—like grapes, as the name implies—brightly outlined against the dark leaves.

The tree won me. A landmark, it spoke of childhood and nostalgia. The orange trees I later discovered in the back added to the incantation. Yet the deal seemed doomed to failure. Everything that could have went wrong. The whole process staggered station to station—a *via crucis* without resurrection in view. When transactions became truly bad I tried to pull out. Why insist? Complications multiplied themselves with inappropriate redundancy. Still, somehow, I sensed the tide would change. I would end up by the grapefruit tree, sooner or later.

I moved in at the beginning of February. That's when, from the window against which I pushed the piano, I noticed the face on the trunk. First I thought someone sculpted it. I was told bohemians and hippies once inhabited the house. Perhaps some artistic soul carved it into the cambium.

But those features—brows, eyes, nose, lips, high cheeks—were natural, an effect of creases and bumps in the bark. Weirdly, the face—nicely framed by the window—only appeared when I sat at the piano and looked up for inspiration. Light and shadow, a particular angle of view.

March arrived. The air filled up with scents of citrus blossoms. The balm inebriated me like a sensuous sea, a dynamite mix of memory and hope.

In the following months I learned about the life and death of grapefruit—more than I wanted to know. The tree was a stunning producer, but I couldn't harvest. Practically none of the fruit was within reach. In the back I found a ladder so shaky I didn't dare climb it. Not without help, and help I couldn't find. I looked for eco-charitable groups eager for donations and endowed with the appropriate equipment. Everyone I called was overbooked.

From March to July my tree spat about fifty fruits a day, dropping them from so high they burst on the lawn with impressive thuds. I ate some, juiced some, but couldn't use a half hundred. In the piteous state they were in after meeting the ground, I couldn't give them to people. While I sought ways to avoid wasting I tried to keep up with the mess—each spill quickly darkening, morphing into pungent, fermented, sticky glue. Passing cars smashed the orbs into mushy starfish, sadly liquefying through my fingers. Soon the starfish dried up, separating themselves from the asphalt—nice and clean, like a nut or seed. I carefully removed them.

But I wasn't happy with corpses. I wanted to salvage the bounty. How to get that high? Cherry picker? Helicopter? Balloon?

At night the fruit fell like miniature earthquakes. On the roof, on pavement, on grass, the loud blows jarred my sleep. I imagined knocks at the door. An instant of panic, then a turn to the side, a pillow placed over my head: "It's just a grapefruit," I muttered.

Tiny ones fell, too. If the ripe stuff isn't harvested, babies fall. When I was a kid in the citrus grove I collected them, though they weren't edible. I, at least, thought they were beautiful. Now, among yellow bodies and brown hides, I gingerly picked small emerald pearls.

Pleased in my vain collection I filled a maiolica bowl, proudly propped besides my front door. I enjoyed its calm, composed beauty, contrasting the surrounding mess. Once, an airborne fruit landed in my display with the usual commotion. It splashed all my trophies around and tilted the vase. I understood the tree's sense of humor then. "I'll look for a better ladder," I whispered.

•

I lied. I didn't have energy left for agricultural enterprises. Tossing spoils was all I was good for.

Until a friend built me a picker of exceptional length—a tall stick topped by a milk bottle, slit open. Could I have thought of it earlier? Once the fruit sat into the bottle I pulled down, the bottleneck caught, and the stem detached from the branch. Now I could harvest the lowest third of the thing. Lowest fourth. Lowest fifth. Lowest fringes of fruit.

Enthusiastic about my new collecting capacity, I started keeping a basketful on the backseat of my car, eager to share its content in whatever occasion.

I discovered grapefruit has a fifty-fifty share of lovers and haters. Indicators of who is who aren't clear. Thus I went from a phase of indiscriminate prodigality to a phase of prudent restraint. I decided to limit my offer to those openly showing appreciation. My front neighbor, for instance.

She was the nicest lady. I saw her walking her dog, stopping to lift a fruit from the ground once or twice, caressing it gently. I selected a couple of gorgeous pieces, left them on her porch. Then again. She was first to acknowledge their exceptional sweetness which, of course, made the waste crueler.

She started reciprocating. Once I found at my door a platter of berries, nuts, raisins. Next was a carrot cake, then a slice of pie. I am not a dessert person but it happened to be my birthday. She of course didn't know. I ate, and I cried.

She retired from her job, purchased a better place, moved away. I understood but grieved her departure. Neighbors come and go, I know. Trees mostly remain.

Then a friend found out grapefruit rind contains a detoxicant—something to help eliminate iron residue from blood. She wanted to grate and freeze a large quantity of peel, to then sprinkle it on food on a daily basis, all year round. I invited her to self-serve. She often came with her husband, and ladders. They climbed quietly. I heard a soft rustle through the branches. Then I found a small cluster at my door, as a thank you note.

News of my riches spread by word of mouth. Two guys I had never met asked if they could collect for marmalade. "Of course!" I said. Every rescued fruit was a sigh of relief.

They harvested under a downpour, on a Saturday. Later they sent through the mail a jar of darkish, good-tasting jam. A homemade label accompanied the homemade recipe. Their picture was on it, golden spheres in hand, green branches crowning their faces. I stuck it on my fridge with a mixture of tenderness and pride.

•

I had finally a list of happy takers, and I had mapped a delivery tour. Though my handmade device started falling apart, I struggled to get as high as possible, maddened by the abundance still out of reach. I divided my load in equal bags left at several doors. My errand gave me great pleasure, making me feel like a sunny Santa Claus. A grapefruit fairy.

Meanwhile, a food organization accepted, at last, to collect for the hungry and homeless. Alas, only a young girl arrived, with no ladder. But she had a fruit picker. We gathered the little we could, improving the bounty with a case of oranges or two. Later I got a receipt in the mail— what I had given could be deducted from taxes. Fruit were valued two dollars apiece.

I was stunned: could I live on the proceeds of my crop?

It was what my grand folks had done. The cash for the house came directly from the land, the groves, the trees. Weren't they my whole foundation? I imagined following the ancestral ways, monetizing the overwhelming production I had chanced upon. Weekly, daily farmer markets. Tasty jams in fancily-decorated pots. Liquors. Curds. A whole line of delicacies. Anyone who needed an income would have thought of it. Most would have put the thinking into action.

I didn't. Not sure what was keeping me. Maybe a sense of strange reverence. Was the tree my property? Or was it the other way around?

•

I surrounded the trunk with river stones, the most beautiful I could find. In the ring I planted a fern—her green fluffiness complementing the brown of the bark. I added seasonal flowers—snowbells, pink chrysanthemum. They hid in the creases, by the roots, blooming randomly, impromptu—small winks of surprise. They reminded me of violets I used to dig out, hidden under ivy and grass by the roots of palm trees. Patches of color and smell, tiny appendages of arboreal majesty.

I was four or five, and I stayed at my grand folks most of the year. I squeezed violets into letters I wrote to Mom. All I could trace was my signature, implemented by a spread of purple petals, sweet smelling. The envelope was thick and brittle—I wonder what crumbled out when Mother unsealed it. But it didn't matter as long as it crossed the sea, traveled up the continent, reached her in her busy office. In the busy town—so remote—where she lived.

I lived in the orchards. They were my entire universe.

Grapefruit trees grew on slopes, spontaneously seeded, scrawny and kind of ridiculous with their spare branches and giant fruit. Orange, lemon, tangerine trees occupied acres and acres, terraced up the hills overlooking the ocean. Those trees, under which I spent all day, were tended to perfection. Their bed was neatly edged, devoid of extraneous intrusions. No weeds were allowed. Dead leaves, broken twigs were removed. Brown earth, like a carpet, was kept damp as needed—irrigation a scientific deal. Canopies, rigorously trimmed, joined in tunnels and roofs. Leaves were perky, alive. I accompanied Grandpa for hours while he snapped—with his outgrown, knife-sharp fingernail—pea green, cocky young sprouts from the trunks. They needed constant pruning to save lymph for the main branches, for the fruit.

Grandpa's life was bound to the orchards, organized around their maintenance, their needs, and their miracle. Various harvests at different times of the year, for different qualities of citruses, could go well, badly, or anything in between. It depended on subtle adjustments. On smart choices, alertness, and infinite care. We depended upon it.

•

When I turned thirteen Grandpa died. Unexpectedly, but then you don't usually get a notice. His last years had been shadowed by threats to the land. The town administration wanted to build a mega incinerator on it. Burning garbage. In the place of orchards. Burning truckfuls of garbage. Grandpa fought. He momentarily won.

But as soon as he died (had the town waited for it?) the entire grove was seized. The new plan was to build factories instead—laminating iron—for municipal financial improvement. It was a scam—huge amounts of money were allotted and pocketed, while no factory was ever built. A rectangular foundation lay for decades on top of Grandpa's gutted hill, facing the ocean. Slowly, wild grass swallowed it up.

But the orchards were down in two days. Was it less? The trees were abated by huge tank-like contraptions, and indeed it felt like a war zone. All those trunks lined up—thousands. They could have built a bridge. Or a railroad, spanning from my messy front yard to the motherland I had left behind.

●

Grandpa planted a citrus tree the day I was born. He gave it my name. I am sure he showed it to me, but I didn't pay attention back then. I recall a healthy green thing in its square of earth, lined with other green things—brothers, sisters, cousins. Grandpa planted a tree for each baby. All grandchildren were honored. I am not sure which meaning he gave to the ritual. He had a pragmatic mind and an engineer's sensibility. But he was a fierce nature lover and a caring soul.

I haven't wondered where my tree went. What does a tree matter when thousand are gone in a night or two? When a pair of gutted hills is all that's left under the sky.

●

Since the factories where a scam, the inheritors sued the government. All the paperwork gathered dust as expected, year after year. Then one day our family won. The money was distributed, a share handed to each living relative.

I know a bundle of money can't pay back for a lost grove. But it did pay for this fixer-upper, and for this sprawling giant in the front yard. Grandpa would be impressed. Proud. Perhaps he would have given it a name.

FALL
ZOË RUIZ

My sister says that my father will die soon, and the leaves on the tree turn yellow. When the leaves are gone, my father will be gone, too. I stand on the balcony each morning, drink a cup of coffee, and look down at the tree in the backyard. From the thin branches, leaves drop one by one, unless there is wind. Then they spiral in the air and drop to the ground in clumps of yellow.

·

In the forest, where it is dark and cold, pine trees cover the sky above the creek, and the water reflects shades of green and brown. The rocks in the water shine like silver, and in the middle of the creek, a tree glows yellow. I balance on the rocks until I am standing beside the tree. I hold my breath and reach out my hand. My fingers touch a large yellow leaf and I believe that I am touching my father's death.

·

The sunlight streamed through the yellow curtains and I noticed the whites of my boyfriend's eyes were yellow. It was Valentine's Day. I left him on Valentine's Day. I drove down the 101 to Malibu. I sat on the sand underneath the glare of the sun and wrote him a letter on a legal pad. I was at Zuma Beach while he was in an emergency room in Oakland. That was eight years ago, but the yellow of that day is with me now.

I tear off a piece of white sage and say thank you to the plant on the hillside. I rub the fresh sage into the palm of my hands and breathe in the scent. I walk along the dusty trail for miles, place one foot in front of the other for hours. I pause to look at the forest. Thank you, I say to the mountains. I sweat and feel exhausted and empty. I sit down and bite into an apple. A woodpecker drums its beak on a tree above me and I say, Thank you.

•

In the backyard, the tree is bare and my father is still alive. The man is skeletal. His translucent skin hangs loose from his thin bones. Each of his ten fingers are crooked and bent, and he holds them in the air, above his sunken chest. He has little lung capacity left. He opens his mouth, his teeth are rotten, and he says, Help me. His voice is a whisper, and repeatedly, like a prayer, my father says, Help me.

•

The storm causes strong winds and hard rainfall. Rocks slide from the hillside onto the narrow and curvy road that leads to the forest. Trees and branches collapse onto the muddy trail. The forest is blocked off to the public. The forest is deemed unsafe.

•

Paris is attacked. An attempted bombing and mass shooting takes place at a holiday party in San Bernardino. My father is dying in a room in Burbank. A man with a gun enters a clinic that offers abortion services and kills three people in Colorado Springs. Nine women who work in the adult film industry accuse their Los Angeles-based male coworker of rape. My sister says that she fantasizes about driving off a cliff, that she will be dead before any of us. I do not sleep well these days but then again who does?

•

I listen to the rain and look at the mountains. I take down the dry sage that is hanging from my bedroom wall. I light a match and hold the flame to the tip of a leaf and the whitish-green leaf turns into a bright yellow flame. The flame turns into an ember and smoke rises. I wave the sage slowly around my body. Black ashes fall on the floor and the sharp scent of sage fills my room.

THE PRIEST IN THE TREES
FRED BAHNSON

On the last Sunday in September 2015, the Reverend Stephen Blackmer stopped beside the stand of beech stumps where he had once performed the chainsaw Eucharist. He was leading a dozen or so members of the Church of the Woods on a contemplative walk. With his plaid shirt, decades-old custom Limmer hiking boots, and graying beard sans mustache, Blackmer didn't look the part of a religious professional. He skipped nimbly over roots and rocks, turning around to laugh or make a point. His talk swept from exuberant to pensive to crass; at times he sounded like the theologically astute priest he was, at others like a mischievous wood sprite.

It was the first anniversary of the church, located several miles from the town of Canterbury, New Hampshire. A full lunar eclipse was expected that night, and Blackmer would be turning sixty in a few days. To celebrate these auspicious events, church members had planned a full day of activities: meditation walks, trail work, a Eucharist service, a bonfire, and, for those who still had energy, an eclipse-viewing party. When the group paused along the ridge of beech stumps it was midmorning; they were only halfway through a circumnavigation of the church's 106 acres, which Blackmer described as a "labyrinth on a grand scale." There was no church building, just woods. If you wanted to see the sanctuary, you had to hike.

The contemplative trek would take around three hours, but no one was complaining. Long walks in the woods are conducive to stories. Like the story of the chainsaw Eucharist. On a sunny, twelve-degree day in January,

Blackmer had hiked into the Church of the Woods pulling a sled full of trail-clearing gear: axe, chain saw, oil, and gas. He wanted to clear new meditation trails, which mostly involved sawing up blowdowns and saplings. When he came to the ridge, he found it choked by the stand of young beech, so he cranked up his Jonsered and began felling trees. Over the next hour, Blackmer had a growing feeling that something wasn't right. He hit the kill switch. *Shit, he* thought, *I have utterly sinned and fallen short of the glory of God.* It wasn't cutting trees that bothered him. It was that he had been taking life after life "and had been utterly oblivious to the enormity of that act." He had failed to remember that trees, even scrubby little saplings, are worthy of reverence.

Blackmer's sled also held what he called his prayer kit: Communion bread, a water bottle full of wine, the Book of Common Prayer. Kneeling in the sawdust and snow beside one of the widest stumps, he spread out the elements and set up an altar. That day's lectionary reading was from Isaiah. He read aloud:

> I have swept away your transgressions like a cloud, and your sins like mist. Return to me, for I have redeemed you.... Shout, O depths of the earth Break forth into singing, O mountains, O forest, and every tree in it.

He prayed the prayer of confession, consecrated the bread and wine, and offered them to his fellow congregants—the trees—before partaking himself.

•

Until nine years ago, Blackmer was an agnostic. After

146

training as a forest ecologist at the Yale School of Forestry and Environmental Studies in the early Eighties, he founded and directed two successful conservation organizations in New England: the Northern Forest Center, where he managed a staff of more than a dozen and an annual budget of roughly $1.2 million, and the Northern Forest Alliance, a coalition of advocacy groups that succeeded in both shifting the local logging industry to more sustainable types of forestry and conserving millions of acres of land across Vermont, New Hampshire, New York, and Maine. At the time, Blackmer had no use for religion, especially for *Chris-chens*, as he called them—"those angry, antiscience, antienvironmental bigots." He was fond of the bumper sticker that read BORN PRETTY GOOD THE FIRST TIME.

Then, on a flight to Dublin in 2007, Blackmer heard the Voice. As the plane descended he looked down and saw a church steeple. *Priest*, the Voice said. *You are to be a priest.* He had heard the Voice before, and would hear it many times over the next year, but on the plane it would be the clearest. It was a sound he heard in his heart rather than his ears, but a voice nonetheless, and what it said was not a suggestion like, *Have you ever considered a career in the ministry? You have the right set of skills.* It was a statement of fact. *You are to be a priest.*

There is more to Blackmer's story, both before and after that flight over Dublin, but perhaps the most immediately startling thing is this: not until he arrived at divinity school, two years later, did he actually read the Bible. As a child, he'd read a few chapters of Genesis and heard the Christmas story. When he finally sat down and read the story to which he had committed his life, he was struck by how often the biblical writers engaged the very subject he'd spent his career studying: the land. The places in which the narrative occurred—mountaintops, hillsides, lakeshores, gardens—were not just stages on which the human story played out; they were actors in the story itself. He came to love the Psalms, and the frequency with which the psalmist used metaphors of nature, especially trees. In Psalm 92 the righteous ones "flourish like the palm tree. They are planted in the house of the Lord.... In old age they still produce fruit; they are always green and full of sap." In other Psalms the trees of the fields clap their hands, shout for joy. When humans sing praises, they do the same thing. Nature is not inert. It was a revelatory idea.

In the Gospels, Blackmer found the most intriguing examples of divine encounter in nature. He kept noticing what he called "throwaway lines": after Jesus had "dismissed the crowds, he went up the mountain by himself to pray" (Matthew), or "He would withdraw to deserted places and pray" (Luke). Sometimes Jesus went to a garden. Or a lakeshore. Or the Judean desert. The location varied, but the pattern was evident throughout the Gospels. Jesus went to the temple "to teach and to raise a ruckus," but when he needed to pray Jesus fled to the countryside, to places unmediated by both temples and the religious authorities that governed them. Blackmer came to believe that direct contact with God is religion's raison d'être, but one that's often lacking in church. Of course one can experience God in a building, he concedes. But for at least some people, especially at this moment in history, there needs to be a practice of going into the wilderness to pray. And if one lives in New England, the obvious place to do that is the woods.

Though affiliated with the Episcopal Church (the denomination in which Blackmer was ordained), the Church of the Woods is tied to a nonprofit organization called Kairos Earth, which Blackmer founded in 2013. In biblical Greek, *kairos* refers to an opportune or critical moment when God acts. In its first year, nearly nine hundred people attended services at the Church of the Woods. Of its thirty or so regular members, nearly half have graduate degrees. Many are medical professionals whose finely tuned diagnostic skills tell them that our planet is running a fever. As Wendy Weiger, a Harvard-trained research physician, told me, "Climate change is the biggest public-health crisis humanity has ever faced."

Blackmer believes our ecological crises have precipitated a *kairos* moment. He sees a parallel with the Book of Jeremiah, in which the prophet describes a sense of impending doom as the Babylonians laid siege to Jerusalem in 587 B.C. "I looked on the earth, and lo, it was waste and void," Jeremiah wrote, "and to the heavens, and they had no light." On reading the book in seminary, Blackmer's first thought had been, *He's talking about climate change.*

As Western Christianity undergoes its identity crisis—a reformation or a slow implosion, depending on your leaning—a small but determined number of people like Blackmer are urging the church to seek God in the literal wilderness. They are calling for carbon repentance, but their credo is more nuanced than just slapping a fresh coat of Christian morality onto secular environmental politics; the Sierra Club at prayer this is not. At the Church of the Woods there is no action plan, no hive of online activity promising the earth's salvation if only you *click here*. There is rather a summons, an invitation to carry contemplative practice and ritual enactment into one's local ecosystem and thereby rediscover the awe and wonder that Moses experienced before the burning bush. By wooing Christianity back to its feral beginnings, Blackmer believes, we can finally confront the long trajectory of our ecological sin, and perhaps begin to change direction.

•

It was late morning at the stand of beech stumps. One of Blackmer's congregants, an eighty-year-old retired physician named Peter Hope, had brought his GPS to map the network of trails. If he wanted to cover the distance before nightfall, he would have to get going. He set out walking, and the meditative trekkers followed in silence.

For the first-time visitor, there isn't much to distinguish the Church of the Woods from any other forested part of southern New Hampshire. The previous landowner had cut the most desirable timber, leaving behind the stunted or misshapen trees in a practice known as high-grading. Though the forests are diminished, the bone structure of this land presents a walker with intriguing features: oddly shaped ridges, dells, and vernal pools. Something more than trees or squirrels resides there. The land tells a story about itself that, like braille, becomes legible only if you feel your way across the signs.

Growing on a dead hemlock stump was a dinner-plate-size reishi, a polypore known in China and Japan as the "mushroom of immortality" for its alleged immune-boosting properties. "Hey," Weiger shouted up to Blackmer, "maybe we should apply for a religious exemption to eat psychedelic mushrooms. Like a peyote ceremony!"

Weiger is not the sort who goes in for hallucinogens. After earning her M.D. and Ph.D., she worked for a number of years as a researcher at Harvard Medical School's Osher Center for Integrative Medicine. Ever since living in Nepal in her twenties she had been drawn to meditation, and in 2003 she moved to Maine to pursue a more contemplative life. Once a month she drives the six hours down to the Church of the Woods.

Many of the church's members are either former or current environmental activists. Wendy helped form a nonprofit that fought a protracted legal battle against Plum Creek Timber, a lumber company that wanted to develop 400,000 acres of Maine woods. Sue Moore, who is sixty-nine, was arrested alongside the environmentalist Bill McKibben at a rally against the Keystone XL pipeline in 2011. Blackmer fully supports lobbying and activism, but a common theme at the Church of the Woods is that activism isn't enough. When he considered the difference between Christians protesting a coal plant and secular activists doing the same, he thought, *There has to be something different in liturgy,* giving the word its full extent of meaning in the New Testament Greek. *Leitourgia* gets translated as "worship or service to God," but it can also be parsed as "the work of the people."

This need to find a new path through liturgy and contemplation was true both of seasoned activists like Blackmer and Weiger and of younger members such as Rachel Field, who had looked at the available activist responses to the ecological crisis—secular or faith-based—and found them wanting. For two years Field worked for the Center for the Environment and Society at Washington College, in Maryland, where she and her co-workers banded 14,000 migratory birds a year. She loved the work, but found it difficult to speak about faith in that science-heavy environment, so eventually she enrolled at Yale Divinity School and began attending the Church of the Woods. She was considering returning to Maryland to start a Church of the Marshes, where she might offer up the bread and wine among the egrets and plovers on the tidal flats of the Chesapeake Bay.

The forest trekkers arrived at the Altar, a small clearing where the church holds its services. The altar itself is a white-pine stump festooned with British soldier moss. Field counted the rings and reported that the tree was more than ninety years old, ten years older than Peter Hope. This would have been one of the trees felled when the land was high-graded. Someone placed Indian cucumber on the altar as an offering, another set down the reishi.

The Altar is the spiritual, if not the actual, center of the church. It is here that Blackmer offers Communion to his peripatetic flock. There is a worry among certain mainline Christians that once you start dabbling in nature, you're on the slippery slope to paganism, but Blackmer is no druid. He found years ago that the vague, earth-based spirituality he'd lived with for most of his life wasn't enough, and now considers himself a solid Trinitarian. But that makes it sound as though his conversion was the result of a spiritual shopping trip, when the better comparison would be a boxing match.

•

In 2005, Blackmer had been an environmental activist for nearly three decades, and he found he couldn't sustain it any longer. Despite some successes, the overwhelming reality of climate change made him feel as though the movement was fighting a losing battle. A friend invited him to a vision quest in California's Inyo Mountains, a land of extremes. To the west stands the highest point in the contiguous United States, to the east lies the lowest. Just north grows the oldest tree on earth. An auspicious place to receive a vision.

Blackmer's quest ended in a solitary four-day fast on a mountain, a time full of signs and portents. On his last night, in total darkness, he attempted a walk around the mountain. With no trail to follow, he came to a place where he had to choose between two routes. He asked aloud for a sign, and in the next moment saw a shooting star. "I mean, it was just silly," Blackmer laughed. He followed the star. Groping along in the dark, he stumbled into a deep gully and ran into a rock wall. There appeared to be no way out. "I was scared out of my freaking mind," he said. Feeling his way along the wall, he eventually came to a lone piñon pine silhouetted against a black sky, a tree he had seen before. He knew how to get back. In the small hours of the morning, having walked many miles, he finally stumbled into camp. Blackmer believed that "something utterly profound" had happened in his life, but he had no clue what it meant. He lived with that uncertainty for the next two years and fell deep into depression. That's when he first heard the Voice.

While meditating one morning, Blackmer heard: *The meaning of your journey around the mountain is that you must turn around and go the other way. You must follow the same path, but going in the other direction. This is a spiritual path.* He tried Buddhism, which seemed like a logical fit—he had been meditating for several years—but it just didn't take. Sometimes he woke in the night with horrible anxiety, and the Voice would say, *Rest in the crucible of anxiety. It will destroy you. It will transform you.*

Then came the flight into Dublin.

In the months following the trip, Blackmer resigned from the Northern Forest Center and began to experience visions. He dreamed he saw a triptych of the face of Christ, except the face in all three panels was his own. At the urging of a friend, a fellow forester and conservationist who also happened to be the only priest he knew, Blackmer visited the Society of St. John the Evangelist, an Episcopal monastery in Cambridge, Massachusetts. He spent three days in utter silence and anonymity, feeling like a foreigner. He saw the monks bowing before they passed the altar and thought, *I can't bow to this altar, to the white linens and shiny goblets.* Then he realized that the monks were simply bowing to the mystery. That he could do. On the third day, Blackmer heard the brothers chanting the Psalms and something inside him broke. Their beauty, the chanted words from three thousand years ago, shattered his defenses. He wept. He took the Eucharist for the first time in his life. But when he returned home, he still resisted attending church.

Two months later, Blackmer and his wife were visiting his brother in the cloud forest of Costa Rica. One morning, meditating alone in the house, he heard a knock at the window. He checked and found nothing there. When he sat down he heard a second knock, this time a bit louder. Again, nothing. This happened a third time, and then he heard the Voice say, *Let me in.*

Oh shit, he thought, *it's Jesus.* It was Easter Sunday.

Like Flannery O'Connor's Hazel Motes, who saw Jesus "move from tree to tree in the back of his mind, a wild ragged figure," Blackmer was a man haunted by God. He often laughed at the absurdity of it all. Vision quests, voices, shooting stars? Knocks at the window? He was amazed too at his former self, at the strength of his resistance—"heels dug in every inch of the way." He wasn't going to church.

But after so many rounds in the ring, he surrendered. He began reading about Christianity. He wanted to find out "if there was room for me in this hierarchical, antiquated, rule-bound, antienvironmental faith. Do they have people like me?" The more he read, the more he was convinced the answer was yes. One year after his flight to Dublin, he was baptized. Four years later, in 2012, he finished divinity school. And a few months after that, he purchased, with help from a generous donor, the 106 acres that would become the Church of the Woods.

Following a long respite at the Altar, the trekkers took a fork in the trail. Blackmer stooped, picked a handful of wintergreen leaves from the understory, and passed them around for people to chew. They nibbled, walked, and prayed.

After crossing a century-old dam now overgrown with vegetation, the group paused to observe a young hemlock. Its trunk stood atop an upright protrusion of roots, making the tree appear as if it had legs.

"Maybe it's an Ent," Field said, referring to Tolkien's mythical tree creatures. "Stand back, it might start walking."

They climbed another small rise. "It's an odd piece of land," Blackmer said, "like this funny little ridge we're standing on. But that's fitting, because we're an odd bunch of people."

One of the church's members goes by the name of Sister Athanasius. An Episcopal nun in California since the Seventies, she chose her name when she read about the bishop of Alexandria who was consecrated, in A.D. 326, only after vigorous resistance. Sister Athanasius had not wanted to become a nun, which explains in part why she and Blackmer get along so well. In addition to their attempts at dodging the divine, both speak their minds freely, often employing a most impious lexicon. More important, they are equally smitten with the natural world. On Blackmer's coffee table he keeps a book-length poem given to him by Sister Athanasius: W. S. Merwin's *Unchopping a Tree*. The poem is an imaginative exercise in arboreal reconstruction. The narrator issues directives: how to rig the tackle for lifting the bole, how to reattach the broken trunk, how to glue back every splinter, chip, and piece of moss, until reaching this final, devastating line: "Everything is going to have to be put back."

The walkers came to the boundary of the church's property. Someone wondered aloud why the border still had barbed wire, and Sister Athanasius chuckled and said, "So the prisoners won't escape." Suddenly everyone grew quiet. The Canterbury-pilgrim mood of jocular ease had given way to something else.

Before them lay a bowl-shaped depression, a tiny clearing encircling a dried-up vernal pool. Moose tracks led into the muddy water. A gentle slope rose up and away into thick woods. Fallen hemlock and paper birch lay crisscrossed over the clearing like giant pickup sticks. Trees that had fallen and were not going to be put back. The air was still. Smells of pine, rotting duff, the dank musk of humus. An ordinary forest clearing, and yet more than ordinary. The kind of place that you might chance upon as a child while wandering in the woods, though if you were asked why you tarried there, or for how long, you couldn't say.

Soon Blackmer would send them off for a period of

individual contemplation, but before he spoke there was a long, palpable hush. Sister Athanasius slowly raised her palms to her temples. She gazed at the pools, the bits of sunlight dappling the glade, the dark mystery of the woods beyond. "Ahh, Jesus," she said softly, "just look at that."

The story of Moses and the burning bush is one of Blackmer's favorite texts. In Exodus, the Lord appears to Moses in a bush that burns but is not consumed. "Remove the sandals from your feet, for the place on which you are standing is holy ground." Blackmer often takes that literally, celebrating the Eucharist barefoot. Confronted with the threat of climate change, he believes, we must think of all ground as holy ground. Without such a recognition, there is no way out of our ecological woes. In the Eastern Orthodox tradition, the burning bush prefigures Mary the Theotokos, the God-bearer, who carried the Incarnate God inside her womb but remained unharmed. Blackmer thinks of the Earth itself as a *theotokos*. Would we clear-cut a forest or demolish a mountain or frack a field that bore the living God?

When the little band of pilgrims returned to the parking lot, Blackmer pointed out the church's sole "relic," a bent and broken aluminum ladder leaning against a tree, left behind by the loggers when they high-graded the place. It reminds him of Jacob's Ladder, another favorite biblical story. Genesis recounts how Jacob lay down upon a stone to sleep and dreamed of a ladder that joined heaven and earth. Upon awakening, he exclaimed, "Surely the Lord is in this place—and I did not know it!"

A common theme in Blackmer's conversations is that we've lost the face-to-face connection with God, the awesome, fearsome encounter that so often occurs in wild settings. Art, music, a beautiful sanctuary—all of those can be soul-stirring. But they can also obfuscate one's connection to God. Nature strips away the human intermediary.

A hawk cried overhead. Peter Hope ambled over with trekking poles, backpack, and GPS unit. It was midday now, and after walking the property that morning with the contemplative hikers, he was off to take readings on the remaining trails. By the end of the day this eighty-year-old man would have trod seven or eight miles over this land of mounds and folds. Traversing the *theo-tokos*, praying with his feet.

•

Since the Industrial Revolution we've scaled up development to a tremendous degree, and even under the most optimistic scenarios we're going to be dealing with climate change for centuries to come. Blackmer foresees a time of unimaginable suffering and grief. His faith tells him that on the far side of that suffering stands the tree of life, symbol of the resurrected world in which humans will have found their place in creation. There is no path to that perfect world, however, that does not involve hardship and death. "We're not going to skate through this one untouched," he told me.

Blackmer's understanding of the Second Coming is not one in which Jesus returns to fix everything. His eschatology leans toward the Eastern Orthodox understanding of *theosis*: deification. Through the slow work of prayer and contemplation, a person becomes more like Christ, and Christ comes to dwell more completely within that person. "That's the way Jesus becomes present," he said. "It's through *our* transformation. A spiritual death. And a rebirth." What must die is the materialist worldview in which physical reality is viewed as just stuff: "The world is not merely physical matter we can manipulate any damn way we please." The result of that outlook is not just a spiritual death but a real, grisly, on-the-cross kind of death. "We are erecting that cross even now," he said.

Rachel Field also knows that humans are causing climate change and that the results will be catastrophic, but she wonders about our ability to stop it. She sees the human role as that of a witness, a provider of hospice care for the ecosystems we've damaged. Coming to a place that has been as heavily logged as the Church of the Woods is one way she can say to the land, *Yes, we did this. And we are not going to leave you.* She knows that this earth, this cosmos, will endure and will transform into something beautiful even if humans can't survive on it. "Every time a creature is lost, a piece of God's glory is leaving," she said. "But it's bigger than us."

Though Blackmer freely acknowledges that some are called to activism and that such work is sorely needed, he himself has left that role behind, at least in the usual sense. Activism, in his view, too often becomes a mask for hiding undigested fear or grief. His work now is to change people's consciousness rather than to affect policy.

Hearing Blackmer talk, one might wonder how a shift in consciousness can save a beleaguered planet. As environmentalist groups like 350.org have shown, it takes direct political action to achieve tangible results, such as the protests that managed to stop the construction of the Keystone XL pipeline, or Blackmer's own efforts to preserve millions of acres of New England forest. It's difficult to imagine achieving those results through an internal shift, but for Blackmer, the emphasis is on the activist's starting place. The question is not whether one takes action, it is from what heart and mind one does so.

The church's *leitourgia*, the work of the people, is first the work of prayer. The once-thriving Canterbury Shaker Village lies only a few miles east of the Church of the Woods, and for Blackmer the proximity is no coincidence. The Shakers' connection to the land and their devotion to prayer left a spiritual presence that is still palpable. "Prayer transforms places as well as people," Blackmer said. "You can actually feel it when you walk into a place where people have prayed for long periods of time. It is as if prayer has changed the molecular structure of a place." Thus altered, the woods become a kind of inner sanctum in which we are faced with what the theologian Rudolf Otto called the *mysterium tremendum*. "The semi-darkness... of a lofty forest glade," he wrote in *The Idea of the Holy*, "has always spoken eloquently to the soul, and builders of temples, mosques, and churches have made full use of it."

The work of the people also includes the Eucharist. For Blackmer, "It is the act of taking into ourselves the body of He who died and went through death and came back." Death and grief transmuted into love. That expression of hope in the midst of death is where, for Blackmer, the Christian faith comes into its own. "All of us go down to the dust," he said, quoting the burial rite from the Book of Common Prayer, "yet even at the grave we make our song: Alleluia, alleluia, alleluia." Death does not have the final word. Joy does. "That's what Jesus was all about," Blackmer said. "And if we forget that, then shit—we're a sad, pitiful bunch. And we're sure as hell not leading anybody to the Promised Land." When he presides over the liturgy each Sunday, this priest in the trees, a sixty-one-year-old man still green and full of sap, carefully spreads his elements across the white-pine stump. He offers the first morsels of bread and the last sip of wine to the earth.

That Sunday evening, when most of the crowd had left the Church of the Woods, a dozen members huddled by the campfire and watched the lunar eclipse. The moon rose red above the trees. A super blood moon. It faded as it climbed, its face slowly adumbrated by Earth's shadow. The fading orb seemed to glow from within. Just before the full eclipse, a luminous plane of light appeared on the moon's edge. For a brief moment it grew bright. Then it was gone.

·

Though it began in a desert, Christianity is a faith haunted by trees. The story opens in a garden, in the center of which grows the tree of life. Ignoring that tree, Adam and Eve make for another—from which they pluck our downfall. The primal couple are hungry for knowledge and knowledge they get, but they soon find it's a mixed bag. They eat the fruit and "the eyes of both were opened," and lo, the beginnings of human consciousness. Of the tree of life we hear no more until the final chapter of Revelation, where we find it growing on either side of the river in the center of the New Jerusalem. Its leaves "are for the healing of the nations." Between the Bible's arboreal bookends stands a third tree, the cross at the center of the Christian story. Given their narrative prominence, the biblical drama stands or falls with the trees.

"The bulk of a tree," writes Tom Wessels in *Reading*

the Forested Landscape, "is mostly dead wood." Other than the leaves, the only living part is the cambium, a group of cells a few millimeters thick that resides under the bark. The trunk may be lifeless and inert, but it's still needed to provide structure for the growing cambium. The bulk of Christianity—whether it be ancient cathedrals or big-box megachurches—is mostly dead wood. The cambium of faith resides unseen, just beneath the surface, ever growing in new directions.

I had already been thinking a good deal about trees long before my visit with Reverend Blackmer. I'm surrounded by them, for one thing. Transylvania County, where I live, is aptly named. *Trans,* "through"; *sylvan,* "woods." Trees thrive in this part of western North Carolina because it is a temperate rainforest, containing some of the greatest biodiversity in North America. The landscape here feels maternal. It swaddles you in its gentle folds, its swaying branches, the humid air of so much life breathing in, breathing out. Here I've taken to pondering the symbiosis between these forests and the Christian faith I attempt, and often fail, to practice.

That August, in Transylvania County, it began to rain. Right on through to Christmas, it rained: fifty-nine inches in all. Normally we average around seventy inches of rain a year. As the atmosphere warms, increasing the air's capacity to hold moisture, that amount will surely increase. It already has. Two years earlier we had received 112 inches of rain. A few days after Christmas, on a day like so many other days that December—rainy, seventy-five degrees—I followed my three young sons down to the creek that runs near our house. The boys had been building a mud dam and were eager to show me their handiwork. On a winter's day when we should have been sledding, my sons and I quatted beside a creek in the warm drizzle and played in the mud.

There is a word, coined by the Australian philosopher Glenn Albrecht, that describes the longing for your own home, not homesickness from a distance but the yearning you feel for a place in which you still live but which has become unrecognizably damaged by some extractive industry: "solastalgia." We now speak of "shifting baselines" and the "new normal"—euphemisms that often the blow of climate catastrophe. Perhaps this is our work now, to abandon the false linguistic signposts that lead us astray—"stopping" or "fixing" climate change—and instead find new words and stories and metaphors that will help us confront what is already upon us, and devote ourselves to what we might yet save. "The powerful metaphor," Bill McKibben has written, "will be more useful than the cleanest engine." As the Church of the Woods has discovered, such metaphors are already waiting in our religious traditions, claiming a power far deeper than the utilitarian "ecosystem services" or even the language of democracy. The question climate change poses is how to confront the enemy within, and that is not primarily a technological or political question; it is a religious one.

We have high-graded the world, taking the best and leaving the scrubby undergrowth. We now find ourselves chastened by the scope of our destructive power, yet still hungry for the awe and wonder we once felt before creation's magnitude. The Babylonian invaders are approaching, and we have no choice but to face them—which is to say, face ourselves.

The search for God in a sacred grove recalls the

Israelites in their tabernacle in the Sinai desert. That searc
cannot be contained by human walls, despite the solidit
that Chartres or Notre Dame or the National Cathedr:
might suggest. If Christianity is going to confront climat
change, perhaps it needs to rewild itself, go feral. What th
faith has to offer first is not protest or activism, thoug
it may lead there. It is *leitourgia*. The work of the peopl«
And the work of the people now is this: Keep the lan«
holy. Keep the carbon in the ground. Renounce the myt'
that this earth is a random assortment of bio-geophysic:
processes that can be prodded, manipulated, fracked, o«
drilled for our own purposes, however nefarious or benign
Approach with awe the *theotokos*, the bush that burns but i
not consumed. Perhaps we begin by taking off our shoes.

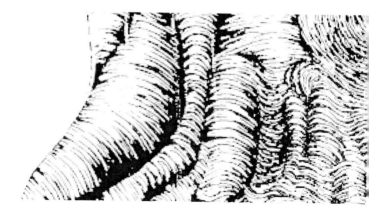

WHAT GOES DOWN
KAY ANN SHORT

For years, we dreaded the death of the venerable cottonwood that cast its meandering limbs across our irrigation ditch to the flower garden on the other side. Rooted on one bank, its trunk leaned nearly horizontal over the other, as if to form a bridge between them. The trunk itself spanned fifteen feet in diameter and was covered with a bark ridged a hand's width deep. Our arborist friend said such thick bark grew only on the oldest variety of cottonwood here on Colorado's Front Range, making our tree a hundred years old or more, following the digging of the Rough and Ready ditch in the 1860s, fifty years before our farm was established.

Standing upright, the cottonwood would have been the tallest on our farm. But as the tree aged, the weight of the boughs began to pull the roots from the eroding bank below, leaving less root structure each year to anchor the tree along the ditch's edge. The more the cottonwood leaned, the less water and nutrients could enter its system, and so the trunk rotted from the inside out, weakening the tree's ability to feed itself. As the cycle continued over the years, we watched the cottonwood tip closer and closer to the flower garden below.

But amid its decay, the tree was full of life. Birds sang and nested above, while squirrels chased their mates below. Raccoons ran up and down the hollow space inside the trunk, emerging on upper branches from rotted knotholes. Once I saw four baby raccoons perched along a limb far above my head. When I returned with a friend, five babies stared curiously from the bough; when we came back with yet another friend, six masked faces looked down as if to say, "See, they keep multiplying."

Despite such signs of life, we still couldn't deny that the tree was dying. When the hard winds blew in the spring, long branches fell onto the flower garden and into the raspberry patch, some big enough to worry about. We were tired of picking up deadfall, but removing the tree wasn't possible either, not without considerable expense and time to clear the remains.

To help lessen the weight upon the tree's remaining roots, we hired our arborist friend one May to trim larger boughs from the tree's north side where they seemed to hang more heavily. We thought that easing that side would help rebalance the tree and strengthen the remaining roots in the ditch. He pruned as much from the tree as he dared but feared that taking too much would leave too little for the tree's survival. Such pruning, we hoped, would extend the tree's life for many years.

May winds blow hard along the Front Range, hard enough to topple motor homes, overturn trailers, and push cars off the highway. Hard enough to blow water towers across the plains. Hard enough to worry about.

Three nights after the pruning, the wind howled and shook the house, but it didn't occur to us to worry about the tree. It had just been pruned, for one, and its mass still seemed indomitable. Barn roofs, yes, and the chicken house, yes, but that tree didn't even cross our minds as we listened to the wind shake the world.

In the morning, John went out to check for damage on the farm while I made a pot of tea. When he came in the kitchen door, I could see from his face that something had happened. "I've got some bad news," he said, but his next words surprised me. "It's the tree." I waited, expecting him to say that a bough had fallen on the tractor barn or more scraggly branches had dropped onto the roses. That wouldn't be good news, but what came next was even worse.

"It fell on the flowers. It *covers* the garden. I don't know how we're going to clean it up."

In two weeks, we would celebrate Stonebridge Farm's fifteenth season as a community-supported agricultural farm with a pancake breakfast and outdoor concert. Friends were coming from out of state. John's family was arriving from Oregon. We already had lots of work to do before the big day. And now this.

I went out to survey the damage and didn't know what to cry over first: the crushed roses, the immensity of the work required to remove the branches, or the felled tree immutably spanning the ditch. No way could we move it. Even if the tractor were strong enough to pull it aside, there was no place from which to pull. We could remove the branches canopying the garden, but the giant trunk would have to remain.

Had our pruning unintentionally unbalanced the tree, shifting its weight on roots already vulnerable and weak? If the winds hadn't come so soon, perhaps in time the tree could have recovered its equilibrium, anchoring again more firmly in the bank. Our attempt to save the tree may have killed it, or at least hastened its end.

No human eyes had witnessed our cottonwood's grounding, the tree straining to balance in the fierce spring wind, giving in to the push and rocking to earth, the birds in its branches flying upward at once in the bough's final sway as the roots released and the trunk thundered to the ground, the impact so heavy it collapsed a metal gate trellising a rose.

But the Y of the trunk's main branches fell perfectly around the metal arbor under which we had stood when we committed our lives to each other. The arbor remained intact, the birdhouse at its apex hanging as before, the nest inside undisturbed.

For two weeks we worked whenever we had a spare moment, spending hours and hours together in the garden, John with the chainsaw and me in gloves pulling the cut limbs across the bridge to stack in a hundred-foot row six feet high, readying the remains for our friend's chipper. As we cleared the arching limbs and masses of small branches from the flower garden, we found other small savings as well. The stone rabbit wasn't crushed but cradled by two lesser branches fallen at its sides. Another trellis lay flattened on the ground but otherwise survived unharmed. We did lose the roses' last round of late summer blooms, but the plants would come back the following season and in future seasons, their growth more vigorous from the sun shining through the space where the tree used to stand. The trunk itself would make a naturally formed bridge for squirrels, raccoons, and children to scamper across.

And from the small ball of roots still fastened to the soil on one bank to the only branch left on the trunk at the other, enough nourishment is sent for new leaves to grow, a small but generative offering to the tree's insistent memory.

One day in the mountains, sitting on a log by the edge of a shallow, sandy lake, John and I first heard, then watched, he falling of a towering lodge pole pine, one we had just passed under on our hike around the lake. No wind had urged its fall. Rather, its decline was decades in the making until it moved with its own breath, heaving its trunk to the ground, where it shuddered for seconds and then lay still. We wondered whether our footsteps had precipitated its descent, just as we had unintentionally hastened the collapse of our cherished cottonwood.

When a tree dies from natural causes, its boughs reach down to the earth as its roots are released from the soil and raised toward the sky. As yoga teaches, what goes down must come up. What first grew upward from a tiny seed must some day fall back to the place of its planting.

Now when I pass the empty space on the bank as I walk to and from the fields, I try not to grieve the loss of shade that canopied my way. I've almost stopped mourning the cottonwood, accepting instead what's left. Nothing lasts forever. Above and below, before and after, we are always poised between different and the same. Only when we accept the passage from one to the other can equilibrium be found. Our old tree is gone, but with the sun across the roses and the trunk a bridge between, new roots find place again.

TREE RINGS: A TIME-LINE
T. HUGH CRAWFORD

2014 Every schoolchild learns that trees, as they grow, lay down new wood each year, so the age of a tree can be determined by counting the growth rings, officially called dendrochronology. Not only do those rings mark time and weather (*temps & temps*), they are subtle ridges to the hand and form supple patterns, both geometric and chaotic, warm and arresting, fragile and strong. Wood remains a constant in 21st century culture, still forming the basis for much of what we do, how we live, and how we mark out our days.

1722 John Harrison finished the Brockelsby Park tower clock, a timepiece that still functions after almost 300 years and is built almost entirely of wood. Harrison eventually received much of the prize money set aside by the British Parliament in the 1714 Longitude Act for service to the crown for finding a practical solution to the longitude problem. His solution was a clock—the H-4 chronometer—which to the modern eye looks like a large pocket watch, but that device helped to usher in the modern era, global capitalism, and the industrialization of time. Brockelsby Park was a farm clock. It measured the rhythms of feeding, milking, plowing, and reaping. Although it did not require the precision of the H-4, this clock did demand adjustment and regulation. One of Harrison's innovations included using tropical woods with a high oil content to reduce friction and eliminate the need for lubrication. Of equal importance, was his understanding that a well-regulated clock was not the result of the interaction of uniform, homogenous material, but instead by compensating for the variations those materials produced. A bimetallic pendulum counteracts the different rates that metal expands in temperature fluxes, and Harrison's wooden clock exploits the varied properties of dozens of wood species and their interactions with other woods. Closed and open grain expands and contracts at different rates, its stability determined not just by species but also by the angle of the saw cut, the direction of the rive. Compensation in clockmaking is not a philosophical or theological concept, but it is fundamental for measuring time and, perhaps, eternity.

1056 The Wooden Pagoda of Yingxian, the world's oldest multi-story timber-framed structure, was built. The trees for a timber frame—felled by axe, squared by broadax, and smoothed by adze—form a structure through massive beams and time-tested joints. Heavy timbers slot tenons into mortises, dovetail tie-beams to headers, and peg girts to posts. These beams carry the full load of the structure without nails, screws, or metal fasteners. The joiners work with care, selecting wood with structural integrity, cutting mortises with long handled chisels and mallets. It is exacting work, slow and patient, but it is also communal. A craftsman may linger in solitude for hours over a kerf-wedged dovetailed through-mortise, but when it comes to raising the frame, he is part of an agile choreography of joiners, timbers, and joints, working in concert to raise a frame that will, given proper care, stand for a millennium. After the joiners finish, the beams, in compression and tension, flex and creak through the days, continuing their own dynamic dance through time.

1665 In Eric Sloane's imaginative recreation, an English family prepares to sail to the New World, packing a cutting of an apple tree, a variety called "seek no further." Sloane's *A Reverence for Wood* is a paen to tree products, beginning in 1965 with the dismantling of an old barn and proceeding back century by century to detail the importance of wood in American life, eventually arriving at the colonial period. The constant in his story is the 400 year life-span of the "seek-no-further" apple tree planted in Connecticut on its arrival in 1665. Apples were fundamental to the American colonies for more than just pies, providing sweetness, vitamin C, and alcohol. Early American settlers consumed unimaginable quantities of what today we call hard cider—a drink deemed safe and palatable for all in the family. As the legend of Johnny Appleseed makes clear, the United States was settled agriculturally with apple seedlings, some wildings and many from cuttings propagated on wild crab stock. Sloane's apple tree was grown from the latter and, although an individual apple tree cannot live 400 years, this seek-no-further was also self-propagating. Planted on the crown of a hill, it became the first great American time-lapse photographic episode. Growing, dying, tumbling over, and re-sprouting from trunk shoots, Sloane's tree slowly walked down the hill, producing its 1965 fruit at some distance from its original colonial position.

350 BCE Aristotle writes his *Physics* and initiates the Western way of thinking about stuff. Technological objects are formed matter (hylomorphism), a world made up of compliant, malleable matter upon which humans impose

their designs. *Hyle*, Aristotle's word for matter and the foundation of all physical interactions, actually means wood. This bit of etymology prompted Henry David Thoreau to question the notion of art determined by form alone, noting that Aristotle defined art as "The principle of the work without the wood," and going on to observe that "most men prefer to have some of the wood along with the principle; they demand that the truth be clothed in flesh and blood and the warm colors of life." As a hewer of the arrowy pines he cut to build his Walden house, Thoreau knew *hyle* not as malleable material but instead as a knotty, twisted living being that can only be known through patient, careful engagement.

1894 On the death of his father, George Sturt took over management of the family wheelwright shop in Farnham, Surrey. George, ever the intellectual, wanted to explain in objective, technological terms what his workers knew through centuries of practice, gestures with wood that spoke directly to them, but only faintly murmured to George. They would fell large trees, section them, and place the rounds in a barn loft, waiting years for them to season, only then discovering if the wood was either sound or frow as a biscuit. Time in Sturt's shop, or at least the time of his workers, seems glacial, and his book, *The Wheelwright's Shop*, is his remembrance of things past, though it is a past of trees: the slow revelation of their strength and affordances. The wagon timbers they formed with axe and adze only resemble the dimensional lumber sold in home centers today in name, those 2x4s expressing their time in decades if that.

2013 Summer in the New England woods was a constant hum—cicadas—a sound both deafening and soothing, heard only every seventeen years. The floor of the forest was a diagram of holes, 1/2 inch across with hundreds in a square yard. Millions of insects, first leaving behind crisp exoskeletons, then waiting quietly, drying out, only to fly crispy and crisply to treetops in order to eat, mate, trill, and die. In 1856, Herman Melville published "The Apple Tree Table," telling the story of another emergence, this time three unnamed insects waking up and chewing their way out of an antique table brought down from a cold attic and warmed by the hearth of Melville's huge chimney at *Arrowhead*. Apparently a famous or at least common event in the era (also mentioned at the end of Thoreau's *Walden*), Melville chooses to frame his version as a ghost or at least ghostly story of uncertain and frightening noises requiring late night exploration. On the capture of a beautiful, iridescent bug, the narrator and his naturalist friend compute the time from this insect egg being laid to its emergence as 150 years. Melville's characters speculate on the miracle as possible proof of the truth of Christian spirituality, but, beyond theological speculation, time and the table remain. Waiting in that wood were creatures whose temporalities are simply different from that of humans. The trees in New England waited seventeen years for 2013. They were transformed for a few brief weeks, then lapsed into primeval silence, waiting out another seventeen.

1379 New College, Oxford is founded and College Hall is built with a massive oak-beam roof. In the late 1800s, those roof-beams became infested with beetles, so the school's dons cast about trying to find 40 foot oak timbers of sufficient heft to replace the existing roof. Someone suggested checking with the college forester to see if there were any ancient oaks in the college's woodlots. As the story goes, the queried forester smiled and informed them that a stand of oaks had been planted when the hall was first built with the express purpose of supplying those timbers when needed. The perfect parable of planning for the future, the story has been contested (the forest land was not acquired by New College for a number of years after the college hall was built). Nevertheless, it resonates: the college maintains forest land for production with exceedingly long-term plans. Even though the trees were not explicitly planted to replace that particular roof, those oaks were nurtured over hundreds of years, and, when needed, timbers of sufficient strength and size were available. An ancient version of just-in-time management.

1996 Gary Snyder publishes his long poem, *Mountains and Rivers Without End*, and puts wood-time in perspective:

A spoken language works

for about five centuries,
lifespan of a douglas fir

1964 A young University of North Carolina forestry student researching Bristlecone pines breaks off his core-borer in an attempt to determine the age of a tree. He secures permission to cut it down, only to discover 4844 growth rings. He had cut down Prometheus, the oldest living tree on earth. The mythic Prometheus was bound to

a rock for all eternity; his evergreen namesake was bound
to a rock, perhaps not for eternity, but a damn sight longer
than human understanding extends. You cannot think
wood without thinking time.

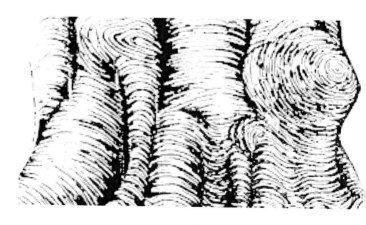

THE LINE OF NO TREES
RENÉE E. D'AOUST

The line of no trees stops us. My mother and I have just walked out of the shaded corner of our property. Our neighbors are massive corporate landholders. "Forest Capital." Private equity. Forest Capital clear cuts are happening all over northern Idaho.

Mom gasps. I reach for her right hand, wrap it over my arm, so the bird weight of her forearm rests on my own. I used to take the weight of fellow dancers in the studio or onstage, a hand, the back of the neck, but now I take the weight of my mother's shriveling arm. I stroke the hand I call "your claw"; her claw lacks innervation and turns in on itself, fingers curling the way a cat's claws curl around a toy. The radiation that saved my mother in 1977 also caused this.

When my mother lost her first breast, she joked, "Now I'm half liberated."

From the age of ten onward, I witnessed her fake boob regularly fall out of her bra, splashing into Sirius's dog dish. That's how I grew up thinking that feminism intertwined with dog food intertwined with breast cancer. Surgery, radiation, and chemotherapy made my mom free, I believed. Cut, burn, poison.

Twenty-nine years later, when Mom lost the second, becoming flat-flat, we tried dark humor. Mom said, "Now I'm totally liberated."

We didn't laugh; it wasn't in us. Breast begets bone begets sarcoma. Yet I always see a mist of yellow surrounding my mother. It's her aura, we say. Sun-color as the life-color of woman. And smell her lavender scent. My lemon-lavender mom.

Mom's current oncologist says, and I paraphrase: "I'm sorry for what we had to do to you in 1977 to treat breast cancer. We were very aggressive. And I'm sorry that the radiation you received as an infant probably caused cancer."

My mother tells me, "Before this oncologist, no medical professional had ever apologized to me. Not even my mother."

My mother's mother, my grandmother, had her daughter, my mom, irradiated as an infant. My mom was a day old. The belief, for it was belief, not science, was that an enlarged thymus caused SIDS. Irradiate and kill the thymus to save the infant. Cause cancer in the woman. We are here today by the grace of radiation cancelled and radiation scheduled.

"It was accepted medical practice," said Dr. Saxton, my grandma.

If it had been, Dr. Saxton, my grandfather, would have allowed the full three days of radiation to occur. He cancelled the series. This is a man who served in WWII. He did his time in the psychiatric ward. He came back from electroshock therapy to be the head of thoracic surgery at Vancouver General. Mom was born before WWII, before these events. My grandfather had the strength of vision, of knowledge, of character to cancel my mom's infant radiation series before—*before*—he had been taken to the core of himself. And come back.

My mother didn't even know she had been irradiated as an infant until the first tumor showed up. In her thyroid. To Grandma's credit, she immediately told Mom what had happened. Mom's thyroid was cut out, and the tumor was benign, but the actual thyroid had to be replaced with little pink thyroid pills for the rest of Mom's days. Later, pink ribbons joined those pink pills on the bathroom counter.

When I was an infant, Mom stopped nursing me because of her thyroid surgery. I refused milk formula; insisted on pineapple juice. To this day, I love pineapple juice more than milk. It's best if it comes out of a little tin can with a pop cap top. Mom had Grandma's information, but all records had been destroyed. When people wax poetic about Canadian health care, I think of my mom and those destroyed records. Apparently no infants were ever irradiated in Canada.

Here is the ground at the edge of our stewardship forest. In a clichéd movement, my mother and I cross our fingers. We pray that the larch and western white pine seedlings—thousands soon to be planted by a crew on this industrial forest that borders our land—will win out over bunnies nibbling roots and deer eating shoots. We want Rothko's burnt green to turn to Dalí's slippery glade.

"Look at that opening," says Mom. "The light pouring through."

The adjacent trees are gone. The light is here. We stand in the light.

The old trail we took up Middle Mountain: gone.

The ski trail we took down Middle Mountain: gone.

The deer path winding sideways across our land and over old cedar stumps and round the massive one-hundred-year old Western White Pine: gone.

The White Pine stands, a lone testament to survival. Mom approaches the logger to see if she could salvage the tree. "I like that tree, too," he says. "And no mill can handle that size anymore."

Sun bright. Woody debris bulldozed into slash piles. Slabs of half cut discarded tree butts everywhere.

"Oh, God," Mom says. She holds her free hand up to her eyes.

●

I remember the skin on her right forearm was still taut and that her fingers looked chicken strong, though shriveled. I should say wild turkey strong. A gaggle of wild turkeys walked across the clear cut. At that time, Mom could still walk to this corner. She was still bending over and picking up forlorn sticks. Unlike me, my mother never succumbed to anger, or to holding grudges. She wondered at the trillium in the forest glade. She never met a stick she didn't like.

Even those who manage forests will admit that a clear cut shocks. Even when the euphemistically called regeneration cut is the preferred cut, the torn landscape tears a heart. When I remember this scarred view, I also feel my mother with me. I don't remember her flat chest. I remember her claw.

The clear cut, which borders our land, has yet to fill in. What cuts now is to know that I will never stand with my mom again. So my memory has the sound of logging trucks driving away, thunking down the gravel road, and the tire chains thwacking my heart. A hearse didn't drive my mom away; Dad said it was a van. A white van. Dad remembers he told me it was a dark-colored van. And Joan Baez sings, "The Green Green Grass of Home."

My mother: gone.

My mother and I stand in a graveyard museum of stumpage covered by bear grass. I write of our bodies, of our woods, of a boob falling on infinite loop into Sirius's doggy bowl.

"The deer will come for cover in our woods."

"They are welcome."

Gradually, in two or three years, when I look at this different topography, I will be able to look at the places that were so scarred I could not look and breathe at the same time. Soon I will see shrubby undergrowth, and the wounds will recede, covered by saplings and woody shrubs and hard wood.

When I walk over this once-scarred ground, I will be hard-pressed not to slip on an unseen log or bruise my shin because I didn't raise my leg high enough to step over the unseen log. In what was once forest and will be again, I'll come back after the planting crew does their work.

I will think of the scars across my mother's chest. I will think of the scar down Mom's leg from the removal of thigh tissue that was used as chest tissue because sarcoma tumors were cut out of her chest four months before Mom died. I will think of how each new wound uncovered and covered the last. Across Mom's nonexistent breasts.

My mother and I stand. I write of our bodies, of our woods, of our compassion. There were two breasts. Now there are none.

The trees are gone, but you encircle them. Gradually, the earth reclaims her duff. Practice makes living possible. Again, there is green. There is always new green.

PINEWARD
LORI BRACK

I was born the day my parents planted two pines, balled roots dropped into two holes just before the labor pains came. I grew up knowing tree words (bark, branch, needle, trunk), as a toddler grows up pointing to parts of her body and naming them elbow, nose, knee. As I grew, so did my lexicon until by the time I was in school I could say from experience cottonwood borer and poplar, leaf vein and sparrow.

Trees litter a life like long pairs of dropped needles I loved to pick up from the ground and split at their woody connection to feel the joints give. Trees taught me how to look closely and how to separate, how to emerge for a season and then regrow. But it was the Norway pine dictionary I took with me—the tree under which I grew up with its colorful bark and oval cones. Each new tree and its terminology never grows quite as fleshly as the first book of the world from which the pines and I sprang.

Psithurism: sound of wind in branches
The two birthday pines grew tall and straight and I can't remember a time when needles did not scent shade, when shade was not stickied by sap. I have studied the pictures of me at two or three buttoned tight into winter coat and hood, standing in a back yard bare of tree shadow, and logic tells me that at least awhile, the pines I thought of as mine must have been shorter than their eventual shaggy height. We lived inside the daily sound of wind-brightening trees, rare out there on the cold and dry Kansas plains, a

shushing made of branches and needles bobbing outside the window, enticing me to believe I could see the gale.

Evergreen: an adjective and a metaphor
When I was five or six, my mother washed my long hair every Saturday in the kitchen. I would crawl onto the countertop and lie flat on my back, hang my hair into the sink. Because I was impatient, she distracted me by singing the parts of Joyce Kilmer's "Trees" she could remember. Though it made reaching every part of my head more difficult, I would turn to look through the kitchen window and stare up into the pine, wait each week for my favorite line: "a nest of robins in her hair." Her fingers scrubbed my scalp and then pulled a comb through the tangles while I looked hard for that nest, the one I imagined was there but obscured by long-needled branches, the nest that was simultaneously being composed against my head, the one that meant somehow I was also the tree.

Resin: sticky tree ooze
After years of growth, one of the original pines was cut down to make way for my mother's dream of a screened porch. The porch gave our prairie home the air of a vacation cabin, shaded as it was by the remaining kitchen-window pine, the only pine on our street of postwar ranch houses and their optimistic fruit trees or spindly maples.

I turn the spyglass of memory and refocus on pines that lengthen and contract in the telling.

My cat, tacky with pitch, slept on my bed and left tree scent behind. One year, the pine gained a redwood bench around its trunk, partly the work of my father who nailed each section in place. When I sat there, my pants came away with sticky spots, needle debris glued to my thighs. As long as that last pine oozed its gummy gold, sifted winter snow, sheltered black-capped chickadees my mother called "snowbirds" and remained, my life was vouchsafed. Even when I roamed far from the center and lived in the desert or the city, I imagined I felt it out there standing strong in January and sending roots deeper in July.

Hardiness: ability to survive temperature changes

As it turns out, Kansas is the only state in the lower 48 that does not have a native pine. I see only two possibilities: the seeming illogic of maps means something to trees that refuse to creep over borders, or this place makes a pine tree shun it. One Kansas horticulturist believes the reason is weather extremes—frigid winters followed by hot, windy summers—that test a pine's resilience. Pines, it may be said, can adapt to either, but withstanding both is out of the question.

Somehow the pine I thought of as mine thrived even where it should not have been planted. One afternoon I stitched sharp pine needles through cherry tree leaves, tearing dashes into the leathery flesh. My palms itched with stringing, suturing oval leaf to leaf, the pine reminding me it kept control of what can be said of the desire to pierce, to connect, and to splinter.

When my son needed room to grow, I chose a house with a flowering crab outside the bedroom window. The spring we moved in, the tree was covered in white blossoms, faintly sweet, or maybe only my imagination of sweetness. I spent afternoons on a blanket holding and releasing my son's squirmy or sleepy toddler body, looking up into branches that drew shapes from a Japanese print on the sky. Grass grew right up to the trunk, the crabapple's branches loose enough to let in light. In fruited summers, a neighbor would drop over to eat the small, sour apples straight off the tree, and a stranger sometimes called to request picking, pausing to apologize for her jelly longing. Each year, inside a smooth hole high up the trunk, hatched starlings' hungry cries punctuated the afternoons.

My son did not grow up under a pine, but the crabapple tree matured with him until it was storm felled when he was seventeen, a tree that offered its interval, and like my pine carved parentheses around mothering.

Deciduous: impermanent

My mother didn't want trees in the front because each evening, barring clouds or blizzard, she would open the dining room curtains onto the west and watch the sunset blaze or fade against the long horizon. Even though I never mimicked her ritual, she taught me to pay attention to the sky. In some of the weeks before her death, I stayed with her, taking on little tasks she gave me while she spent her days drowsing or staring into the middle distance from the couch. She gave me a big job, too, in her last summer— to arrange for the dead pine, its branches dry and needles brown, to be cut down before it attracted fire or fell on the roof.

The day the tree men came, I stood alone on her screened porch and watched them rig up, saw off the lower branches, disassemble the redwood bench. As they readied the chainsaws for the trunk, I invited my mother to come outside to watch. Her response was a gentle roll of her head propped on the couch's arm. I asked her again as the saws started up their loud growling. She shook her head once more, passing on the undercutting of trunk, the snap and boom of limbs. Alone and by lengths I discovered a patch of sky I had not seen in decades, watched the end of my last birthday tree. Between the men's trips to their truck, I slipped out and rescued one branch the circumference and length of my arm, three brown pine cones, and one spray of needles.

I keep them still, put away in a box that my son will come upon one day. On the outside of the box in black marker: Pine Tree. I've never unfastened the lid.

Komorebi: leaf-filtered sun
He has directions, my son, to put me beneath a tree as I'm dying. He's to roll a cot under a fall or spring tree and let leaf shadow play over my blankets, let needles fall on my hands, once more, let me look up.

THE USEFULNESS OF TREES
MERCEDES WEBB-PULLMAN

A celebrated bonsai master from Hiroshima gifted a white pine bonsai from 1625 to the United States in 1976, as part of a bicentennial gift from Japan. Such a tree should be honored with a name. After all, we quickly memorized "Little Boy" and "Fat Man." Perhaps trees *do* have names, if only we spoke the same language.

•

I visit bonsai chat rooms, tree-themed forums, searching for people who speak the same language. I say things like: They're like our lungs. Quietly in the background they pump away, each one an automatic Pool Maid, constantly scrubbing the air clean; without them we'll all die.

I say things like: We've always lived with them, worked together with them, used them, even sometimes acknowledged and worshipped them. Pivot, axis, and sphere—from Druids to the Cabala we've used trees as symbols of knowledge and alchemy, those hydraulic water stacks that all day rhythmically pump sustenance from the soil, up through non-return valves, to exhale into the air a million silent sighs.

I say things like: Solar powered, they circulate water taken up from where roots intertwine; all life begins there in that dark strata that sustains us and holds our destruction. Some read universal patterns, others understand there is nothing else; our need is not returned, the tree exists only to feed itself.

The nursery was only two miles from Ground Zero i
Hiroshima in 1945, yet that miniature pine survivec
was later offered by Master Masaru Yamaki to celebrat
America's first 200 years. Some who commented on hi
actions thought it was a brave and magnanimous gesture, t
give such a priceless treasure to those who had so recentl
been his enemy. Perhaps caring for trees cultivated grace
perhaps mercy.

○

I've seen an old growth eucalyptus forest after it was clear
felled for wood chips. Cheaper and easier to take dow
every tree, apparently, and leave behind what's not wanted
It made me think "Holocaust"; death in orderly heaps
incremental and organized, grisly remains of stringy bark
grey box, red box, manna gums, the habitat for so man
life forms destroyed.

The whole skyline was changed. The horizon hac
fallen, as if the earth was closer than I thought. This wa
the right track, but all the trees were gone. There were onl
snagged-up piles of branches, like bones left to burn. Tire
tracks of logging trucks led to a ridge above the Badja; all
the trees were gone, apart from some discards too hard to
move, a broken remnant.

•

The artist in Japan, having carefully ground his ink, will
take paper made from these trees and paint what he sees;

bare mountains—all the trees will be gone.

Master Yamaki's family home and tree nursery were blown apart by Little Boy, but his family survived the blast. The tree was protected by a courtyard wall.

I think of the wall outside a bank in downtown Hiroshima, close to the explosion's center, where the outline of an incinerated person was flash-fused into the steps.

For almost four hundred years Master Yamaki's tree has been carefully tended: watered daily, inspected for insects, rotated for sun twice a week, repotted when necessary, taken inside each winter, brought back with spring.

America is honoring Master Yamaki's bonsai tree's history this week, as Thursday marks the 70th anniversary of the Hiroshima bombing.

•

Trees, of course, have a different awareness of time. I've stood in New Zealand forests amongst kauris more than a thousand years old, and redwoods of the same age in Californian. I've learned the meaning of the word "reverent."

I'm sure they don't feel that way about us. We must appear as May flies to them, come and gone in one of their days, inconsequential. Tree time is more like mountains, mostly slow and ponderous.

Olive trees still bearing fruit in Palestine were planted in their groves in Roman times. A pear tree planted in Plymouth Rock by Pilgrim John Endicott was a hundred years old when George Washington was born. Now, almost four hundred years old, it still bears fruit.

Even the brittle gums outside my back door in Numeralla exist in their own zone. Some hot summer afternoons the gum tree leaves glitter as breezes stir, pass with heat ripples through the air. Diamond lights flash and sparkle from the oil protecting the leaves.

Yet they are all easy prey for us.

•

It takes inconceivable time and pressure to make diamonds from cataclysmic earth-movements. I prefer the delight that arrives with a summer breeze.

•

In an Edmonds "Sure to Rise" baking powder tin on a wall stud by the woodshed door, Dad used to keep some kauri gum, warm smooth lumps of amber. He told me they were ancient tears cried by the trees as they died.

Some sticky drops had trapped and preserved spiders, ants, flies. The insects crouched, seemingly about to move. I'd hold them to the light and dream about tears that lasted forever, and what would make a spider cry, and whether their tears could contain other, tinier spiders. Grief inside of grief.

•

Both sides of my family, though in different countries, chopped down what trees were already there, to plant grass for dairy herds. On one side of the Tasman they cut through landscapes of red gum, jarrah, and ash to build their homes and dairies, while on the other, they slaughtered kauri and kahikitea, totara and rimu.

Rain forest trees still surrounded my grandmother as she milked her cows but they didn't mean much to her except *green*. She liked them best cut down, cut up and used.

She arrived at her funeral in a dead rimu.

WHAT THE WILLOW SAID AS IT FELL
ANDREA SCARPINO

And what of the willow tree? One hundred years beside the lake. Girls played in its long-armed cape, braided branches like hair, mothers turned its switches into pain. Mallard ducks, Mute Swans, geese built nests with matted leaves. Night of the hurricane, my child body asleep. Sideways rain, lightning: one long, loud crack and the willow split in two, one half in the lake, one half through the roof, broken windows, plaster knocked from the walls. What the willow said as it fell: *Take this body. Make it whole.* And I woke with a crown of leaf and limb, bark-thickened skin, sap down my arms—salicin, aspirin. *What is remembered in the body is well remembered.* Mother's voice through my room's darkness: part crying out, part inhaled breath—

TREE OF HEAVEN
MATTHEW GREWE

Dear Children,

In this house where we live, people made bathtub gin during Prohibition; there are streams under the street, one neighbor says. When mom and I moved in, your grandparents gave us a dogwood sapling to plant in the front. I rode the bus up the street one night and distantly saw, through the length of the bus and out the windshield, fire in our street. The house next to ours sat burned and open to the sky for two years; the weeds in back grew taller than me. The tall plants and the raccoons and possums that sheltered in them reasserted the forest effortlessly. Sun and rain and not much time.

This may be when the tree took root. Or it may have got here before us. Our *Ailanthus altissimus* exercises the strengths of its kind: it does not concern itself with soil quality. It is indifferent to street pollution, needs little water and has no fear of insects, cold, or disease. It can grow ten feet in a year.

This is the tree from *A Tree Grows in Brooklyn* which reaches toward the sky from a crack in the cement, lives through the grind and crush of the tenements, gives symbolic starch to the story of Francie and Neeley, children of immigrants who likewise survive. You have seen me cut it down to its roots and seen it spread back up from the ground again, unperturbed, determined.

I grew up ten miles from here in the suburb of Plymouth Meeting. We moved there when I was four years old, as the house had room for gardens and for more children. Your grandmother knew the area already, having moved there when she was very young. If a family living in a small Philadelphia rowhome in 1959 could get someplace with a backyard and a driveway, near a newly built school, that is what they would do. An acknowledgement of that era can be found inside one of the entrances to the Plymouth Meeting Mall, which developers built in 1964-5 on the site of a tree nursery. There, in a wall-mounted display case, is a cross-section disc of tree, wider across than either of you are presently tall. Metal pins mark certain dates on its growth rings: the Revolutionary and Civil Wars, the completion of roads and railways, and, on the outermost ring, the beginning of mall construction. The tree was nearly two hundred years old when it fell. Imagine how the ground shook.

The rest of the tree was long-gone lumber and dust by the time my family came to Plymouth Meeting, but I was small then, with a small child's ability to construct an entire world out of the things that are present and immediate. My first memory of my family's house is a tire swing in the horse chestnut tree. The phone wires picked up the frequency from the AM radio towers across the street, so there was always some mixture of static, music, and speech when I put the handset to my ear. Once a pheasant exploded into flight out of bushes at my feet, but I took it as something that happens. A great horned owl sometimes perched at night in the pine tree on the corner and watched the road and radio field spread below. I learned to climb the yew tree next to hers, its branches spaced like ladder rungs but with a live spring and suppleness I could feel in my hands and feet.

194

Your grandparents fixed up the run-down house and made a peaceful place. You can understand why they worried when, as an adult, I moved to the city. This was before I was attacked from behind on the street or heard the gunshots of multiple fatal shootings, like the time a man in the street, holding a gun in the air, would not put it down, and the police fired so many shots we were certain the sound outside had to be firecrackers. This was before I realized that, to many of my neighbors, I look like the police myself.

The two of you ask lots of questions about skin color, and homeless people, and why a police car is flashing its lights. You are more curious than troubled, but by the time you are old enough to read this, you will have found concerns of your own. In my boyhood case, Ranger Rick, the earnest cartoon/raccoon environmentalist whose magazine I read, raised my hackles concerning destruction of animals and their habitats. A neighbor's huskies had also attacked and mortally wounded the family cat, my old companion. I saw that savagery was just down the street, waiting to break from its pen, and not even your grandmother, brandishing a heavy coal shovel, was a guarantee against it. When developers bought the woods behind the house and brought the heavy equipment to bear, it only caused me to wonder more what kind of place we lived in.

That summer the underbrush, which we knew to be full of wineberry canes—we had picked their fruit into large colanders and buckets in the years previous—was clawed and dragged away by heavy machinery. For the trees, there were no saws or lumberjacks. A bulldozer eased its blade to their trunks, throttled forward, and leveled them into the dusty cloud that filled that summer.

I, just about old enough to explore those woods alone, could do nothing but glare and seethe. Your nana rushed from the house and down the road one day when she saw a bulldozer bellying up to a huge pine (nowhere near the building sites and in no one's way). Her persuasion of the driver and the sparing of the tree was a certain victory, and it indicates your grandparents' care and will, but its effect was largely symbolic. The woods were gone, and in was Tara Court—a cul-de-sac tribute to someone's teenage daughter, we always imagined—and its faux Colonial homes. Zoning regulations made for large but ornamental front lawns, and sale agreements forbade residents to use clotheslines or cut their own grass. I could perch in the yew tree and scan what we called the Development for minutes at a time and see nothing move.

Your grandparents took us camping, hiking, canoeing, and I learned to climb other trees at home. There were chickadees and cardinals in winter, robins in spring, and a pair of orioles who nested in the oak every summer. We bought live Christmas trees and planted them when the ground thawed. Your grandpa split and stored firewood under an old shed at least one Development neighbor found to be an eyesore. We took in strays, like the bare-boned cat trying to sneak through the mall doors to the Chick-Fil-A, the dog ditched at the church parking lot, and another cat left on our woodpile. He sat there, like a peace offering from somewhere out of the Development, next to a pastry box full of cat food.

As we grew up, your uncle and aunt and I did yard work for Dr. Corson up the street. He lived in a house built by his grandfather, who had planted trees of all kinds around the property. Dr. Corson loved his trees and taught us many of their names, but I was more familiar with the trees' shapes and textures. I worked in their shade when I could.

Dr. Corson was a retired dermatologist, but one alike in spirit to William Hamilton, who imported the Tree of Heaven to this continent out of horticultural passion. Hamilton's Philadelphia mansion and grounds, called Woodlands, held the finest, fullest collection of native and exotic plants and trees in North America. That he would receive a specimen from China like the Tree of Heaven was a matter of routine: while President, Thomas Jefferson directed seeds and plantings from the Lewis and Clark expeditions to Hamilton's care.

His visitors would ferry across the river from the mercantile, political city and enter a sanctuary of cultured talk and fine cigars, gardens and hothouses filled with thousands of specimens, with views of the river winding toward the Delaware Bay and the sea. Hamilton noted times of day and season when the light and breeze allowed for the best experience of the place.

A desire for that kind of knowledge troubled me as I grew up. When people asked me where I was from, they didn't know Plymouth Meeting was named after the old Quaker meetinghouse or that certain homes were Underground Railroad stations. I didn't know myself about Abolition Hall, built over a carriage shed to host conventions and speeches by abolitionists such as Frederick Douglass. People knew about the mall[1], and in particular

1. The mall apparently owns some notoriety in building circles from the Plymouth Meeting Mall Fire of 1970, which burned a third of the place before the sprinkler system of a department store stopped its advance.

about its flagship Ikea store. In effect, my home was best known for unassembled particleboard furniture named after things and places in Scandinavia and made almost everywhere else.

More big box stores came and the local lumberyard and hardware store closed, and the people seemed just as untethered as the place. Your great grandmother sold her nearby house to my uncle and then effectively disappeared. My playmate from across the street, with whom I had shared my climbing trees, told me extravagant lies. Your uncle and I then started to observe—informally but steadily, over many years—that when the police stopped drivers on the four-lane road nearby, those drivers were most often black men, none of whom, as far as we knew, were residents of Plymouth Meeting.

I chose New England for college, just far enough away. I ran in the woods and learned, after some bruised knees and scraped hands, to watch the path ahead and the roots and the rocks at the same time. I heard the phrase "sense of place" in an Early American Literature class and sought some through fieldstone fences and along the coast and on Sunday afternoons walking Boston. I enjoyed my friends but missed my family. Neither the worldly types I met nor those who had barely left their bit of New Hampshire or Maine had any idea about Plymouth Meeting, so I said I was from near Philadelphia. The phrase "from the suburbs" may have passed my lips at some point, but I preferred "from the city limits" for its semi-accuracy and what I imagined as a dose of credibility.

I spent a few months of school in Washington, D.C., surrounded by other earnest 21 year olds also living city life for the first time. I was exhilarated and helpless: the

apitol Dome from the window but homeless men always
utside the door, then the tourists arriving for the cherry
lossoms. I wore a thrift store wool topcoat with sleeves
vo inches too short and tried to keep up with the white
apers and luncheons and business cards.

I graduated, spent two weeks backpacking in the woods,
nd came home to start work. The job was in an office
ark, a twenty-five minute commute away. We researched
rants for relief and development in the building next to
he headquarters of TV Guide, which was known for its
afeteria. I would email or phone a person helping AIDS
rphans at a small church somewhere in southern Africa
r providing credit to poor women in rural India and
hen have lunch on the slate patio under the trees. Mostly
wrote reports, so I took afternoon walks to keep from
apping at my desk. After I returned from a work trip to
ndia, it felt strange to walk those smooth, tree-lined lots of
mported German cars. I could still smell the city streets on
ny clothes and could picture, in afternoon quiet, a woman
valking a dirt road, her arms full of water containers, and
well in the distance.

A friend took me to church in Hunting Park, a working
class Latino North Philadelphia neighborhood in a city
vith ever-fewer jobs for working class people. The songs
nd prayers were those of people who did not assume
comfort and material prosperity. They needed God and
one another. I needed to be someplace that was not mostly
for white people and not mostly about me. Your mother
and I met there.

She already lived in Germantown, and we were married
here on a mild New Year's Day. On their way to the church,
the wedding guests drove past a corner memorial—stuffed

animals stuck to the staple-riddled wood of a telephone pole—for a young man shot at the convenience store blocks from where George Washington lived for a time and around the corner from Freedom Square, the site of the first anti-slavery protest in North America. I found work teaching GED classes and watched people grow when they had some space and some nurturing. When I took the train out of the city after work to meet your mom, I had to remark at how green and tree-cooled it felt along the suburban roads. My daily bus ride squeezed through tight at times crumbling blocks of small rowhomes, where the struggling street trees seemed to restrict the space more than liberate it.

Our city is not the one envisioned by William Hamilton, but then even the world he positioned around himself did not last very long. Within a generation of his death, Woodlands was sold to become a cemetery, the mansion remaining but with loops of headstones and elaborate mausoleums curling around it. The hothouse collections disappeared; the remaining trees are likely the grandchildren of those Hamilton planted. What would become West Philadelphia grew in and around, a contested space which manufactured, boomed, peaked, white flighted, de-industrialized, gentrified, ending (for now) with a mass of universities and hospitals at its heart instead of a house and its gardens.

The Tree of Heaven spread through the city's every convulsion even as a thick band of train tracks came to sever Woodlands from its shining S-curve of the river. It replicated under its own considerable power and with the help of tree nurseries, which sold saplings of the new Chinese ornamental as quickly as they could be grown.

City planners in Europe planted the Tree of Heaven along their boulevards for its avidity and its tolerance of grim conditions. New York City and Philadelphia followed the fashion. An era of fascination with Chinese decoration doubtless inspired their choice (Chinese immigrants would later bring the tree to the West Coast of the United States, but they had a medicinal use for its every scrap). This was before the term "invasive species" and before the tree would be removed from official use, scorned by botanists in their tree encyclopedias, and spread from one side of the country to another—and some of Canada besides.

Brought on the wind to our patch of front garden, it has claimed a spot of gravel and dusty tan soil, wedged against the bricks of the house—misery or doom for most living things—and seized its opportunity. I cut or break it down and turn toward the (admittedly haphazard) care of our household, turn back some weeks or months later, and it has sent eager shoots up toward the sun, and may have gently leaned a leafed branch against the porch, or atop another plant in the garden like a heavy arm.

One man in our city, who must have his troubles, believes the Tree of Heaven destroys buildings and people's minds and harms infants in the womb. He has self-published a book about this and written letters, demands for action, to more than one President. He is not wrong in that the "Ghetto tree" thrives in empty lots where homes once stood and around abandoned factories where people once worked. A sapling wide around as my small finger resists pulling but can still be removed without tools, if you brace yourself and lean your weight back on it. Left alone, it roots deeply, seeds heavily, poisons the surrounding soil to push other plants toward its own growing periphery.

I cannot dislodge ours, and it might take poison to see it gone. Meanwhile, the deciduous street tree across from our house was leafy last year, dead this year, and a stump and a trace of sawdust on the back of the car when we came home one day.

Dr. Corson also recently died. On his deathbed, he talked and joked with you children until he became short of breath and needed to rest. At the memorial service, in his side yard, we sat by his cypress trees. He never did convince a Franklinia tree to grow, despite many years of trying—the species having never much cared for anyplace other than the section of Georgia forest in which it was first discovered. I grieve for him every time I go by the house, and for what he left behind, which will be sold and developed into as many houses as the drainage of the clay soil will allow.

Up the road from Doc's house, the field and grounds around Abolition Hall will become townhomes in a year or two. In a few years more, the emerald ash borer will have spread across Pennsylvania and will reach the ash tree by the side gate of your grandparents' house. The beetle will burrow into the tree's bark and destroy its ability to nourish and water its canopy; within two years of that time, the tree will be all but dead.

As for us, now and until we have a good reason to go, we live in Germantown, and we do wonder what kind of place this is. There is trash and heat in the street this summer, and another stuffed animal and candle memorial around the corner. You and I have also watched the demolition of a 200-year-old house up the block. It was empty fifteen years and collapsed its chimney bricks onto the sidewalk. The workers broke it down and hauled it away, but the imprint of its rooms and staircase remain on the wall it shared with the neighboring house. This will likely be covered over, but we have seen it, and in the absence of commemoration, we know.

To seethe at all of this is your right, but I hope you will be better than me and merciful wherever you go. Look at the young men who sell drugs down the block, who now have small children and treat them tenderly. See the house next door under slow, deliberate, eternal repair. Consider the dogwood tree and its shade over the front garden. Sit on the front porch in the heavy summer air. Watch for signs of life.

A TREE OF CRAB-APPLE VARIETY / MY BIRTH
JACKLYN JANEKSELA

This is the story a mother told me about her birth and birthing process. She told it to me from inside a fort we had made with handmade quilts and threadbare sheets. She told it to me as if it were from a storybook, with both a wide open mouth and a closed one. By the colors and smells of dawn that peeked in from a crack between the blankets, I could see her shadow reflected more than her earthly shape.

•

And she pushes until it is no longer within her, but without her. It is birthed by strained pelvic bones, tendons squeaking to the sound of midnight mice. Everything tight and waiting, until it exits her body where it has been learning how to extend or retreat, how to turn flower into fruit, how to break without being broken. It is not an easy birth, this one. But she has been preparing for it, despite being so young. When, for the first time, her brother swings on a branch, she braces herself for the joy of swinging, the near accumulation of flight. More than just birds scurry.

During those first weeks, twigs spiral cloud-bound— the blinking of a leaf as if her own eye. These trees have no names, but are hard to bear, hard to handle, hard to stomach. It is with this bark that tribes make the traveling tea. Or it is the bark of that tree? For reference, look at the palm of her hand, study the wind currents, watch how things curl. The recommended dose is two branches worth, ut she's only had one. Trees crouch to hear her story. *There are other ways to come or go*, she whispers. To travel, take a trunk and make a boat, a vessel of Nordic proportions.

With time, things sprout like spuds or eyelashes or both.

It isn't until the spring that she notices the cicadas, he carcasses croaking even well past life itself, well into he fall. Some bodies are plucked by the non-delicate fingers of the non-adults, some are brushed by the broom of mothers, while others remain steadfast to her limbs wanting to become bone, or at least cartilage. She never pushes away, not a single one. Her branches open like nets or net castings or falling stars or Midwestern landscapes.

The tree splits horizons and constellations, but only if she squints her eyes. It is so much easier to master this technique at night, but she's bold enough to practice it in non-night moments, too. Sun emissions tendril from sacral centers. Stars appear when she closes her eyes—like feather tips like medicine like shaman. She sees other things too, but she can't explain everything. The words are not yet a part of her. She is but a sapling, a young girl, without period.

The tree split a spirit once. She watched the ghostly rays disperse into dandelion pods and then milkweed vines. Something similar happened when she examined her fingers—the brittle leaves clicked like nails on a desk.

It is there like it had always been, since they remember—in the middle, right there. Do you see it? It's almost impossible not to. It almost covers the whole house. Its shade the biggest of the block. It starts with that one— the crab apple blossom; the pear and oak would come later. The family ordered a multi-arboreal lawn and she would be the one to bear each and every one.

No ravens come pecking at their trees. But the pine next-door are divine.

Never does a cat climb the tree, as far as she knows. They come to lick the skins of fallen crab apples, shiver fur when vampire teeth puncture the flesh. Leave the seeds for a squirrel or a field mouse.

The amount of bees and wasps mounting the crab apple stamens overwhelm her. Not for fear, but for lack of time to study each one—to ask their names, to have a chat. Her brother jumping ship, is later found resting his nose against the screen door. He fears what natural reproduction could to do him. The honeycomb so far away yet reflecting in his hair. Once, tiny twigs stole a few flaxen threads and gifted them to a robin who was rushing to make a nest before the end of May. But the cat who never climbed that tree certainly climbed the ones next-door. Bird-hungry and curious.

Someone or something born and chirping, but not a bird. It is a heart of another bud, the crescent of a waning moon prospering the vulva of another flower. Someone or something says: Sister, and the mother of the first one agrees. No one touches the tree but the tree. Those two branches outstretch to imitate legs. Birds ready to land or a woman hungry for any number of genders. She unfolds like laundry sheets tucked away in a wooden armoire, slight of lavender and ghost musings.

The tree remembers from which the sapling plunges and sways magic fingers but are really whiskers of some neighboring cat or kitten.

The tree sighs between non-melodic lyrics, between popcorn kernels, and non-foreign irises.

It is her turn to birth again, to present the present with the crying mouth of a baby called she.

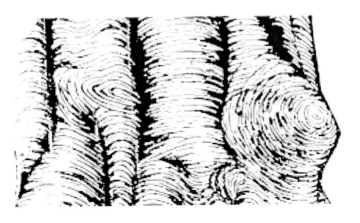

WORD-AND-WOOD WORKING
WENDY CALL

I set up shop wherever I go: notebook, pen, laptop, and prompt: a book, a postcard, a view of water or wall, a note scribbled on a paper scrap. My word-factory might happen at a friend's kitchen counter, roadside picnic table, bus stop, beach towel, or boring meeting.

For the last several years, I have often made my desk in national parks: a chair at a visitor center, a trail-side bench, or a patch of bare ground. At a half-dozen parks in all four corners of the continental United States, people's question is nearly always the same. They smile shyly, lean toward me, gesture at my laptop, and ask, "Are you online?"

At Mount Rainier's Nisqually Vista, it happens again. A tourist from Japan breaks away from her group, walks up to me, and says carefully, "Oh, is there wifi?" She points toward the sky. "Signal?" She points down at the ground. "Here?"

I stare at her, shaking my head slowly.

I wander a Mount Rainier forest trail, seeking a desk. Signs endlessly instruct. No bikes. No pets. Don't go off-trail. Don't crush the flowers. Don't trample the soil around the trees. I end up working on a tree stump. I have never before even climbed a tree stump, though they are ubiquitous in the Pacific Northwest. This one spans fifty-seven inches—its width nearly my height. The nearby Douglas firs of similar girth are neck-craningly tall, their lowest branches many stories above the ground. This particular stand of firs is just inside the park boundary, where nineteenth-century loggers plied their trade. Moss carpets the stump; trillium frills its skirt of roots. Hesitant saplings grow at its edges: the largest only four feet tall, their trunks the diameter of my thumb. A thrush's song spirals; a breeze flows over the tree canopy like a wave. The soil around every old tree has been trampled trail-smooth; we love our trees to death.

Though I aspire to honor these trees, I trade in their destruction: pulp for the pages on which my words are printed, hunks of wood at which I sit to write. Stumps, like this one, are my nurselogs.

A trail of sawdust and sweat connects every desk at which I've turned my trade. In twenty-five years, I have sat at hundreds of desks, but owned only four. A college professor gave me the desk that had traveled with him since his college days. For a decade, it was the only piece of furniture that moved with me from the Midwest to the Gulf, then Pacific, then Atlantic Coasts. I loved its heavy walnut planks, worn smooth by decades of words hewn from its surface.

I left that desk behind when I moved to Mexico, where I worked at a plywood desk given to me by the friend who had loaned me his house. The tropical termites that burrowed into the house's cement walls also invaded my desk. The desktop angled down toward the center seam, creating a hammock for my books and computer. Each time I sat down to write, a layer of wood dust gathered in my lap. The termites and I worked in tandem; they spun wood into dust as I spun dust into words. At night I imagined my computer crashing to the cement floor, my wood-pulp desk-hammock finally collapsing.

I wrote to a friend back home about my dilemma. Should I buy a plastic, non-biodegradable desk that the termites couldn't eat? Should I buy another plywood desk, knowing termites would devour it within six months? Or should I invest a tropical hardwood desk? It would cost me six weeks' rent and cost the planet a rainforest tree, but would last, termite-free, for the rest of my life.

My friend wrote back, saying only, "You mean there are *termites* living in the *desk* in your *room*? I can't quite fathom that."

I bought the hardwood desk.

Somewhere in Mexico's Chimalapas rainforest sits the stump of an old-growth guanacaste—a sacred tree—that became my desk. Fifteen years later, my guanacaste desk has traveled with me from the Gulf, to the Atlantic, and finally the Pacific Coast. Now, our guests write at it, while I work at a white-pine desk from trees felled on a Massachusetts tree plantation. A genealogy of tree stumps—at Mount Rainier, in Massachusetts, in Mexico—sustains my words.

HOME IS A CLOSED SKY
MACKENZIE MYERS

2016: I like to think it started with the old, hundred-foot Eastern white pine that crashed through my uncle's roof last summer. The massive trunk shredded the shingles, shattered the skylight. It shook him, a forty-year-old man who is just mentally developed enough to live in a house by himself but not enough to hold down a job. It scared him so badly he slept at the house of a family friend for weeks until my mother coaxed him back and scheduled the trees to be cut down.

The pine was one of a group of five, which stood across from my bedroom window at my childhood home in Michigan. I don't know about my brother, Eareckson, who shared the same view, but as a child I looked out at the trees every night. Some nights the pines were guardians and some nights they were hazards. In storms I eyed them uneasily, my child-brain unable to triangulate the distance of their fall. My mind could discern only two options in the event of a storm ripping the trunks from the ground. Either the thickest part of the trunk would go right through our kitchen and living room sometime in the night, quietly devastating the places my family spent most of our time. If not: the tree would terrify on its descent, but only brush the tips of its crown on the back of our patio fence, leaving my home unscathed.

1888: President Grover Cleveland signs United States homestead certificate #6009, granting John Bathke, a

German immigrant farmer, one-hundred sixty acres at th[e] "north west quarter of section twenty nine in townshi[p] thirty six north of range four west of Michigan Meridia[n] in Michigan." It's the last day of May when he signs thi[s] and if there were white pines on the property granted t[o] Mr. Bathke, they would have been spouting yellow polle[n] that blanketed every blade of grass below. They woul[d] have been sprouting new cones, sporting bright fingers o[f] growth on the tips of their branches.

But there weren't pines on Mr. Bathke's new corne[r] of the world. Not yet. It was farmland, and open, an[d] probably full of the timothy hay that is still in the meado[w] behind my uncle's house.

According to a local resident whose hobby is famil[y] histories, the pines—thirteen in all—were planted shortl[y] after the Bathkes were granted their land.

This means at the time of death, these pines wer[e] about 125 years old.

2016: Just one of those thirteen pines, in its 125th year, would have intercepted an estimated 4,059 gallons of stormwater through its needles, roots and bark, conserved around 173 kilowatt-hours, or about half the electricity it takes a window air conditioning unit to run for one month (according to an energy co-op in south Kentucky), reduced atmospheric carbon by 521 pounds, or slightly more than the carbon emitted each time I fly from Traverse City, Michigan to Sacramento, California.

The big pines spent decades insulating the house in winter, providing shade in summer, slowing wind speeds and structural wear. They kept years of nitrogen dioxide (a main culprit behind fossil fuel-burning engines choking down the ozone layer), volatile organic compounds (gasoline, benzene, house paint, formaldehyde), sulfur dioxide (e.g. volcano belches), ozone pollution, and tiny particles of material from sticking in our lungs, our skin, our mouths, our hair.

The pines, though clearly capable of physical devastation, were not just imaginary sentinels.

1998: About a century after the Bathkes moved on to their land, we moved on to it too—though in a shallower layer of time, and on two-and-a-half acres versus one-hundred sixty. The summer before I started kindergarten, we said goodbye to the scorpions and tarantulas and lawn regulations of New Mexico's Holloman Air Force Base, and returned to my parents' original stake in the ground: northern Michigan. We moved into a blue house with white borders around the windows and lichen taking up a permanent residence on the north side, darkening the paint by a shade or two. When we arrived, the front lawn was so overgrown I disappeared in it on the way up to the porch of my new home. The swaying tops of timothy hay served as the only indicators of my movement.

I don't remember the vegetation of New Mexico. From what my mom says, there wasn't a lot to remember in the first place, besides yucca flowers and the browning grass in the front yard. I don't remember taking one final glance at the lawn when we loaded up the U-Haul and our tiny teal Cavalier—Dad and me in the truck while Mom drove with baby Eareckson behind us. I don't remember watching the landscapes change as we wound northward through the panhandle of Texas, the pan of Oklahoma, Missouri, Illinois, the smile of Lake Michigan on northwestern Indiana, and finally, finally across the state line, northbound.

I don't remember my disappointment in hearing we still had six hours to go from the state line, not understanding that the "Welcome to Michigan" sign was not synonymous with "Welcome home."

2001: I don't remember learning what grew or hibernated or lived and died around me in Michigan. Growing up, I was surrounded by field guides with cracked spines in both my living room and at a nearby biological research station where my mom worked. We had copies of *Sibley's Birds of North America*, some books specific to Michigan, umpteen *Petersen* guides for natural entities both living and not. I knew what birds landed in our yard, what waterways surrounded me, but if not for the books, I might believe this information was written in my genome, a fingerprint that came with me out of the womb.

White pine is one of the few things I do remember absorbing. Mrs. Spencley's fourth grade classroom had an entire unit devoted to Michigan. We learned about the area's indigenous populations, the Chippewa, Odawa and Potawatomi; legends behind the Sleeping Bear Dunes on Lake Michigan, the Song of Hiawatha, the copper mines and lumber towns that both helped and harmed our collective history. We learned the state flower: apple blossom. State bird: American robin. State fish: brook trout. State motto: *if you seek a pleasant peninsula, look about you*. State tree: Eastern white pine. *Pinus strobus*.

"You know it's a white pine if it has five needles," Mrs. Spenceley said. "One for each letter of the word W-H-I-T-E."

That was the introduction, the handshake with what would become a constant presence until I left the nest at 21, what greeted me outside the window nearly every morning until that point. I looked for its cones—as long as my hand, slightly curved, covered in sap-crusted scales. I looked for its bark—smooth and light in youth, but like alligator hide on mature trees. I looked for its general shape—windblown but majestic, fluffy but sculpted. Eventually I learned to identify the white pine in the same way we learn to identify good friends—not by employing mnemonic devices to remember their names, but by becoming accustomed to the way they speak, the way they move, the way they make my heart leap into my throat when I see them after months of separation.

2006: Once I learned them, I loved them. My uncle's pines were around a hundred feet tall and therefore difficult to play in, but the smaller pines in our sandy yard kept Eareckson and me engaged in what we thought was give-and-take. We admired them; we carved our initials into their bark. They held our bodies up from the ground; they kept our frisbees longer than we wished they would.

My brother and I had a swing-set like normal kids. We had soccer balls and footballs and bikes. But the trees are where I remember spending most of my time outdoors with Eareckson. Each season meant something different in terms of pines. Summer meant collecting shovelfuls of rusty, dead needles from the ground for Mom to mulch her gardens. Autumn was for traversing crooked farmstead posts and the Bathkes' barbed-wire to gather precious amber liquid—a tincture of dried needles and rainwater—for use in spells when I was young enough to believe in them. Winter meant quiet mornings spent snowshoeing, when snow formed pillows on the boughs.

Spring was climbing season. The ground was too wet to play on without Mom having a conniption, so we took to the skies. On the south side of our two-and-a-half acres was the small stand of white pines only about twenty feet tall, and we climbed those halfway, acting out any number of scenarios. Some days, we were pirates scuttling up the masts of our neighboring ships. Some days we were spies, scaling skyscrapers. Other days, we were siblings commiserating about the kids at school or how our parents refused to buy us an Xbox. Several of the pines were permanently tattooed with our presence, carved with Eareckson's Swiss army knife, which we tossed between us tree-to-tree.

Eventually, those trees took on something bigger than a two-inch blade. Eventually, pine blister rust moved in—a fungal disease that grows inside the cambium and bursts, like little bombs going off inside the bark, releasing its spores to surrounding white pines and diminishing the tree's structural soundness. Eventually, the tree would turn rusty orange from top to bottom, needles thinning on the way, at some point looking not unlike a trunk on fire.

2010–2013: In college, every time I come home from Marquette in the Upper Peninsula, four hours away, some new patch of sky has opened up. The wind sounds different, too. Five years prior, the *shhhhh* of the wind blowing through the trees was heartier, more forceful, like exhaling hot breath on a cold window to draw pictures on the frost. The trees swayed for entire afternoons, thrashing, alive with movement.

Now, when the wind blows, it's hollow and higher-tched, having nothing to grab on to. It rushes right past e branches at the top, making me wonder at the time hat the trees will look like in a few years and if they really ill fall, sooner or later.

014: Of course it's only coincidence, but blister rust hits y uncle's pines around the time I move away to graduate chool, thirty-five hours from home, in Portland, Oregon. I oard a flight at the end of August, heading from Traverse ity into the middlespace, already suspecting that Portland ill never be home. The minute Grand Traverse Bay drops ut from under my feet and the shoreline disappears, I fall sleep to keep from sobbing.

Late in the evening, I arrive at PDX, fortunate to have place to stay and a ride. After we load the luggage and hit he highway, neon lights of bars and strip clubs whoosh ast us in the dark, blurring in my vision. The white-and-lue *Pure Michigan* license plates are now light blue plates livided down the middle by a green conifer. Lines of raffic, red lights in the right lane and white lights in the left, tretch out beneath overpasses. Instead of Sault Ste. Marie, Mackinaw City, Gaylord, Kalkaska and I-75, there are signs for Seattle, The Dalles, Bend, Eugene, I-5. The drive is ike veering down a waterslide, twisting in the dark with a looser knowledge of my position in the world after every turn. It amazes me that this feels familiar to anyone, but over six-hundred-thousand call this place home, including the woman next to me, the friend of a family friend and my only connection to the city. She explains our route. We exit the highway onto what she says is Cesar Chavez, 39th Avenue, a main vein running through town.

"It's really easy to get to the airport," she says. "You take the 75 bus up Chavez, which is close to my place. Then you'll head to Hollywood Transit Center and take the red line to PDX." It's nearly laughable; I've only just arrived and she's explaining how to depart.

In the morning, there are Douglas-firs outside the window.

2015: Come spring, the small white pine stand across the driveway, where Eareckson and I used to pretend we were pirates, is culled because of blister rust. Its remains are spidery fingerprints of stumps ground into the earth.

Only after coming back home for the summer did I discover my near-constant awareness of which organisms surround me. The signatures of my coordinates are in constant assessment: am I near the ocean or Superior? Douglas-fir or Eastern white pine? Scrub jays or blue jays?

In leaving, I found that my stability is determined by the thickness of an area's forests, the proximity and size of its waters. I'd heard Portland was green and lush and full of trees, but compared to what? Miles of the Hiawatha National Forest? The 13,000 acres, mostly wooded, that the field station of my childhood owns in northern Michigan? Without a car I was locked inside the city's skyscraper hallways, the sky closed there like at home, but by the claustrophobia of artifice, not the comfort of boughs.

At the end of the year, around Christmas, we're hit with an intense windstorm. Reading a book in the living room, I hear a crack like a lightning strike and then a crash comes from the meadow north of our house. Mom is walking in the meadow, so I throw down my book and run outside in my bare feet. The top half of a tragically straight pine, one that was across from my uncle's pines but around the same age, lies mere yards from her. She stands with her hands in her pockets, staring.

2016: When I finish my master's degree and come home for a final Great Lakes summer before moving to California to join my partner—who is also from northern Michigan—the sky outside my window is open. White clouds suspended in blue over naked land.

Nearly all of the white pines in our yard are gone. The big ones and the small ones.

Nearly.

On one of the last mornings before my move to Sacramento, Mom and I have coffee on the cedar swing under a cherry tree. The fragrant mulch beneath our sandals is what remains of the big pines' trunks cut in spring; the brush pile lining our property, now home to squirrels and chipmunks and mice, is what remains of the branches.

"We live in such a beautiful place," I say.

She corrects me, elbowing my side and looking over the top of her glasses with a grin. "You mean *I* live in such a beautiful place."

She's right. My walls are repainted, my bed was sold, my pines are gone. Mom and Dad are remodeling the house soon, so who knows what any of this will look like in a few months. As we sip our coffee in the only-August-but-already-chilly morning air, she tells me again how she plans it all to look. On the way to get a refill, she gets sidetracked, excited, showing me where she'll plant what, how the cutting garden in the back will fill in nicely with different flowers on a rotating seasonal schedule, how the willow tree she planted will someday droop down over the adirondack chairs, how they want to put in a horseshoe pit behind the dogwoods.

As we move along the property, clutching our empty mugs, she stops at a clearing where they buried the powerline that runs diagonally through our slot of land. When the company removed it, poles and all, it left a space between the trees, letting the sky in. We then get to talking about the honey locust that grew all along the edges of the road when she was a kid in the seventies, an era between when this was the Bathkes' and when it was mine. While I'm busy examining the locust stems for spines, she eyes the clearing and says,

"And then I put these guys here. I'm hoping they'll fill in the gap."

When I look over, she's patting the top of a scrappy little white pine, smiling.

THE SCENT OF A DAPHNE
KAREN K. HUGG

It was early September, my second semester of horticulture school, and class was about to begin. I stood outside the door on the narrow sidewalk that ran along the building. The day was warm and the door propped open with a wedge. Flies buzzed in and out. Students chatted and shuffled through notebooks while friends hugged at seeing each other again. I hadn't made any friends yet, but that didn't bother me. I had other things on my mind. Like the situation I had to explain to Tim, my professor.

He was an outdoorsy 50-something with wavy, gray hair dressed in boots and a canvas jacket. "What's up?" he asked.

It was actually what was down. Down in my life. As in down and out, or beaten down, or in a downward spiral. My husband, Ethan, had just had an operation, not to remove an organ or clean out dangerous tissue or repair a ligament. The surgeon had installed a port in his chest, a small flat disc with a little tube connected to his artery so chemotherapy drugs could be injected into his bloodstream. He was about to be poked with a lot of needles a lot of the time and surgically inserting a port was easier on his body than poking the same veins again and again.

"My husband has cancer," I said. It felt strange to say that. I was 34 years old. Ethan, 35. I explained the diagnosis, the treatment appointments, the waiting, Ethan's unknown prognosis. My uncertainty at learning horticulture. I asked Tim whether I should withdraw from Deciduous I.D. and all the other classes I was registered for. I'd miss some sessions, I knew that.

Tim had glasses that automatically darkened in outdoor light and, despite the cloud cover that day, they had darkened to charcoal gray. "Well, it's too early to drop out," he said. "Take the class and see how it goes. If it gets to be too difficult later on, I'll give you an incomplete."

Incomplete. The word rang like a gong as I walked away. Ethan with advanced colon cancer was headed toward incompletion. Dying when? A year, two, five years later, at 36, 37, maybe 40 if we were lucky. Robbed of the opportunity to live a middle-aged or elderly life. And me—the loss, the fear. I imagined myself a young widow living in our old house, alone. Floating in a fog. Hope was a word I had never understood, but now had a new appreciation for.

After class, the day turned sunny. I went to the parking lot and got in my car. It suffocated with stagnant heat. I felt trapped but knew I couldn't open the windows. I turned the ignition and made the obligatory turns I needed to get back to the highway. In intermittent spurts, I cried as I drove the 11 miles south to the city, trapped in thick traffic, pressing the brakes before a slight acceleration, then stopping again before going forward, stopping, going, again and again as I inched along, imagining what it would be like to drive a car into a grave.

•

In weeks to come, I walked on soaked grass and puddled concrete in the rain, writing the Latin names of trees and shrubs under an umbrella: *thuja plicata, pseudotsuga menziesii, tsuga heterophylla*. These were the trees of the Pacific

Northwest. The giants whose car-sized girth loomed over a person in Seattle's public parks and Cascade mountains. Tim argued for the importance of knowing the exact spelling of each botanical name. A requirement. An agonizingly particular requirement.

I lost myself in that act of spelling, a discipline I'd always respected but never delighted in. The minutiae of the exact order of letters in a Latin binomial took my focus away from illness. I pictured how *Acer palmatum* "Sango-Kaku" looked written on the plant list handout. Making certain to add the final e on *Aceraceae* and other tree family names. My favorite name to write was *Metasequoia glyptostroboides*. Or should I say, my favorite to speak. The rhythm of it delighted me. The "oi" and "ee" sounds at the end felt bright and cheery. What the Latin actually meant was sometimes self-evident, as in "meta sequoia," and while Tim informed us of many meanings, I can't recall the meaning of the prefixes and suffixes of "glypto stro boi des." Still today, I love that it's as mighty of a word as a giant tree's name should be. And that it is one of the most deeply colored trees of green-blue needles and reddish, gnarly bark speaks to its majesty as well.

The majesty of all plant traits, not just their names, astounded me. The more I learned, the more passionate I became. When I'd walk to the class's meeting spot from my car, whether in the university arboretum or at a local hospital, the worries of how much Ethan had eaten that day or whether he'd suffered through a work meeting faded away. It still haunts me to say the pinging worry of losing the man I admired most in the world disappeared. I simply studied trees: examined their bark, their leaf patterns, the shape of their crowns, their fruits, their seeds. I counted

the number of buds in a cluster, learned the differenc
between fresh twig growth and last year's brown. How
tree could feed itself despite a severe gouge in the trun
Life was simplified and focused in a time when I wa
overwhelmed by a large, dooming complexity. I wasn't
caretaker, I wasn't the unfortunate soul whose husban
had cancer. It was as if horticulture had created a safe wa
around my psyche so I could exist as only Me.

Until the day we visited the zoo.

The zoo's gardens alternated between dull swath
of boxwoods and barberry to more enticing border
of salmon-branched dogwoods and delicate laceca
hydrangeas. Sugar maples and cherries grew overheac
Tim led us to a Hollywood juniper and we gathere
around the seemingly windswept tree, taking notes on it
botanical attributions. He pointed to it with his signatur
wrapped umbrella, noting the spiky ball fruit. He gesture
to a fragrant daphne at its feet, rattling off *Daphne odor*
"Aureo-marginata," a name so new to me then, alon
with its most prominent features, before encouraging u
to smell it. People clustered around the low shrub, takin
turns inhaling its fresh, spicy scent.

I waited at the back of the group. We were a rugge
but goofy bunch. Mostly in our 30s or 40s, former hi-tecl
and Boeing employees, landscape business owners, a few
undergraduates, a few unemployed, wannabe designers anc
arborists. Becky, the only student to commute from further
south than me, owned a small CSA farm. She and I, along
with a few others, were the last to smell the daphne and I,
unable to pull myself away from the brief, neutral moment
of inhaling a flower, was the last student still crouched
down, alone, when the others had moved on.

Or so I thought.

Angela was a woman I knew by sight. She was a thin, petite, 30-something with long, black, curly hair and a narrow nose that at the last minute swooped forward. Her eyes were close-set with long lashes. She had tiny, dangly earrings. Groovy earrings. The kind of earrings I wouldn't dare wear but that looked interesting and tasteful on her. Suddenly, that face was next to me, at my low level, close in the cold winter light.

"Hey," she said. Her voice had a nasal reediness. "I heard from some folks that your husband is sick."

I blinked. I wasn't prepared.

"I wanted to tell you, I can't believe how strong you are. It's amazing you're coming here and doing this. I admire you so much."

Her hand, a bony, small hand, rested on my forearm. The feel of it, the touch of it, the reaching out of a not-quite stranger, ruptured the pain I carefully compartmentalized into my gut every day.

I set my hand atop hers. My voice huffed in the wind, lost its resonance. I breathed in but couldn't get air. "No," I whispered. "No." I shook my head because I couldn't form the words—my mouth muscles were lax when I wanted them to move. My face was hot. "I'm really not, I'm just…"

Her face crimped with sympathy.

In a squeak, I whiffed out, "It's just…I have no other choice."

My body broke into a sob. So did hers.

Our fingers interlocked, this hand of a person who I didn't know a minute before, together, neither letting the other free. She'd punched through my wall, the wall that separated my two lives, and the crash was loud and unexpected.

The sounds that followed were her words of encouragement, my confessions of terror, and a lot of sniffling. We got up and strolled into the aviary, which the class was cutting through to study another section of plants. There, with the colorful birds swooping past our heads, we stood under a net, talking. The mural of a Northwest scene, trees and sky, sprawled before us in the snug, curved room. We stared at the painted pond and talked about Ethan's condition, how the cancer had migrated to his liver, and the inexplicable chaos of how this had happened to a young, healthy man. A thrush with a blue back landed on a staged branch before the mural, then cocked its head in that jerky, bird-processing way. It watched us with one eye and waited for our next move. We stood together, speaking in low, quiet tones, uneager to catch up with the class. For the first time in many months, I felt at peace.

•

Cancer sat in my life like a boulder that couldn't be budged. So I went around it as best I could. Ethan and I dutifully attended chemo appointments by day, sitting in vinyl chairs and chatting with the center's "spiritual advisor" (the multi-denominational counselor who helped patients cope with impending death) as the toxins went into his bloodstream. At night, we pretended to be a normal couple. We took walks. Ethan rode his bike a few blocks. We avoided sugar, bought a bunch of baseball caps. We went to Sonics games, our friends standing to cheer at an unexpected come-back while Ethan sat in his seat, ready to regurgitate his dinner. We did that for eight months. Then we endured colon surgery, more chemotherapy, liver surgery, more chemotherapy. Yes, it was long and if it hadn't been so intense, it would have been boring, which, at times, it was anyway. Treatment lasted 15 months.

Meanwhile, Angela and I became friends. We took more horticulture classes and passed our exams. We went to lunch. We muddled through our Diseases class, the last looming biggie before graduation. I'd pick her up and we'd drive to campus, talking out the difference between bacterial leaf spot and fungal leaf spot, griping about how Walt's quizzes were too difficult. Later, when I started working on clients' yards, she helped me on jobs. And on the weekends, we tried to plant and rearrange our gardens so they looked like the sanctuaries of our dreams.

That I had a dream was a good sign. I wanted to make my garden into a psychological refuge and so did she. One afternoon in summer, I went to her house, a bungalow in a suburb with an elegant, finished front yard and small back one that needed work. Adjacent to the yard was a tall house that overlooked her deck. The meager *Arborvitae* trees lining the fence had offered no privacy for seven years and scant ornamental interest. We agreed to remove and replace them with equally uninteresting Leyland Cypress trees, which at least would grow tall enough to screen the neighbor's house. So we took our shovels and picks and dug a hole around the first tree.

As we uncovered roots, she grabbed her loppers and sliced through them. Then she'd stick her hand beneath the root ball, feeling for an anchor root, the chest of her flannel shirt scraping against the filthy dirt ball. I'd dig out more soil, then lean the tree back to reveal its hidden tendrils. More sawing, more digging until the tree's last root either snapped or was cut and we threw the poor conifer on the brush pile.

We conquered three trees that morning, then ate lunch. Over tacos in her kitchen, we talked about Ethan's latest scan. It was clean. But we had four more years of clean scans before the doctor declared him healthy and no longer in need of monitoring.

"You never know. Things could go either way," I said. "We're only a year out."

"Well, how does he *feel?*" The word "feel" came out in two syllables, like "Fee-ul."

"He feels great. He's pretending he can play softball on Sundays."

"Wonderful," she said. That reedy voice and assured tone sounded like a grandma, a grandma who's just seen the result of a child's craft project and is satisfied.

We went back out before our bodies cooled and our muscles tightened. We dug out five more trees. The tree in the center of the fence line, the lucky one that received the most light and sun, stubbornly clung to the ground. We dug a huge trench and lopped off its thicker roots. We scraped away more dirt with our hands like archaeologists clawing for artifacts. One root, directly beneath the tree's root ball, had grown straight down. Angela crawled under the ball and stuck an arm underneath. "I can feel it, but the pruners can't cut it. It's too big."

"Hold on," I said. I went to my truck and got out a root saw, then got in the trench and stuck it in the soil, sawing blindly. After sweat poured off my forehead, I stopped and said, "It cut it through, but it still won't give." I got up and she jumped down.

I rocked the tree backward. "Can you see anything?"

"Yep, it's hiding under there, little bugger."

I went around and jumped in the hole, then wrapped my arms around the prickly evergreen as if I were wrestling bear to the ground, sideways.

"Here," she said. She walked behind the slanted conifer and threw her little body onto it, legs split as if riding a orse. "Is it giving?"

"No."

She hopped off, took a few steps back, then ran and apt onto the tree again.

I giggled at the absurdity of her determination, at the bsurdity of my own. At the absurdity of spending our ime ending the life of a perfectly good tree. We waited for he root to snap, but the tree only shook with our laughter.

Eventually, we felled the *arborvitae*.

•

Now, 12 years later, I realize Tim was right. Not only did I not have to take an Incomplete, I finished the horticulture program and became certified. If I hadn't stayed in the Deciduous I.D. class, I would have never been friends with Angela. And now I lie in bed every night with a healthy husband, often in awe of serendipity. Sometimes it occurs because of chance, like who dies from cancer and who doesn't. Sometimes it occurs because of choice, to take a class or not, to reach out or not. I wonder sometimes who I *haven't* become friends with because I didn't choose to reach out or an unknown person chose not to reach out to me. Angela chose to go in close, to not retreat, teaching me that one of illness's gifts is friendship. I can still imagine that day with vivid clarity, she and I under the June sun, she riding atop a tree and me hanging on the side, clinging to a scratchy, green cone pointed like a rocket toward the sky, laughing at our weird task, both ready to launch into a mysterious future.

TEN TAKES ON THE PALM
PAUL LISICKY

1. The sandy soil, the boggy ponds: whenever I feel that inexplicable sense of geographic safety (say, in parts of Cape Cod, coastal North Carolina, or Florida), I understand soon enough that I'm looking at a replica of my childhood backyard—or the woods and marshes nearby.

And yet I once wanted to be elsewhere. Or at least I wanted my plants and trees to be elsewhere. I wanted them to grow in daring shapes, tips pointy as shovels. I wanted them to be scary, a little closer to life as I knew it, which felt to me both beautiful and a little brutal. Don't children always know that consciousness is more extreme than their parents remember? On childhood trips to Florida and California, my eyes went first to the palms. Palms weren't bound to restraint or to the pressures of some unnameable force, the codes always changing, impossible to decipher. I'd look a little like a palm if I were allowed to let go.

2. Empty signifier, totem of better times, the better life. Plant six in the ground outside a bayside bar, and you're not in Ocean City, Maryland, anymore but someplace sexier, looser, where the people aren't required to wear a lot of clothes. Maybe after three drinks Ocean City is Belize. Those palms say: you can be outside all year. You need not hibernate or live against the cold from November through March. Duty, drudgery, self-punishment: what for? Think of the vitality on its way to you. But the scudding clouds, the washed-out beiges of the buildings, the deciduous trees across the lagoon: why do the palms look so wrong?

You can't even see them without intuiting *doomed*. They have but 160 days before the bud browns, the fronds burnt after the first hard freeze. Trucked off to the landfill, disposable as a paper towel. Come next spring, the cycle begins all over again: another six trucked in from hundreds of miles away. Even if you're not a fan of palms, you have to admit any living thing deserves better than that.

3. A worthy tree? You might say a subtle tree, a tasteful tree, with branches instead of pleated fronds. A tree that changes, with leaves that color, dry, and drop: this is what intelligent, evolved people are expected to value and cherish. Time, the passage of. A soul that doesn't attach, a spirit that loves, nourishes, lets go. Why put stock in an embodiment of joy, emblem of ongoing life? Tree of denial, tree of escape, indifferent to history and suffering, with none of the asceticism and severity of the conifer, which also keeps its green.

4. But strip the palm of its louche associations and what's left? A tree with a trunk so smooth and gray you think of the skin of seals, dolphins, manatees. Stand a few feet away, look up, let your neck fall and marvel at its architecture, the fronds leaping out from the bud. They look like they want to reach the sky. Only weight and gravity pull down the ends. In this way a date palm is a fountain. Or fireworks. Or even someone praying: "...in a gesture both hieratical and profound," as Flannery O'Connor puts it in "Revelation."

5. More man-made than plant. A sculpture, a lamp. A wig: doesn't the palm exist for that mop on top? Clip off the fronds and what's left is a decapitation,

which is why we can't bear to see them shorn after a hurricane. The palm looks a little like us, simple as that. Of the two kinds of frondage, the palmate and the pinnate, the palmate's lobes fan out from a common point. The structure an open hand, its fingers radiating.

6. In ancient times, the palm's associations were victory, fertility, peace. When Jesus entered Jerusalem on his donkey, the celebrating throng both waved fronds before him and carpeted the ground in his passage.

No surprise then that *palm* is but one letter away from *psalm*.

7. I've seen unwatered palms, nutrient-starved palms, unclipped palms, but never an intrinsically ugly palm. Over three-thousand varieties of palms exist, yet there's a remarkable consistency in each. They want to look like their siblings. Perhaps there's something unnerving about a species so bent toward sameness, endlessly reproducible, as if from an assembly line. Perhaps in the palm we humans see something we don't like to see about ourselves.

8. The Cuban belly, The Sago, The Butterfly, The Pindo, The Coconut, The Mexican Fan, The Canary Island Date, The Royal, The Queen, The Bangalow, The Betel, The Silver Saw, The Puerto Rican Thatch, The Lady, The Kentia, The Chilean Wine.

9. Every hour a palm frond crashes through the windshield of some parked car. Falling fronds paralyze and kill, plummeting from a height of a hundred feet. After Santa Ana winds, dark fronds litter the boulevards, snarling traffic. There they look a little like centipedes on steroids

until the trash collectors haul them away to be chipped.

In Miami and Los Angeles, city officials talk of replacing palms with sycamores or more practical specimens. Shade cover is the issue; no one can cool off from 101-degree heat underneath the palm. Certain longtime residents can't wait to see them gone. To them, the palm drinks up the aquifer. To them, the palm is so ubiquitous it might as well be a concrete telephone pole. And yet people born elsewhere can't bear the thought of their removal. What is Southern California without palms? some say. Where is the romance in that? Echo Park might as well be Wisconsin, and our myths of self-transformation are just myths.

10: Is the palm a grass or a tree? Flowering plants, botanists say, are either dicots or monocots. Palms belong to the latter, which are grasses: wheat, oats, barley, corn, lilies, onions, orchids, bamboo. Turf gone colossal, extreme. No bark. Cut through a palm and you don't find growth rings. No, think household sponge, but denser, harder, without the expected moisture. And they can't resist death the way an oak takes care of itself by sealing off an injury. The palm is vulnerable in the way that your lawn is vulnerable if you splash gas on it, or forget to turn on the sprinkler system in a hot spell. Could the joke be on us? Has the palm fooled us into thinking it's a straight razor when it's always been a butter knife?

AIRING OUT
STEFAN OLSON

I see it every day now on my walk to the University. House owners drape rugs from porch railings, yard workers clear the matted leaves and groom the grass, and two border collies keep watch from a boulder behind a wrought-iron fence. After months under a cloudy sky, now it's the season of stretching out, whatever form that takes. The elms are budding, the dandelions sprouting, and the spiders in my apartment have migrated to the space beneath the eaves. Spring has arrived in Missoula, Montana, and with it the pollen and bicycles, the snow melt rushing between the banks of the Clark Fork: it is time to pull the shrink-wrapped plastic covering my windows and let this place air out.

•

When I moved to Missoula, my mother saw potential in my little studio: the bedroom was painted a warm orange and the kitchen a soft yellow. It was clean, cozy, and move-in-ready with a bed and two cast-iron pans. I saw potential in the backyard. Large, misshaped logs bordered a dirt path ran from the back gate to the patio. Raspberry bushes grew beside a small garden box that wasn't square with the house. Thistles and clover littered the grass.

•

I, too, have begun airing things out. I bought some

patches and thread to mend a pair of work jeans. Got my grandmother's sewing machine from the 1960s up and running. I flushed my car's transmission fluid for $119.99 and I stopped by the auto parts store for a synthetic oil blend, high-quality oil filter, and spark plugs for my motorcycle. Bob, my cashier, was surprised I'd found what I'd needed without help—"We don't usually see people back here in the spark plugs." He questioned why I wasn't buying motorcycle-*specific* oil. We tend to repeat the motions that have already worked for us.

•

I bought my father a hatchet at our town's auto parts store for Christmas when I was seven. Next to our garden spades and garage brooms, he stored a rusted John Deere maul—just wide and heavy enough to split logs—and I'd thought the hatchet would be a nice addition. I'm not sure I've ever seen my father chop wood with that maul. He usually bought a cord of split logs every other fall from a reservation family that sold from their pickup alongside the highway; I'd help unload, and Dad would tip them. He did buy a Stihl chainsaw a few years ago, but it can only take the small limbs in our backyard. He's always told me to just "have at it."

•

I've always been drawn to purposing wood. My first spring in the apartment, I built a 150 square-foot garden box using recycled lumber. I also cut scrap boards from the garage and hammered together a flower box for my stoop. That was a nice study break. Instead of preparing for a new semester, I taught my neighbor how to lay a stone walking path. He set the last ten feet alone; the path veers to the right, there, and sits an inch below the patio. It bugs me every time I see it. But the place is a rental, a temporary fixation I put hundreds of dollars into just to feel at home. I stacked the old logs with space to dry, and that felt right.

•

I was eighteen and newly single the first time I was furious. I threw the TV remote at the wall, busted it to pieces, and woke my mom up in the middle of the night. My heart rate wouldn't drop below 140 for another twenty-four hours. I snapped at Dad that I just wanted to chop a tree to chips. We were in the kitchen and I'd slammed the door. He threw up his hands and yelled, "Well, go already if it'll calm ya down!"

•

I'm a month from moving out and at a loss for ways to distract myself. Job applications and graduate thesis drafts are due, but I'd really rather not. The grass is growing and onion shoots have already popped up in the garden; the raspberries bushes are three-feet tall. I won't be here to taste the harvest. Yesterday I looked to the woodpile and decided it was time for a new axe.

•

Each October, a handful of us former camp staff meet at the site for a weekend of splitting wood. The summer staff burns through about seventy aspen, sixty-feet tall, but it's been a few years since they've been able to fell, split, and stack that many on their own. We pack our sleeping bags, pork butt, and cases of Mountain Dew and double-park on a Friday to fill the camp's wood boxes to their brim.

A long-time site director, a real Paul Bunyan-type, nitpicks over every tree and log. Mattern, as he's known, taught me the ins and outs of splitting and stacking. It was kind of his thing—that and welding metal behemoths, like the 500-pound sauna stove, "Hades," or the 12x8x10-foot steel wood drying rack we call "Princess" to Mattern's chagrin. If a log had knots, wasn't squared, had a little mold rot, or was the slightest bit too long, it went straight to the twelve-foot-tall incinerator, "Ozzie." Mattern welded it together out of a farmer's old fuel tank. For a time he made us build *holzhaufens* to dry the firewood—a German approach of stacking logs in a cylindrical tower that circulates air in the hollow and dries the wood quicker. After a long, loud week with the campers, I used to spend hours quietly circling a *holzhaufen*, laying logs until its base had risen beyond my reach. When I circled the evening campfires playing guitar, I'd feel the heat singeing my hair and then sleep well knowing the logs had come from my stack, burned long, and comforted the kids before bed.

Mattern once told me that he often thinks about The Gospel of Thomas when he splits wood. This gospel is one of the Gnostics believed to predate the four heavy-hitters in the Bible. It contains only a series of sayings attributed to Jesus, and he never proclaims himself to be the Son of God. My favorite is, "Jesus said, 'You see the sliver in your friend's eye, but you don't see the timber in your own eye. When you take the timber out of your own eye, then you will see well enough to remove the sliver from your friend's eye.'"

•

My favorite hour to split wood is at sunrise before the frost melts. During the last alumni wood-split, I woke before my friends, started the coffee, showered, and walked the gravel road under yellow oak leaves to the hydraulic splitter. Two days before, I'd flown home from Montana to see if I could pull myself out of a rut, a spontaneous depression whose cause I couldn't figure out but knew the drone of the splitter could mute. The frozen logs popped apart, and the work went fast. Later my nephew sat on the stack and watched. I flew back righted, myself.

•

My sister usually has a handle on what I should be reading. This past Christmas she gifted me a best-seller, *Norwegian Wood: Chopping, Stacking, and Drying Wood the Scandinavian Way* by Lars Mytting. It's chapters are on "The Cold," "The Forest," "The Tools," "The Chopping Block," "The Woodpile," "The Seasoning," "The Stove," and "The Fire." I read that many Norwegians greet their splitter when the steel is still cold enough to burn their fingers. The moisture trapped inside the logs condenses overnight, and when the hydraulic arm pins the log between the end-plate and the wedge, the wood snaps clean and straight with hardly a splinter. I've wondered if my Norwegian blood is what draws me to the woodpile. Is it possible that dormant ancestral knowledge passes through generational fibers? My sister inexplicably has red hair.

•

I settled on a hickory-handled axe from Ace Hardware. Technically, it's a single Michigan-style wedge axe, but it's what you expect an axe to look like: long, narrow steel blade; a slim, untempered butt; and a three-foot stained handle. The only quirk about it is the slight curved knob at the handle's end.

•

This wasn't the first axe I'd bought for splitting wood. A year prior, my Tennessean friend with a southern accent was watching a professor's cottage in the Rocky Mountain pine forest, and we decided that there was no better way to pass a cloudy January day than by chopping down a tree for the sitting room stove. I was surprised when he told me he'd never chopped down a tree. So I picked up potato salad, a case of light Canadian beer, and an eight-pound splitting maul. I let cockiness prevail and passed over the six-pounder, thought eight would explode even the most stubborn of green pine. I'd forgotten the physics of the equation: the faster you swing that blade, the more force you'll strike the log with. A heavier head might be slower and have less force than the faster, lighter steel. But we made do.

We found a bare 50-foot pine on the hillside with plenty of undergrowth to take its place, and took two-minute turns, watching the other's precision sharpen with each crack. We clipped the branches for kindling and gave our rotator cuffs a workout by sectioning the trunk with a bow saw. The Tennessean and I drank the snow-chilled beer because you drink, smoke, and bullshit when you work in the woods. After three hours, we'd moved thirty feet of logs through the knee-high snow and decided that placing the 500-pound trunk on our shoulders was the quickest way to move the last fifteen feet. When we split, we were silent. That's a time for yourself, for whatever is churning in your insides that you won't mention over light beer.

For me, every crack was to the girl I'd been seeing for the previous four months, the one who had a boyfriend and slipped into each precarious position with a whisper of "we shouldn't" before pulling down the neckline of her V-neck t-shirt. You'd have thought she'd have wanted to finish quickly, but she was one for prolonged foreplay, the kind that makes you think it means something, and sometimes she says it does, like when you tell her you're done with it all, but fifteen minutes later she's storming away screaming at you, and when you're done with the yelling and insults and block her phone calls, she calls eighteen more times. She then shows up crying and apologizing, or other times she'll threaten to cut herself, so you speed across town and pull the knife from her hands. Every crack of that axe into green wood is like the cracks she took at your face in an alley when she said she wanted to talk to you. Every crack is for every scream is for every orgasm is for every tear and every blood drop. Every crack is for going ahead if it'll calm ya down. Drop the axe and find your beer.

•

That eight-pound maul disappeared last fall. So I bought the Michigan single with Lars Mytting's book in hand. The Norsk journalist drove fjord backroads and pulled over whenever he heard the distinctive crack echo through the forest. The elderly woodsmen showed him their stacks, their fifteen-year-old steel, the groves of new tree growth. As I turned from page to colored photograph to mini-profile and learned about the innovative carbon-neutral stoves and the splitting axes that popped off a single log without disrupting the larger section, I became convinced that my affirmative response to a friend who asked, "Where do you live that you have to chop wood? It can't be for fun," was validated, was normal, was right.

But, "no," Lars Mytting told me in chapter "Chopping Block" subsection "The Wood Age." A Swedish University of Agricultural Sciences study found that "an interest in firewood can be related to a man's view of himself as a provider. Young men who had not yet started a family had almost no interest in wood whatsoever." Swedes—and by neighborly association Norwegians—did not have an interest until middle age, and retirees with nothing else to do spent the most time of all at the block; neither of these apply to me. My draw is conditional, not hereditary.

•

At four in the afternoon on a Friday, I made a pot of coffee—because it matters what you drink by yourself—and I tucked my gray t-shirt into my work jeans so I wouldn't catch the handle on loose fabric. With the new Michigan single I popped the logs into the air from the base of my stone walking path. I aired it all out, whacked away the job applications, the revisions, and the once-again left-behind heart. One after another, misshaped sections split into identical logs and the new pile grew orderly like. I wiped sweat from my brow and readied the final.

•

Lars Mytting says that as soon as you decide to split a log, it's already over.

•

I swung the axe with all my might and sliced it through its marrow, wedging the blade deep in the chopping block. From the very center of the log, I plucked a perfectly straight, one-inch diameter core: the tree's first growth, one ring, the heart of it all.

EUCLID'S ORCHARD (FOR BRENDAN PASS)
THERESA KISHKAN

Come now as the sun goes down.
See how evening greens the grass.
Is it not as though we had already gathered it
And saved it up inside us...
      —Rilke, from "The Apple Orchard"

I never imagined we'd abandon our orchard. It was one of the first things my husband and I planned as we worked on the house where we hoped to raise our children and write our books.

We spent a year or two learning the lay of our land—where the sun rose, where it set, and when; where the warm hollows were, where we might sit and look out to blossoming trees in spring. John dreamed of walking under their gracious boughs and I hoped for a wide gate so we could back our pick-up truck right into the orchard to load up the fruit. Dreams of space and abundance, the scent of apple blossom and then the jars of preserves on the pantry shelves to take us through winter. In anticipation, I bought a big willow basket to hold the future's apples.

We hired a backhoe to clear the bottom land at the foot of the bluffs where our house stood. A half acre, perhaps, a gentle slope, fringed with alders and a few cedars. Rocky, but with pockets of soil—and anyway, we reasoned, we could build up the planting areas with manure, seaweed, and compost.

Those first trees—bought from a man who collected heritage varieties and had an apple tasting weekend at his orchard on Norwest Bay Road in West Sechelt: we tasted, then ordered a Melba, a Golden Nugget, a Cox's Orange Pippin. The trees were tiny and we planted them reverently, shrouding them in old gillnet salvaged from the dump. Later we bought a Transparent, too, for early pies and sauce. Pears—a winter variety, and one for eating out of hand in late summer. Two cherries; a golden plum, a green-gage, an Italian prune. Hazelnuts. Each tree had a cage made with sticks and gillnet. But eventually we fenced the whole area, a long process, which required that some post-holes be created by building up cairns of rock and then cementing the posts into the stone. We used green wire. We used chicken wire. We used strands of wire connected to a battery in order to give any animal trying to enter the orchard an electrical reminder not to trespass. The truth of our location, though—below a mountain, in woods threaded with game trails—slowly dawned on us.

It wasn't until our big dog Lily came to us, in her second year, after her original family moved elsewhere, that a combination of fence and canine reliably kept deer and bears from the trees. The deer liked them any time of year. The tiny buds and leaves, then the fruit. The bears liked to drag down boughs and tear fruit from them, leaving huge piles of golden scats everywhere. Even the grouse liked to climb out to the ends of the branches and nip at the buds and green fruit. Eventually the Roosevelt elk discovered the trees. But Lily slept with both ears attentive to the slightest noise from the orchard and often at night we'd hear her barking, hear the barking grow fainter as she pursued intruders deep into the woods. Sometimes she slept in the grass under the trees. She took her job seriously.

•

On the transitive property of equality: Things that are equal to the same thing are also equal to one another. (Euclid's First Axiom)

I don't remember when coyotes arrived at the north end of the Sechelt peninsula where we built our house in the early 1980s. There were coyotes in Vancouver, certainly, but not on our part of the coast. People said that a healthy cougar population kept them away. And in those years, there were regular reports of cougars passing through schoolyards, hovering on the beaches, prowling the hiking trails along the spine of the peninsula. We heard one once when we were living in a tent with our first baby, building during the day and collapsing onto the foam mattress within the canvas walls at night. We heard it scream—yes, it *was* blood-curdling—and our dog, Friday, a big English sheepdog cross sleeping under the tarp by the entrance to the tent, began to dig under the plywood platform we'd built so that the tent would be off the damp ground; she wanted the safety of the small space between earth and plywood. Now I know it was probably a female lion in estrus, alerting males to her availability. But in the darkness, it was as wild a sound as I've ever heard.

Coyotes were spotted south of us, in Gibsons, perhaps in the early 1990s. How did they arrive? Our peninsula is connected to the mainland by mountains, too arduous for road-travel; and people arrive here by ferry, crossing Howe Sound from Horseshoe Bay, a distance too far for a coyote to swim. But perhaps a pair, a pregnant female, even a family intrepidly heading out for fresh territory, could find a way through the mountains. After the initial sightings in

Gibsons, we began to hear reports of coyotes mid-Coast, then at Halfmoon Bay, and finally we began to see them occasionally where we live near the northern end of the peninsula.

During the summer of 2005, we were driving back and forth from the little village near us over three evenings for a music festival we were involved with, and each night, coming home around 11, we saw a pup in exactly the same place by the Malaspina Ranch, hovering in the area where coltsfoot and wild hazelnuts grow. In our car headlights, we could see it was pale, alert, and obviously waiting for a signal from nearby parents to let it know it was safe to return to whatever it was doing. Which might have been eating stranded fish in the muddy bay below the old barn across the road.

And driving back from dinner with friends late one night, we saw a coyote family feasting on a deer recently hit by a car on a wide part of the highway. We stopped to watch and the adults backed away, but only a short distance, their teeth bared, not willing to risk us taking the carcass from their young. It was abundance to be defended. If we'd opened the car doors and walked towards them, I think we'd have regretted it. It was a window into a wild moment, mirroring our own care and concern for our young, who were grown up by then and living far away.

•

Things which coincide with one another are equal to one another. (Euclid's Fourth Axiom)

All my life I've felt at home in language. I began to read when

I was five, well before I began primary school at the age of six. Fifty-two years later I still remember how I would rush to my room, having just read a library book in grade two, and try to write one myself. The stories involved horses, perfect families, ranches tucked into box canyons, or else camping trips on the edge of rivers or beaches resembling the ones my own family camped near during those years. When I got older, I still tried to write stories, spinning out the intricate webs of words until I ran out of them, unable to finish. When my children were small, I loved to gather them around me so we could read a book together. One sustaining memory has us immersed in Arthur Ransome's *Winter Holiday* over the Christmas season when we had an unexpected flurry of snow. That story tells of a group of children quarantined from school because one of them has mumps. The lake they live by has frozen, so they spend the days skating and traveling its length on an improvised ice sledge. On our own holiday on another continent, many decades later, we remembered the book as we skated another frozen lake. The Ransome book was also about childhood languages—the children use Morse code and other kinds of signals to communicate—and about an igloo (that spiral of snow blocks), an expedition to an imaginary Arctic, camping on an ice-bound houseboat, and the dire rescue of a sheep. My children hauled out our collection of sleds and tried to recreate the book's adventures. They were lit by the warmth of a good story and used its codes to make their own, in action if not in words.

We understood one another in those days. The books, the movies we watched together, the challenges of locating constellations in the story-laden summer skies. It never occurred to me that other vocabularies would enter our lexicon and that I would comprehend less and less of the codes my children were using to navigate their way through the world.

Especially my younger son Brendan who, from the time he entered adolescence, became more and more fluent in the language of mathematics. His high-school teachers praised his abilities and his exam scores were often perfect. The school directed him towards the sciences, in part because they had strong teaching in that area and in part because no one thought the humanities were truly an option. Except his parents, both writers with English degrees. When Brendan went to university, we advised him to take a range of courses in his first year so he could find out if he really wanted to study physics and math or if he might veer toward history, perhaps theatre. Math and physics it was, though, and when he went on to do graduate work in Toronto, he concentrated on math. I tried to understand the nuances of a partial differential equation but felt as though I was reading Sanskrit.

The boy who once counted stars as he reclined on the dry moss of our orchard, windfallen apples in hand as he translated the density of the Milky Way into individual points of light, who walked the alder path with his grandfather and explained his theory of negative numbers as the dry leaves rustled at their feet, began to travel to conferences all over North America and Europe. I was so proud of him for doing well in his chosen field but the field existed in a dimension foreign to me. Could I touch its ground? Was a line something I could trace my finger along, ease my needle along with its tail of cotton thread? And did the line end or keep going to infinity?

To produce a finite straight line continuously in a straight line. (Euclid's 2nd Postulate)

I've made dozens of quilts over nearly 30 years. I begin each in a kind of heat of creation, ideas and colors clamoring in my imagination, my hands almost shaking with the urgency to sew. And yet, I am anything but skillful with the tools of quilting. My own are pretty low-tech—scissors, a cutting mat and wheel, packets of quilting needles, three wooden hoops of varying sizes, and a frame of PVC pipe with clamps to fix a section of quilt into a taut surface for stitching. I have other bits and pieces I almost never use—a thimble, a leather finger protector, books of patterns which are somehow never the patterns I want to make. I invent my own, badly, and scribble them onto scraps of paper— old manuscript pages, envelopes, the pieces of light card that come in pantyhose.

If equals are added to equals, the sums are equal. (Euclid's 2nd Axiom)

In mathematics, Euclid's orchard is an array of one-dimensional "trees" of unit height planted at the lattice points in one quadrant of a square lattice, the square lattice being a type of lattice found in two-dimensional Euclidian space. It's taken me most of the fall to actually grasp what this means.

And then it turns out I've imagined it as something far

more complicated than it is. After asking Brendan about the difference between the one and two-dimensional spaces, he sends me an email two sentences long:

> *I think two dimensional just refers to the lattice that the orchard lives on (like in a real orchard, where the surface of the ground is 2 dimensional).*
>
> *One dimensional refers to the trees themselves (which extend vertically from the two dimensional ground).*

Euclid didn't know the earth curved, that it was a globe loose in the universe. That lying on the grass in our orchard, we were turning as the earth turned, around our own dear sun. The warmth of it on our faces, the bees alive in the apple blossom, the drift of violets in the dry grass, a woodpecker drumming in the woods nearby—all this was momentary as we moved towards night. But we could anticipate the beauty of it again and again, light bending around a star.

I want to find a way to sew the graphic representation of Euclid's orchard. For years I've quilted to find a way to explore texture, to try to bring a one-dimensional space into something resembling two: runnels of cotton pierced with small stitches; stars slightly embossed on a bed of dark velvet. I think of these surfaces as a kind of landscape relief, something for the hands to read as though reaching down from the sky to learn something about the earth— hills of brown corduroy, cabins built of strips of colored fabrics, a red hearth at each center; an indigo river alive with the ghosts of salmon, their eggs glittering among the stones below them.

I want to re-create those neglected trees rising from the surface of the ground, the clovers and wiry grasses around their trunks, the spring daffodils I planted in hope, and all the teeming biota under the earth: worms tunneling through the porous soil, the burrows of field mice, the root systems of the native wildflowers. I want the nematodes, the protozoa, fungi, the broken rocks, minerals, the decaying organic matter creating the humus needed to keep the soil healthy. I want to commemorate the dream of an ever-thriving orchard, alive in our stories when we gather now together ("Do you remember the time we slept on the moss?" "Remember walking up the driveway and surprising a herd of elk that winter, snapping off the lower boughs?").

•

Some mornings in late spring I walked down the driveway and saw the lattice of chicken wire strung with dew-covered spider-webs, glistening in the sun. The chicken wire was composed of cells like the hexagons bees create from wax taken from abdominal glands of the worker bees and softened in the mouths of house bees. The wax is shaped by their bodies into circles which quickly form into hexagons. Mathematicians such as Pappus of Alexandria attributed this to "a certain geometrical forethought" on the part of the bees—*Bees, then, know just this fact which is useful to them, that the hexagon is greater than the square and the triangle and will hold more honey for the same expenditure of material in constructing each*—but modern physics suggests that it is less calculated. Bees make cells that are circular in cross-section, all packed together like bubbles. Surface tension in the soft wax pulls the cell walls into hexagonal, threefold junctions as the wax hardens. I think I am with Pappus on this one, though. Try dropping circles of wax as close to one another as possible onto a flat surface and watch what happens. I've done this, several times, dropping wax from a beeswax candle (for authenticity) and the results are *not* hexagonal threefold junctions.

The pear blossoms smelled of sandalwood. Pressing our faces to branches heavy with flowers, we'd breathe in small insects, brush pollen from our noses.

On early summer mornings, our orchard was like a corner of a Botticelli painting, tiny violets and daisies and wild roses, heart's-ease and self-heal, wands of Columbia tiger lilies, four or six blooms to a stalk. To paint them, to have some long-longed for gift to capture each in its specificity, the opening sequences timed for bees, other pollinators: the art of utility yoked to beauty.

We added strands of barbed wire between 4x4 posts after deer kept getting in between the green wire and electric. But the deer persisted. The bears, too.

There was that gate, generously wide so we could bring in our truck with that big willow basket, for when the trees produced the harvests we thought might be possible. I filed recipes for apple preserves, for plum jams, for bottled cherries in exotic liqueurs. One year I scavenged enough pears to process in mason jars and we had pies of Transparent apples encased in buttery pastry. Some years this happened, that we managed to harvest enough for ourselves against the constant predations of bears.

When Lily barked at dawn or dusk, when we could hear animals crashing in the woods near the orchard, or within it, we'd go down with sticks and pans to make enough noise to raise the dead. Or scare off the living.

Finally we gave up, though the chicken wire and the green-covered wire still surround the trees, gaping in places where the animals muscled their way through. We returned the battery, almost unused, because the bears didn't care about electric fences any more than they were afraid of barbed wire. They didn't give a fig—and when they discovered the fig tree by the house, they ravaged the young fruit until the tree grew too tall for them to reach and because the trunk grew against the side of the house, they didn't care to climb it. But down in the orchard they'd usually eat every pear on the trees and then shit out golden pulp as their own parting barb.

•

That all right angles are equal to one another. (Euclid's 4th Postulate)

I've been making quilts for over two and a half decades, a quarter century, a process expressed as a series of fractions, reduced to the lowest common denominator: hours of the day stretching into weeks, then years. A basket of cloth, a bedcover, a bag of scraps.

I realized soon into the world of quilts that my carelessness with measurements and my slap-dash way of planning would cause me grief. "All right angles are equal," said Euclid. I assume that cutting those angles precisely would mean that a quilt would become a series of beautiful and elegant geometries. Instead, my stars, some of them the Variable star, composed of triangles within squares, aiming for yellow constellations in dark skies, are lopsided, the imprecise points of stars forced into clumsy arrangements. Another style of star, the Ohio, usually turns out even worse. With every new quilt, I promise myself I will slow down, take my time—the time needed, each step conducted with care and attention to detail, no matter how small and seemingly insignificant. And with each new quilt I am again in the middle of a chaotic equation (though not differential), cutting at random, my notes scribbled on the back of an old envelope. How many triangles will I need to make these stars? How many strips of light cotton, then dark, to build the log cabins, each with a tiny red square dead-centre: the hearth?

We built our house wall by wall, framing them on the ground, then lifting them into place. And the wood stove blazes in the middle of the kitchen, drawing us to its heat, to sit on chairs with quilts on the backs for extra warmth.

•

The cleared area where we planted our orchard was not geometrical. Or wait, maybe it was. *Is*, because it's still there, though the alders grow closer, the limbs of cedars, once trimmed, lean over the collapsing fences, the salal and huckleberry reclaim what was truthfully theirs. From the air, would it resemble a trapezoid? I try to envision it, the points which might be considered corners. Angles. Is it faintly scalene? I realize I know far too little about everything. Math. Quilts. Coyotes. The requirements of fruit trees. The complicated tangle of inherited traits.

I thought it was too late to learn something about mathematics. All my adult life I've had dreams in which I am about to take an exam in math, an important exam, but I can't find the classroom. Or else I realize I haven't even attended the classes all term, all year, a number of years. In the dreams, I recriminate myself, walk towards the exam heavy with dread, knowing that I will never graduate because I can't even begin to do the math. I wake, feeling hopeless.

Then Brendan suggested I take a course. Or at least sign out the Great Courses offering, *Joy of Math*, taught by Arthur Benjamin, from the local library.

Turns out Benjamin's a good teacher, a magician, an international performer of mental calculation. Mostly what intrigues me about him is that he took the time to deconstruct simple mathematical principals and to show the fledgling student (I was 59 when I watched the 24 lectures on my computer screen) the complex structures in a way that highlights their beauty and interconnectedness. Arithmetic to prime numbers to combinatorics (at the heart of those questions about the possible outfits you can figure out if you have three pairs of shoes, four skirts, seven blouses, and two cardigans. And maybe two pairs of jeans. A very useful skill for packing a single carry-on suitcase for extended travel...). Prime numbers, Fibonacci numbers to algebra (which finally made a kind of sense as I watched), proofs to geometry (which I've always sort of liked because of how quilts are so often based on geometric forms within blocks, but made not by pencil on paper; rather by hands sewing cotton, easing corners together, working out how to represent a tulip with rectangles and triangles). And then pi. Beautiful pi: π. I wanted to think of it as a pie, literally, because that was something I knew about, could bake if the bears left enough apples, hold a knife over top and plan the cuts to allow the greatest number of people to receive a (more or less) equal slice. Pi always made me tremble in my boots, but how reassuring to learn that it's a constant, a ratio (a circle's circumference to its diameter), and not something wildly arcane or terrifying.

One day, while taking a break from the *Joy of Math*, I was reading the *Vancouver Sun* obituaries on a quest to find six degrees of separation in at least one of the entries, when I saw the obituary for my eight grade math teacher. (*Things which coincide with one another...*) He was a charming man but shares responsibility (with me, of course) for derailing me from any kind of deep interest or understanding of mathematics. He had a wandering eye and assigned the prettiest girls in the class—I wasn't one of them—to the front row, nearest his desk and the blackboard. He flirted with them so emphatically, leaning over their desks to explain the problem on the board so quietly that the rest of us knew we were doomed. At noon he drove around in his convertible with the top down and an array of lovely young girls arranged on the seats like beauty queens. He taught me important things but they weren't math.

The degrees of separation became the possibility of connection. That summer of 2014, I felt confident enough to try to grasp some new ideas, to understand in particular how every linear transformation can be represented by a matrix, and every matrix corresponds to a unique linear transformation. My transformation might be in language—a new language—and maybe an expansion of my heart and spirit. My feet, long planted firmly in mud and compost and the piles of manure I'd have delivered every few years, might find themselves venturing onto some other pathway. And it would help me to understand how an orchard, and the legacies of genetics, could be given a new context in a quilt. I was thinking of how to turn my attention, newly-attuned to mathematic pattern, to fabric—its dimensions, its willingness to be shaped and manipulated into something at once practical and encoded. An equation for love and for the years devoted to growing trees, sons, a daughter, and then understanding the point at which one had to simply let them go.

•

One autumn evening, under brilliant stars, a white coyote crossed the highway as we drove home from Oyster Bay. Its eyes glowed and its ears were beautifully shaped, like receptors—every sound of the night entering them: owls, the skittering of mice under dry grass, a raccoon leading her kits to eat apples in moonlight, even the skeins of snow geese heading south in the darkness, muttering and calling, their navigational system a form of quantum entanglement.

•

I am interested in mathematics only as a creative art. (G.H. Hardy)

I ordered a copy of G.H. Hardy's *A Mathematician's Apology* in a moment of nervous energy, thinking: I will continue trying to learn about the history if not the practice of math. And it turns out I didn't need to be nervous. Hardy was a mathematician who wrote elegantly and clearly about youth, the beauty of pure math, and who said, late in life, that his biggest contribution to his field was his mentorship of the Indian mathematician, Srinivasa Ramanujan His book is an essay, really; a reflection on having given his life to the pursuit of something for which he was not interested in extending a practical application. "It is a melancholy experience for a professional mathematician to find himself writing about mathematics. The function of a mathematician is to do something, to prove new theorems, to add to mathematics, and not to talk about what he or other mathematicians have done."

I read it with a kind of surprised delight. His mind constantly made connections between math and music, math and poetry. He was interested in pattern. And I realize, with some surprise, that this is why I take such pleasure in following his sentences—each well-constructed and leading the reader logically through his thinking.

Pattern has been an abiding concern of mine, too, one I am constantly looking for ways to explore. In language, in my orchard, in fabric as I imagine ways to build a whole of small fragments of cotton. I don't use formal patterns but try to let colors of the materials and the ideas I am interested in determine how I will cut and piece together and shape into something practical.

This is where I part company with Hardy. I want my quilts to have a function, perhaps because I am a woman and for thousands of years women have used the necessary materials of daily life to create art. Subversive art, in many ways. How could a table cover or a bedcover or a basket for collecting seeds and roots be considered art at all? And therein lies the subversion. Women, some believe, created string by twining short sections of stem and root and fiber together. And string functioned as yarn, as thread, as anything that might be twisted and woven and made into something durable. If that was your job and you were a woman, then you found ways to make it beautiful. You dyed and compounded pigments, you wove, you knit, you wrapped your children and yourself in lengths of fabric you might have stamped or printed or appliquéd, and you grew food, cooked it, served it, and it was beautiful, though no one called it art. The women, though, knew what it felt like to have our hands immersed in rich wool or finding our way through a complex schema of linen thread, of silk yarn, of pounded nettle fibre, with a whole palette of grasses and reeds for imbrications.

I am driven to make a quilt using the patterns I'm finding in mathematics. I can't sew well enough to piece together DiFinetti's triangle but I am thinking about ways to explore these ideas. To look at them for their graphic interest (and behind that, the subversive notions they reveal to me about genetics, parenthood, the correspondences between life and science and art) and to try to draw together the beautiful and the durable. Or to track the grid of trees planted for optimum light and air, but as lovely as a trellis in a medieval manuscript, holding a vine close to a stone wall for its warmth, but making an intricate lattice-work of branch and leaf.

•

In retrospect, I wonder how we knew the coyotes had arrived in our area to stay when we saw them so infrequently. Other big animals occurred ephemerally in the forests and mountains surrounding us. Cougars passed through. Wolves too—tailing the herds of Roosevelt elk re-introduced in the early 1980s in part to try an innovative way of maintaining the brush growing under the big Cheekeye-Dunsmuir power line.

We knew about the coyotes because they left scats on our driveway, in the hollows of moss in the orchard, on the nearby trails we hiked regularly, and even along the highway we walked to collect our mail at the community boxes about half a mile away. Every time we walked, we saw the scats. If we were on a trail, the scats were in the middle. The animals wanted anyone using the trail to know they'd been there. On the edges of the highway—a sign that the animals had mastered the knowledge of traffic—the piles were right on the human-worn margins.

And they were—*are*—fascinating. Coyotes are ominivores. They eat rodents, frogs and other amphibians (but not toads because their skins are bitter), reptiles, fish, crustaceans, birds, larger mammals that they can either kill or scavenge, grass (which helps them to digest fur and bones, I've read, and which also serves to scour parasites from their intestines), birdseed, and all kinds of fruit and vegetables. Once we watched a young pup hold salal branches down with its foot so it could reach the ripening berries, plucking them delicately one at a time. We've noticed more fur and bones in spring, when rodent populations are highest. And sometimes the scats seem to be composed entirely of grass. Once, the head and neck of a garter snake, scales still intact. Bloody flesh gives them a darker color. Fruit—crabapples, wild cherries, even elderberries—give them bulk. Seeds and fur make them grey. And if they're lucky enough to find a source of dry dog or cat food, the scats resemble those of canines.

Even though they were mostly invisible, we knew they were around and felt lucky when we saw them. Luckier still when we heard them. We live far from the nearest village and can usually hear emergency vehicles coming from a distance. But if there are coyotes in the immediate vicinity, they begin to howl before we hear the sirens and by the time the ambulance or police car is near our house, on its way to the ferry or to deal with a collision on the highway below us, there's a cacophony of siren and coyote accompaniment. A wild orchestration for voices and synthesizer—longitudinal waves coming toward us, bending and refracting the long length of the highway. Sound nowhere and everywhere.

•

The Dualities: a meditation on correspondence.

I read Edward Frenkel's *Love and Math: The Heart of Hidden Reality*, entranced by the ideas of a unified theory linking math and physics because it gave me courage to think that other things could be connected if one could only find the right language, the right equation. I have no idea what automorphic functions are and when I try to figure them out, I quietly give up. But not before I find sites online which offer—again—the most beautiful graphics, with colors and feathery patterns and I want so much to make something of this. Not mathematics, but something resembling how I feel when I look at its vocabularies, its imagery.

Frenkel's book is filled with anecdotes—partly a memoir of his relationship with physics and math as well as with significant mathematicians, living and dead (and truly the dead ones are as lively as the ones still with us). There are recipes in this book (for borscht), memories of conversations, jokes, deeply serious analyses of current research and future possibilities, and even an account of the genesis and making of his film, "Rites of Love and Math," in which a mathematician discovers a formula of love. He quotes from Henry David Thoreau: "The most distinct and beautiful statement of any truth must take at last the mathematical form. We might so simplify the rules of moral philosophy, as well as of arithmetic, that one formula would express them both." And I thought of Euclid again: *Things which coincide with one another are equal to one another.* Though I suspect my own apprehension of an equals sign is not necessarily the same as a mathematician's. But in my reading, I've come across the work of the 16th century Welsh physician and mathematician Robert Record who is credited with introducing algebra to England and also with first using the equals sign in his book, *The Whetstone of Witte*: "… to avoid the tedious repetition of these words: 'is equal to,' I will set (as I do often in work use) a pair of parallels, or Gemowe lines, of one length (thus =), because no two things can be more equal."

Of course, I thought. That makes such sense: parallels.

•

You can draw a straight line between any two points. (Euclid's 1st Postulate)

For the longest time, I couldn't think how to represent the ideas that catch my attention. Not wholly, because although I know, for instance, that an algebraic equation is a combination of numbers and letters equivalent to a sentence in language, I read those sentences as clumsily as a child might try to sound out a simple passage from a primary reader. In grade one I was praised for being able to decode the word "something," a word I'd not yet encountered in my library books or volumes borrowed from my older brothers' shelves. The sentence, in a Dick and Jane reader, was "Mother makes something." In our reading circle, in the front classroom of the Annex at Sir James Douglas Elementary School on Fairfield Road in Victoria, I sat in one of the two plaid dresses my father bought me on a naval trip to Hong Kong and used my finger to keep my place not just on the page but in each letter of each word, symbols becoming meaning in the chalky air of that classroom with its generous windows looking out on Garry oaks and houses on the lower slopes of Moss Rocks. I never had that deep illumination with the math lectures though I enjoyed brief moments when I realized what relationship was at the heart of a differential equation or how the Fibonacci sequence worked.

But some of the graphics are beautiful. An arrangement of stars and squares illustrating dominant and recessive phenotypes. An ancestry tree showing that the reproductive numbers of drone and worker bees in any generation follows the Fibonacci sequence. I choose 12 of my favorites and then spend more time figuring out how to reproduce them on fabric. Should I appliqué? Should I use colored pens on plain cotton? Should I free-associate and simply create abstract versions of each concept? Try to reproduce a grid echoing our original orchard? None of these are quite right.

Then I remember that an ink-jet printer will print on cloth, and after tracking down a source of specially prepared cloth (which seems more practical than trying to pass regular cloth, stiffened with freezer paper, through a printer), I buy some.

I decide to use a cotton print to border each block—it is a little like the illustration of Mendel's theory of how hereditary characteristic are passed from parent to offspring. I decide this will be a quilt to hang on a wall. The special treated cloth is stiff and I don't think it will drape softly enough for a bedcover.

Making this quilt is like the long process towards learning even the most basic concepts in mathematics. I sit with the cloth. I look at the printer. I wonder. I ponder. My heart starts to race. I hear the voice I've heard all my life when something new presents itself. Who do you think you are?

•

One day a single light brown coyote came out of the woods and walked by my window. It had all the time in the world. It passed the wing of rooms where my children grew up. It passed the windows they looked out at night, first thing in the morning, drawing their curtains to let sunlight in or the grey light of winter, in excitement, lonely or sleepless, in good health and bad, dazzled with new love or sorrow, at the lack of it, on the eve of their birthdays, new ventures, on the eve of leaving home. I went to the back of the house to see where the animal was headed but it did what coyotes do, a trick I wish I could also learn. It dematerialized. Vanished into thin air.

•

I'll use red thread for this quilt, this assemblage of

geometric investigations, algorithms, spirals, and ratios, an orchard's grid in plain and printed cotton, small stitches to draw layer to layer, capillaries to help the blood of our relationship circulate through the images and actual fabric of my thinking. Red thread, long strands carried by the needles I will prepare, three at a time, to allow me to push and pull the red lengths in and out, to meditate between the past and present, to contemplate the future, to secure with tiny knots the end of each fragment of thought.

●

I love looking at Pascal's Triangle. I don't understand a lot of the language used to talk about it but the way I understand it, simply, is this: each number is the sum of the two directly above it (or below it, depending on how you are viewing the triangle). In a way, it's like genetics, except that contained in the numbers (those binomial coefficients) are other sums: the grandparents, the great-grandparents, and those falling back into history, into pre-history, but who might emerge in the integer at the top of the triangle in some form undreamed of by the two below (I am looking at the triangle from the bottom up...).

This is the way I'd like genetics to work, in a way. Two numbers adding up to one, a system that is predictable and easy to plot on six rows of Pascal's triangle. But of course human beings are nowhere as tidy as numbers, though we can chart the DNA sequences within the 23 chromosome pairs in the cell nuclei and within mitochondria.

●

A mathematician, like a painter or a poet, is a maker of patterns. If his patterns are more permanent than theirs, it is because they are made with ideas. (G.H. Hardy)

At my desk, I look up to see two large brindled coyotes lope out of the bush and across the grass in front of my study. In the past I've heard coyotes in the area they've run out of and suspect there's a den there used year after year. Once, reading in bed late at night, my husband and I heard a pair mating—the rhythmic grunts and growls, the high-pitched squeals, a passionate duet, tempo changing until all we could hear was an urgent expressive finale, and then silence. Though running, these two also seemed at ease in their surroundings, coming out of the woods where there's a rough game trail used by deer and elk, and crossing the grass as though they'd done it many times before, on their way to the orchard. I called my husband to see but by the time we opened the back door, they'd disappeared.

•

The stray, the unexpected variable.

One apple tree remains under my care. It's a Merton Beauty, bought as a tiny plant at a produce store in Sechelt. An organic gardener had grafted interesting varieties to dwarf rootstock and I chose one almost at random. Merton Beauty is a cross between Ellison's Orange and Cox's Orange Pippin. For years ours sat sort of sullenly in a little circle of stones near the garden shed, caged in chicken wire. I'd water it, give it the occasional mulch of compost and drink of fish emulsion. A few frail blossoms, an inch or two of new growth. Then it produced some fruit which was delicious. The information I've read about this variety stresses the aromatic flavor of the apples— their spicy taste, redolent of pears, cinnamon, aniseed. I can't say I noticed those particular notes but the skins were pretty, russeted at the shoulders, and the flesh was crisp, with a true flavor of apple. Not the empty watery taste of many supermarket apples, sprayed, waxed, gassed, and stored for months.

When we rebuilt the vegetable garden after the septic field over which the garden was first made needed repairs, I replanted the Merton Beauty within the newly fenced area. I gave it lots of mushroom manure, bone meal, alfalfa pellets, and a long drink of liquid kelp to help it settle into its new home, a raised bed I called Apple Round.

We also have five crabapple trees up near the house. Two of them, growing in tandem, were given us twenty-five years or more ago by John's mother, and each spring they bloom like debutantes in deep pink gowns. Working near them, we hear the bees. Most falls a bear comes for their scabby fruit which is the size of plums. Beside them I planted a lanky crab from my friend Harold Rhenisch; he told me he'd brought it back from Bella Coola. And further down the driveway are two small crabapples, white-blossomed, with tiny apples the size of cranberries. These came from Roberts Creek. Once upon a time I made jelly using a combination of crabapples from all five trees but no one in our house really liked it and there are so many more rewarding preserves to make in fall so the bears are welcome, if they would only not break branches in their eagerness to gather fruit from the high limbs. And grouse, too, like to graze on the frost-bitten apples in late fall.

More than once we've joked about a Thanksgiving dinner of apple-fed grouse but neither of us has the heart (or gun) to make this happen.

So one eating apple and its array of pollinators. And now a stray. Just beyond the sliding doors that lead from our kitchen to the sundeck, coming up from rocky ground, is a small tree that has revealed itself to be an apple. Not a Pacific crabapple—our native *Malus* (or sometimes *Pyrus*) *fusca*—which is what I thought it was when I finally recognized its leaves and bark. I left it to grow up beyond the pink rambling rose tangled among the deck railings so we could enjoy its blossoms in spring. Last year it had fruit, and they weren't crabs but fairly large green apples: there were four of them and when it seemed they might be ripe, when they came easily off the branch when twisted a little, I picked one to try it. Not delicious, not even remotely. I think now of Euclid: *"The whole is greater than the part."* A tree's beauty is more than the taste of its fruit. But the question of course is how the tree got there. I know that apples don't come true from seed. Blossom from a Merton Beauty, say, is pollinated by an insect bearing reciprocal pollen from another apple—here, it would be a crabapple—and although the resulting apples would be true to their tree, their seeds would be the children of the Merton Beauty and the crabapple. One in ten thousand of those seeds might produce something worth eating. Who are the parents of this stray apple tree? It started growing before the Merton Beauty began its small production of fruit. Did this tree sprout from a seed spit over the side of the deck or excreted by birds or even seeds from the compost into which I regularly deposited cores and peelings from apples given us by friends in autumn? Belle of Boskoops from Joe and Solveigh, for instance, which make delectable fall desserts and cook up into beautiful chutney. Or else a seed from the few rotten apples from the bottom of a box bought from the Hilltop Farm in Spences Bridge, their flavor so intense you could taste dry air, the Thompson River, the minerals drawn up from the soil, faintly redolent of *Artemesia frigida*. This stray is all the more wonderful for its mysterious provenance, its unknown parents, and its uncertain future, for it grows out of a rock cleft, on a dry western slope. I won't dig it up since I have no doubt its roots are anchored in that rock but I will try to remember to water it occasionally and maybe throw a shovel of manure its way this spring.

•

The Fibonacci numbers are everywhere in nature, as a numbering system which allows a pinecone or sunflower to pack as many seeds as possible in limited space, to allow cellular information to flow in an efficient way in organisms ranging from the ovaries of the tiniest fish to the fiddleheads of ferns and the leaves of a tightly-wrapped head of cabbage. Some days I wander the garden as though through an archive, looking at flower shapes and seed pods to find this miraculous system. In my study, I have pine cones on sills and shelves, gathered from beloved places—the Nicola Valley, the side of the highway in Marble Canyon where a fascinating research project is underway in Pavilion Lake, looking at fossil microbialities, some of the earliest remnants of life on earth, and from a shelf just north of Lytton overlooking the Thompson River. And a new place too, the Dominion Arboretum in

Ottawa where I imagine walking with a future grandchild, sharing my love of trees.

"By dividing a circle into Golden proportions, where the ratio of the arc length are equal to the Golden Ratio, we find the angle of the arcs to be 137.5 degrees. In fact, this is the angle at which adjacent leaves are positioned around the stem."

Phyllotaxis is the term Swiss botanist Charles Bonnet introduced in 1754 for the study of the order of the position of leaves on a stem, how the spiral arrangement allows for optimum exposure to sunlight. It's a term that sinks so naturally into my own lexicon that looking at the way the leaves are arranged on a dogwood tree near the orchard gate, I think of my children, my brothers, our parents and grandparents and all the generations of the spiral configured on our own family tree. We are a case study in phyllotaxis, all of us absorbing the light, all of us contributing (*"The whole is greater than the part"*), even in death, to the ongoing life and vitality of the tree. Though by now, who knows its genus, its specific name.

•

Braid groups, harmonic analysis: The whole is greater than the part. (Euclid's 5th Axiom)

A mid-summer evening, clear moonlight. Down in the orchard, the coyotes have gone under the fence with their young. How many? I've seen one, heard several others. I've imagined them on the soft grass, tumbling like my children used to play, rolling down the slope over tiny sweet wild strawberries, over the heart-shaped violet leaves, the deep pockets of moss, while around them snakes hid under the lupines. But now in the quiet, I am shaken out of my dreaming because a coyote is singing a long, low passage. A lump forms in my throat as I look out into the night, the sky dusty with stars, a three-quarter moon hanging so perfect over the hidden lake that I think of a stage-set, an arranged scene created by strings and wishful thinking. A jagged line of dark horizon and the vertical trees, the line of them rising, then descending as the bar changes, a page of music, the arpeggiated chords, the implied bassline. A pause, a comma of silence. Another coyote joins in, then at least two more. It's a part-song, a madrigal. Each voice is on pitch but one is low, another high, and several braid themselves in and around the melody line.

> See, see, mine own sweet jewel,
> See what I have here for my darling:
> A robin-redbreast and a starling.
> These I give both, in hope to move thee—
> And yet thou say'st I do not love thee.

What feast have the parents provided—a flying squirrel, a clutch of frogs, robin nestlings fallen from a tree, a cat from the summer neighbors sound asleep in their beds? *See what I have here for my darling*—I hear the *riso* in the father's line, his extravagant vibrato; and then the *sospiro—in hope to move thee*, as the mother nudges the twitching body towards her eager pups. For she knows, oh, she knows, that by summer's end, her young will have gone their own way, far from the natal den in the woods just south of the orchard, forgetting the braided perfection of the family body and its unravelling, the strands unplucked and loose, and *yet thou say'st I do not love thee*.

•

Twelve quilt blocks wait for me to find an ideal pattern for them. I arrange them on Moravian blueprint, somehow expecting to see logic at work. Do I begin with the first idea I had—the representation of Euclid's orchard, the set of line segments like a trellis to hold the heavy blossoms of fruit trees in May? Or do I find a way to let the blocks tell a story all their own, dense with figurative language? Does it matter?

•

Blossoms ignite on the long, unpruned branches of the stray apple. The bees are in heaven, their faces buried in the open flowers, rising on legs heavy with pollen to find another, and another. Nearby a sapsucker tests the cotoneaster where the young are brought, year after year, to learn to feed on insects their parents have trapped in pools of sap. Leaning over the railings, I try to see the pattern of the leaves on their stems, because it's a wonder the tree is where it is, rooted in a cleft of rock, its branches nudging into light. It's a wonder, how far children travel from a house buffeted by winter storms, spring rain, the sound of loons nesting summer after summer on the lake just below the forest, and for a time the promise of fruit from trees planted in their infancy until the orchard was abandoned to the alders and bears, and to the late-coming coyotes who made their home in its remains.

•

It is the star to every wandering bark/
whose worth's unknown although his height be taken.
(William Shakespeare, Sonnet 116)

Late in my father's life (green-hazel eyes, light brown hair,
a sturdy build, a temperament shadowed by melancholia:
I have inherited the last two) he talked about reconciling
numbers. I believe he had a form of dementia and this was
what he felt called to do, I suppose, though his relationships
with his children suffered and could have used the same
attention. He hadn't used this term before, or at least not
in my memory of him. But he'd been good at statistics
and good at mental calculations. After he retired, he sat
in a big armchair in one corner of his living room and
taught himself celestial navigation. He had a book from
Goodwill and a life-time of buried ability to learn, a mind
that might have been nimble if it had been let free to roam
and develop. And maybe it had always been free, maybe I
never noticed. (He was the grandfather who walked with
Brendan under the alders, discussing negative numbers, the
possibilities of zero.) Maybe it was freedom to sit in the big
chair with columns of numbers, reconciling them—I have
no idea where they came from and why he felt he needed
to do this. He used a mechanical pencil, always used one—
for sums, for crosswords: "What's a Greek letter used in
math to mean a small positive quality?" I wouldn't know so
never answered. And he'd repeat the question, querulously.
"A Greek letter used, oh never mind, I'll look it up myself."
It was the same chair where he sat fifteen years before,
newly liberated from his job as a radar technician, and
made himself simple tools—a cottage cheese lid cut into
a circle and rigged with glass and a tiny mirror became

a sextant; cardboard, string, a plastic straw, and a fishing weight became a quadrant. He had patience for this intricate work but I don't believe he ever did anything beyond finding latitude in his back yard and filling paper with sums. Maybe on the long sea voyages that took him away from us for two or three months at a time—once, six months—to the Orient, Australia, around South America. Maybe he was the sailor who left his bunk and looked at stars at night and wanted to know how to find his way, though by day he worked with radar systems, repairing them, fine-tuning them so the vessels were anything but dependent on celestial navigation. It would have made sense to have learned then, when he could perhaps have applied the knowledge to the dark skies near the Antipodes or approaching Madagascar. But he waited until the early 1980s, after retirement, to sit and work with angles, degrees which became, using the same notebook of graph paper and his mechanical pencil, reconciliations. And I wish now that I'd asked him to show me what a disk of plastic fitted with mirrors could tell a person about where they were on the planet so I could imagine him now, at sea, finding horizon.

•

To describe a circle with any center and distance. (Euclid's 3rd Postulate)

I tried hard to understand the *Joy of Mathematics* and realized that I couldn't, except in the broadest possible way. That at the heart of it is an attempt to relate concepts that might not readily suggest themselves to be connected. Number theory and harmonic analysis, for example. And I can only think of those by relating them to the figurative language I learned as a student of literature. Language departing from its logical usage to urge the reader to emotional and intellectual discovery. On that mid-summer night, listening to coyotes sing madrigals in our abandoned orchard, I should have remembered Theseus in *A Midsummer Night's Dream*:

> The poet's eye, in a fine frenzy rolling,
> Doth glance from heaven to earth, from earth to heaven;
> And, as imagination bodies forth,
> The forms of things unknown, the poet's pen
> Turns them to shapes, and gives to airy nothing
> A local habitation and a name. (V. i. 12-17)

They were our names, our bodies under the heavens, all of us singing together in different voices to tell the story of our orchard, our time here in this place we have inhabited since—for John and me—1981, and the only way to shape the story is through connotation, not ordinary discourse, though I praise the literal, the specific, but by reaching up into the starlight to parse what lies behind it.

I've tried to puzzle through equations: the arrows, the lines and diacritics, the glyphs, the beautiful characters that look like Greek (*are* Greek)—a notation, a way of assigning symbolic value to constants, function, variables. A way of talking about equalities between variables. It's the chicken and egg argument written in the ancient markings of Simonides in wax. Would math work in Chinese characters or the syllabics of the far north? Would flowers still smell sweet if their seed patterns were random? Would a baby ever be born in our extended family without the blue eyes or sturdy legs of a potato-farming ancestor near the Carpathian mountains? Would it matter?

Inside I am stitching a spiral into the layers of the orchard I have pieced together, a snail shell curled into itself. That's what I'll see when I've finished. I begin the spiral at its very heart, keeping my course as even as I can as it opens out and widens. Not the complicated pathways of the sunflower, some turning left, some right, so that an optimal number of seeds are packed in uniformly, or Romanesco broccoli, its arcs within radi resulting in something so intricately beautiful I wonder how anyone could cut into it to eat it. On windowsills, pinecones. The plump Ponderosas, brought home from the Nicola Valley, and a few long monticolas. They're dry, open, but at the base, where their stalk connected them to their trees, two spirals are still visible, like a relaxed embrace, lovers asleep. My spirals are simple, my hands sewing to follow a path from its knotted source, around and around, until I've learned that my pleasure comes from the journey itself, a needle leading me outward, towards completion. A quilt elegant and sturdy, a sequence emptied of its numbers.

And listen: the coyotes are singing, the deep voice of the father, the rather more shrill voice of the mother—anxious that all her offspring eat well and learn to hunt, to care for their safety in the forest beyond the orchard—and the lilting joyous youngsters unaware that a life is anything other than the moment in moonlight, fresh meat in their stomachs, the old trees with a few apples and pears too small and green for any living thing to be interested in this early in the season.

VERTEBRAE TO BARK
COURTNEY AMBER KILIAN

Sometimes I lay awake all night. Sometimes I sleep for days.

Today I step into the dampness of early morning and sit, leaning against my favorite tree, a knobby gray ficus weathered by time and low floating clouds.

I flutter with images of a hike we took—meadow, mountain, field, foot. Skeleton trees sprawled across moist earth, their branches curving into ribs of moss and woodland dwellers.

Hiking is not the same. It takes focus to put one foot in front of another. Walking and talking is multi-tasking. I stumble, twist my ankle, trip over rocks. I move slowly, cautiously. This type of injury shatters your confidence, gnarls you into fits and fragility. At intake for the brain injury rehab program, they write that I have the reaction time of an 83-year-old.

I'm 27.

At night, I wander our house, shuffling my feet through the darkness as if to avoid jellyfish in the warm Baja waters we waded in. I stare at frogs clinging to stucco near our porch light, rock back and forth crying, and listen to screech owls.

I hug my hand around the ficus' exposed root, searching for its basement. For those backstairs that wind in humble cascade through heavy, chocolate soil. I worry what I've done to you. The stolen time, those creases on your face, my puffy, swollen eyes.

The hike's lounging aspen with their punctuated hips, roaming spines, and kissing throats paint the snow in crescent shadows. Our breathing is part of that natural home, part energy of tree and young white wood.

I never saw you fall asleep without a smile, plum-touched veins spindling across your eyelids. But now, you hold your face tight, compressed with worry until sleep takes you, jaw slack, snores rattling from an open mouth, body convulsing in short restless fits.

Lighting begins to change, moving from the gray scales of night to the sheen of morning, the landscape throbbing fuchsia with wildflowers. Vertebrae to bark, I sense the ficus' buried breathing. The locomotion of water through its roots. I want to trace their depth, follow their roads. I slip my hand into soil, my palm listening to its pulse.

One day those aspens will peel like paper, and I'll dip my pen and write across their weathered seams. Ink bleeding, letters becoming words, becoming sentences. It won't matter what they say, just that they were written, bark curling in my hand. Lost thoughts recorded somewhere.

The grasses weave in dance, their white dagger tips bobbing in puppeted flight. In my swirl of confusion, exhaustion, anger, I'd forgotten the mere thing that could heal me in any moment—a simple step outside.

Spine to trunk.

Vertebrae to bark.

Body to earth.

They tell me it's not about recovery, because that implies I will be the same again. It's about adapting and working with the injury. About resiliency. They like that word.

But in this moment I want to laugh at them. In this moment my spine is straight, my muscles relaxed. I am composed of rock and wind and tree. Flesh and bone and bile. Earth, this lifetime and generations past. My heart beats to the drum of the land. I breathe and the land breathes. I breathe and the trees breathe.

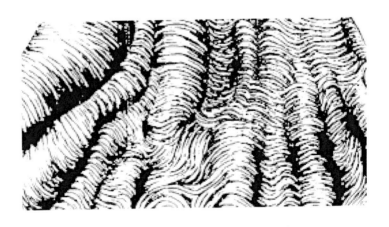

CONTRIBUTOR NOTES

Josh MacIvor-Andersen is a former Tennessee tree climbing champion, the author of *On Heights & Hunger*, and an award-winning contributor to many journals and magazines. He lives on the shores of Lake Superior with his partner, Kathryn, two holistically kickass children, and a fat cat named Baby Kitty.

Bill McKibben is a founder of the grassroots climate campaign 350.org and the Schumann Distinguished Professor in Residence at Middlebury College in Vermont. He is a 2014 recipient of the Right Livelihood Prize, sometimes called the "alternative Nobel." He has written a dozen books about the environment, including his first, *The End of Nature*, published 25 years ago, and his most recent, *Oil and Honey*.

John Roscoe lives near Portland, Oregon, with his two young children, Nora and Evan, plus two cats and a dog. All but the dog are avid tree climbers.

Diane Payne is the author of *Burning Tulips* (Red Hen Press) and has been published in hundreds of literary journals, most recently *Watershed Review*, *Tishman Review*, *Whiskey Island*, *Kudzu House Quarterly* and *Cheat River Review*. She is the MFA Director at University of Arkansas-Monticello. "Trimming Trees" was published in *Whiskey Island Review*, Spring 2016

Brian Doyle is the editor of *Portland Magazine* in Oregon,

and the author of many books, most recently the novels *Chicago* and *Martin Marten*.

M. J. Gette is an MFA candidate in Poetry and Anthropology minor at the University of Minnesota. Her work has appeared or is forthcoming in *Anthro/Poetics*, *BOAAT*, *Carolina Quarterly*, *Tupelo Quarterly*, *Fugue*, *otoliths*, *Indefinite Space*, *Eratio* and elsewhere. She won the 2015 Gloria Anzaldúa Poetry Prize for her chapbook *The Walls They Left Us* (Newfound, 2016), where "Prometheus" first appeared. In 2015 she was awarded a writer's residency with Arquetopia, Oaxaca for a project in architecture, culture and language, alongside the Marcella DeBourg Fellowship, for "giving voice to women's lives." She is currently on a fellowship to continue study of the Kaqchikel language in Guatemala.

Annie Bellerose is a writer and Vermont native who has explored and worked in the Northeast's mountains, earned an MFA in creative writing from the University of North Carolina Wilmington, and now teaches high school English. Her most recent project has been *New Voices on Wilderness: Collected Essays from the Waterman Fund Contest* published in spring 2017 from the University Press of New England. The collection compiles writing on environmental stewardship from nearly a decade of the non-profit's writing contest.

Sarah Bates is a creative writing MFA candidate at Northern Michigan University. Her work has appeared or is forthcoming in *American Literary Review*, *BOAAT*, *So to Speak*, *Washington Square Review*, *The Normal School*, *First*

Class Lit, and *Pacifica*, among others. She currently lives in Marquette, Michigan with her goldendoodle, River.

Steven Church is the author of five books of nonfiction, the most recent being *One with the Tiger: Sublime and Violent Encounters Between Humans and Animals*. His essays have been published in *Passages North, Creative Nonfiction, Fourth Genre, River Teeth, Prairie Schooner, Colorado Review, DIAGRAM, Brevity*, and many others. He's been anthologized widely, including in the *2011 Best American Essays*. He's a Founding Editor and Nonfiction Editor for *The Normal School* and teaches in the MFA Program at Fresno State and for the Sierra Nevada Low-Residency MFA Program. "Tree Eater" originally appeared in *The Guinness Book of Me: a Memoir of Record* (Simon & Schuster, 2005).

Lia Purpura is the author of eight collections of essays, poems, and translations, most recently a collection of poems, *It Shouldn't Have Been Beautiful* (Penguin.) Her awards include Guggenheim, NEA, and Fulbright Fellowships, and *On Looking* (essays) was a finalist for the National Book Critics Circle Award. Her work appears in *The New Yorker, The New Republic, Orion, The Paris Review, The Georgia Review*, and elsewhere. She lives in Baltimore, MD and is Writer in Residence at The University of Maryland, Baltimore County. "Study With Crepe Myrtle" first appeared in *Iowa Review*.

Diana Hume George is the author or editor of ten books of nonfiction, literary criticism, and poetry, including *The Family Track, A Genesis*, and *Phantom Breast*, as well as *Oedipus Anne/ The Poetry of Anne Sexton*, and the Pulitzer-nominated

Blake and Freud. Former co-director of the Chautauqua Writers' Festival, she is a contributing editor of *Chautauqua* journal. George is Professor Emerita of English and Women's Studies at Penn State, and Professor of Practice in Goucher College's MFA program in Nonfiction. A second edition of her book of essays, *The Lonely Other: A Woman Watching America,* was published in 2014.

Jacqueline Doyle lives in the San Francisco Bay Area, where she teaches at California State University, East Bay. Her creative nonfiction has appeared in *South Dakota Review, Waccamaw, Southern Indiana Review, Cold Mountain Review,* and elsewhere. Her essays have earned Pushcart nominations from *Southern Humanities Review* and *South Loop Review,* and Notable Essay citations in Best American Essays 2013 and Best American Essays 2015. A version of "Saving Trees" originally appeared in the *Catamaran Literary Reader.*

Matthew Gavin Frank is the author of the nonfiction books, *The Mad Feast: An Ecstatic Tour Through America's Food, Preparing the Ghost: An Essay Concerning the Giant Squid and Its First Photographer, Pot Farm,* and *Barolo;* the poetry books, *The Morrow Plots, Warranty in Zulu,* and *Sagittarius Agitprop,* and 2 chapbooks. He teaches at Northern Michigan University, where he is the Nonfiction/Hybrids Editor of *Passages North.* He persevered through this past winter via the occasional one-handed cartwheel in his mind. "Hector in the Redwoods" originally appeared in *Pot Farm* (University of Nebraska Press).

"Temple" is from Angela Pelster's most recent book *Limber,* which was a finalist for the PEN/Diamonstein-Spielvogel award for the art of the essay and won the Great Lakes Colleges Association New Writer Award in Nonfiction. Her work has appeared or is forthcoming in *The Kenyon Review, River Teeth, Hotel Amerika, Granta, Granta Finland, Seneca Review, Fourth Genre, Passages North* and *The Gettysburg Review* amongst others. She lives in St. Paul with her family and teaches creative writing at Hamline University.

Amaris Feland Ketcham is an honorary Kentucky Colonel and Assistant Professor at the University of New Mexico. Her work has previously appeared in *Creative Nonfiction*, the *Los Angeles Review, Rattle,* and the *Utne Reader.*

Thomas Mira y Lopez is from New York. He holds an MFA from the University of Arizona and his essays appear in *Alaska Quarterly Review, The Georgia Review, Hotel Amerika,* and *The Normal School* among other journals. He is an assistant fiction editor at *DIAGRAM* and a founding editor of *Territory,* a literary project about maps and other strange objects. "Etiology" first appeared in *CutBank* (Issue 81).

Toti O'Brien's work most recently appeared in *Door Is A Jar, Syntax & Salt, Wilderness House* and *Litro UK.* More about her can be found at totihan.net/writer.html

Zoë Ruiz lives and writes in Los Angeles. She is a staff writer at *The Millions.* Her writing has appeared in *The Weeklings, Salon, The Rumpus, Two Serious Ladies,* and the anthology *California Prose Directory* (2014). She is a freelance book editor and edited *Nothing Ever Dies* by Pulitzer Prize Winner Viet Thanh Nguyen, which was a finalist for the 2016 National Book Award for nonfiction. You can find her on twitter: @ruizzoe.

Fred Bahnson is the author of *Soil & Sacrament: A Spiritual Memoir of Food and Faith* (Simon & Schuster). His essays have appeared in *Harper's, The Sun, The Oxford American, Image, Orion, Washington Post*, and *Best American Spiritual Writing*. His writing awards include a Pilgrimage Essay Award, a Kellogg Food & Community fellowship, and a North Carolina Artist fellowship in creative nonfiction from the North Carolina Arts Council. He teaches at Wake Forest University School of Divinity and lives with his wife and sons in Transylvania County, North Carolina. "Tree of Life" first appeared in *Harpers Magazine*.

Kayann Short, Ph.D., is a writer, farmer, and teacher at Stonebridge Farm in the Rocky Mountain foothills. Her essay, "What Goes Down," first appeared in *A Bushel's Worth: An Ecobiography*, reprinted with permission from Torrey House Press. Her work has also appeared in *Pilgrimage, The Hopper, Mad River Review, The Courier*, and *The Roost;* her essay "Soil vs Dirt: A Reverie on Getting Down to Earth" appears in *Dirt: A Love Story* (University Press of New England).

T. Hugh Crawford is an Associate Professor who teaches environmental literature at the Georgia Institute of Technology. Author of *Modernism, Medicine, and William Carlos Williams* and former editor of *Configurations*, he is currently writing a book on the Appalachian Trail and long distance hiking. "Tree Rings" first appeared in *The Atlantic* (online).

Renée E. D'Aoust's book of essays *Body of a Dancer* (Etruscan Press, 2011) was a ForeWord Reviews "Book of the Year" finalist. She is the recipient of Puffin Foundation, Idaho Arts commission, and Idaho Department of Lands grants, the "Intro to Journals" award from AWP, and six "Notable" essays from the Best American anthology series. D'Aoust has numerous book reviews and journal publications to her credit, including most recently *Brevity*, *Los Angeles Review of Books*, and *Sweet*. D'Aoust is the Managing Editor of *Assay: A Journal of Nonfiction Studies* and a Contributing Editor to *Women Owning Woodlands*. "The Line of No Trees" was previously published in the journal *Ragazine*.

Lori Brack's essays and poems have recently appeared in *The Fourth River*, *Gingko Tree Review*, *Superstition Review* and its blog *s[r]*, *Another Chicago Magazine*, *Mid-American Review*, and others. Her 2010 chapbook, *A Fine Place to See the Sky*, is a collaboration with her grandfather's 1907-1919 farming journals and serves as a poetic script for a work of performance art by Ernesto Pujol.

Mercedes Webb-Pullman graduated from Victoria University Wellington with MA in Creative Writing 2011. Her poems and prose have appeared in *Turbine*, *4th Floor*, *Swamp*, *Reconfigurations*, *The Electronic Bridge*, *Otoliths*, *Connotations*, *The Red Room*, *Typewriter*, *Cliterature*, and *Pure Slush*, among others, and in her books. She lives on the Kapiti Coast, New Zealand.

Andrea Scarpino is the author of the poetry collections *Once Upon Wing Lake* (Four Chambers Press, 2017),

What the Willow Said as It Fell (Red Hen Press, 2016) and *Once, Then* (Red Hen Press, 2014). She received a PhD in Creative Writing from Bath Spa University, and an MFA from The Ohio State University. She has published in numerous journals including *The Cincinnati Review*, *Los Angeles Review*, and *Prairie Schooner*, and she served as Poet Laureate of Michigan's Upper Peninsula 2015-2017. This piece originally appeared in *What the Willow Said as It Fell*, published in 2016 by Red Hen Press.

Matthew Grewe lives with his family in Philadelphia, Pennsylvania, where he specializes in kid maintenance, time spent with friends, and city politics. When not writing for pay, he most enjoys personal correspondence.

Jacklyn Janeksela is a wolf and a raven, a cluster of stars, and a direct descent of the divine feminine. She can be found at *Thought Catalog*, *Luna Magazine*, *Talking Book*, *DumDum Magazine*, *Visceral Brooklyn*, *Anti-Heroin Chic*, *Public Pool*, *Reality Hands*, *The Feminist Wire*, *Word For/Word*, *Pank*, *Split Lip* and Civil Coping Mechanism's anthology *A Shadow Map*. She is in a post-punk band called the velblouds. Her baby is at femalefilet.tumblr.com. She is an energy. Find her at hermetichare.com for herbal astrological readings.

Wendy Call has served as writer-in-residence at two dozen institutions, including five national parks and Washington State's Mineral School, where she wrote the essay included here. She co-edited *Telling True Stories: A Nonfiction Writers' Guide* (Penguin, 2007) and wrote *No Word for Welcome: The Mexican Village Faces the Global Economy* (Nebraska, 2011), winner of the Grub Street National Book Prize for

Nonfiction. Her nonfiction has appeared in forty journals, including the *Georgia Review, Guernica, Michigan Quarterly Review, Orion, Terrain,* and *Yes.* She teaches creative writing and environmental studies at Pacific Lutheran University.

Mackenzie Myers is a native Michigander living in northern California. After spending childhood summers at a biological field station, she loves the natural world as much as words. Most recently, her work has appeared in *Under the Gum Tree,* as well as *Gadfly* and *Traverse* magazine. She earned an MFA from Portland State University in 2016.

Karen K. Hugg is a writer and horticulturalist living in the Seattle area. Her publications include *Minerva Rising, Specs, Hip Mama, Opium, Shifting Borders, Garden Rant,* and others. One of her novels, *Harvesting the Sky,* was a recent semi-finalist in the Del Sol Press First Novel Prize contest. She is the owner of Red Madrona Gardens and writes the blog, *Gardening, Seattle Style.* You can contact her through her website, karenhugg.com.

Paul Lisicky is the author of five books: *The Narrow Door, Unbuilt Projects, The Burning House, Famous Builder,* and *Lawnboy.* His work has appeared in *The Atlantic, BuzzFeed, Conjunctions, Ecotone, Fence, The Offing, Ploughshares, Tin House,* and in many other magazines and anthologies. A 2016 Guggenheim Fellow, his other awards include fellowships from the National Endowment for the Arts, the James Michener/Copernicus Society, the Corporation of Yaddo, and the Fine Arts Work Center in Provincetown, where he was twice a Fellow. He has taught in the creative writing programs at Cornell University, New York

University, Rutgers University-Newark, Sarah Lawrence College, the University of North Carolina Wilmington, and elsewhere. He currently teaches in the MFA Program at Rutgers University-Camden, the low residency program at Sierra Nevada College, and at the Juniper Summer Writing Institute. He is the editor of *StoryQuarterly* and serves on the Writing Committee of the Fine Arts Work Center in Provincetown.

Stefan Olson holds an MFA from the University of Montana. A North Dakota native teaching in St Paul, Minnesota, Olson's essays have appeared in *The Cardiff Review* and *BULL*.

Theresa Kishkan is a writer living on the Sechelt Peninsula on the west coast of Canada. Her work has appeared in many literary journals and she has published ten books as well as three chapbooks.

Courtney Amber Kilian is a writer, gentle yoga teacher, and the founder of *Om & Ink: Live, Breathe, Write*, which offers prompts for mindful creative practice and Yoga For Writers classes. She received her MFA in Creative Writing at UCSD, and loves working with others to inspire their creativity, deepen their intuition, and use writing and yoga as therapeutic practices. Learn more at www.om-and-ink.com and follow her on Instagram @Om.And.Ink.